The Wire in the College Classroom

The Wire in the College Classroom

Pedagogical Approaches in the Humanities

Edited by KAREN DILLON *and* NAOMI CRUMMEY

McFarland & Company, Inc., Publishers
Jefferson, North Carolina

LIBRARY OF CONGRESS CATALOGUING-IN-PUBLICATION DATA

The wire in the college classroom : pedagogical approaches in the humanities / edited by Karen Dillon and Naomi Crummey.
　　p.　　cm.
Includes bibliographical references and index.

ISBN 978-0-7864-9528-3 (softcover : acid free paper) ∞
ISBN 978-1-4766-1967-5 (ebook)

1. Wire (Television program)　I. Dillon, Karen, 1980–　II. Crummey, Naomi, 1973–

PN1992.77.W53W5265 2015
791.45'72—dc23   2015000405

BRITISH LIBRARY CATALOGUING DATA ARE AVAILABLE

© 2015 Karen Dillon and Naomi Crummey. All rights reserved

No part of this book may be reproduced or transmitted in any form or by any means, electronic or mechanical, including photocopying or recording, or by any information storage and retrieval system, without permission in writing from the publisher.

Front cover image of abandoned row houses © 2015 EyeJoy/iStock

Printed in the United States of America

McFarland & Company, Inc., Publishers
　Box 611, Jefferson, North Carolina 28640
　　www.mcfarlandpub.com

Acknowledgments

This book has been a three-year process, from the initial conversation in which we decided to go with our guts and bring *The Wire* into our classrooms, to multiple conference presentations on our experience teaching *The Wire*, to the realization that there was, in fact, a book to be written, and finally to the completion of the manuscript. Now at the end of the process, we must thank those who have helped us along the way.

Foremost, neither of us would have ventured into using *The Wire* in the classroom, let alone conceptualized this book, if not for the professional and intellectual support of the other. A colleague who is also a kindred spirit is a rare gift. We are grateful to another colleague, Kristi Nelms, for her help in gathering the data necessary for our essay, and our students Amanda Gerson, Nikki England, and Max Vitori for their role in data processing. A special thank you to Laurel Pacey who provided early editorial feedback. Finally, thank you to all of our WR 112 students for their enthusiastic participation.

A few personal notes: thank you to Bryan, the first person to say, "You must watch *The Wire*"; to Brian, who listened, watched, and weighed in; to Steve for being patient and such an incisive reader; and to the Busters for their cuddles.

Finally, this book is dedicated to Paul W. Dillon, who would have loved this, and Lorraine and Don Crummey, the first and best teachers.

Table of Contents

Acknowledgments   v

Introduction
    Karen Dillon and Naomi Crummey   1

I. Media

It *Was* TV: Teaching HBO's *The Wire* as a Television Series
    Todd M. Sodano   7

The Angriest Auteur on Television: Teaching Media Authorship Through David Simon
    Alex M. Kupfer   32

Post–Network Era Television, Cultural Hierarchies and Sociological Uses of *The Wire* Beyond Urban Inequality
    Michael L. Wayne   47

II. Writing and Narrative

"Dope on the damn table": Narrative Discourse in *The Wire* and African American Literature
    Paul D. Reich   61

"They're not learning for our world; they're learning for theirs": Changing the First Year Writing Experience
    Karen Dillon and Naomi Crummey   76

Exercises in Revision and Form
    Michael Ennis   93

Closure in the Classroom: "Final Grades"
  C.W. Marshall and Tiffany Potter   108

III. Ethics and Rhetoric

"The gods will not save you": Teaching Ethics with *The Wire*
  James W. McCarty III   127

Good Lives in Tragic Worlds
  Nathan P. Gilmour   143

Wallace's Choice
  Tom Nurmi   160

IV. Education and Literacy

Reading the Scene: Discourse, Literacy and Pedagogy Through *The Wire*
  Daniel Listoe   179

The Wire at a Distance: The Socio-Cultural Determination of Meaning and the Challenges of Online Learning
  Matt Applegate   196

Using *The Wire* to Teach Cultural Competency in Higher Education
  Tia Sherèe Gaynor   212

About the Contributors   233
Index   235

Introduction

Karen Dillon and Naomi Crummey

Like many of the best television shows, books, and films, HBO's *The Wire* did not gain a wide audience during its five-season run (2002–2008) and won no top industry awards (aside from the Peabody in 2004) despite being loved by television critics. And yet, with its raw subject matter, richly layered narrative, and explicit critiques of American socio-economic institutions, *The Wire* offers a perfect cultural text for the college classroom's analytical agenda, making it one of the most teachable television shows in recent years. College classes using *The Wire* as a key or central text are being taught in a range of disciplines—media studies, sociology, literature, writing, education, philosophy—from the highest echelons of academic institutions such as Harvard, Duke, and Berkeley to small liberal arts schools such as Rollins College and even tiny regional ones such as Blackburn College. What Drake Bennet has called "[t]he academic love affair with *The Wire*" (para 4) continues to grow due to teacher-scholars' belief in *The Wire*'s ability to open discourse among academic disciplines and to reify for students the intersections of work, class, poverty, and race in the epicenters of contemporary urban institutions. Moreover, *The Wire*'s teachability lies in its powerful contemporary rhetoric; simply put, it is one of the most moving and provocative contemporary American narratives, one worthy of being analyzed, criticized, pondered, and appreciated by new as well as seasoned scholars.

The cultural and academic value of popular culture has always been contested, but academia increasingly embraces it as a crucial site for analyzing the reflection of our cultural values. Despite this, however, there remains a kind of Bourdieuian bias against television in particular as a cultural text worthy of rigorous academic study. Our own (then) provost's response to our use of *The Wire* illustrates this traditional view of television as a "low brow" cultural form not suitable for the classroom. When he heard that a television show—knowing nothing about what *The Wire* in particular had to offer—would become the core text for the second semester of our first year writing sequence, he wrote in one of our end-of-the-year reappointment letters (quoted with his permission):

> I have to comment on the use of *The Wire* as the "televisual" text for WR 112.... I admit that my response was not enthusiastic. I suppose that I am not unlike the champions of oral tradition who greeted Gutenberg's new press with skepticism. Like many others, I imagine that changes in the core media we use for communication and presenting ideas will somehow degrade the quality of our thinking and our culture. The saving grace for me, of course, is my complete confidence in you ... and thus I was able to set my fears of the decline and fall of western civilization to rest.

Though consciously hyperbolic, the provost's words reflect a common perception in academia of the inherent cultural value of one form of media over another. This perception, as confessed in the letter, stems ultimately from fear of the expanding boundaries of the academic landscape. Like gargoyles guarding the sacred print texts shelved in the ivory tower of academia, such academics lament the inclusion of television and other popular media into the canons. Those who consider film, television, and internet-related media the specific purview of disciplines like media studies fail to see the rich narratives and rhetoric in such media that should be the bedfellows of sociology, literature, philosophy, and writing, for example.

Speaking to television's place in the hierarchy of cultural value, Thomas Doherty, in the article "Storied TV: Cable is the New Novel" for *The Chronicle of Higher Education* (2012), claims, "Long top dog in the media hierarchy, the Hollywood feature film ... is being challenged by the lure of long-form, episodic television," what he calls "Arc TV...finely crafted, adult-minded serials built around arcs of interconnected action unfolding over the life span of the series" (para 3). Doherty likens the narrative world of Arc TV such as *The Wire* to "the social matrix of a Henry James novel, where small gestures and table manners reveal the content of a character molded by convention, class, and culture" (para 9). Perhaps the best example of this is the opening scene of season four in which all of the season's major plot points and central themes—education (in school and on the street), codes of communication and power, mobility across socio-economic boundaries, individuals and their place within a community—are laid out in a seemingly innocuous two-minute scene in which Snoop and Chris, enforcers for drug kingpin Marlo Stanfield, purchase, with cash, an almost seven hundred dollar nail gun at a suburban hardware store.

Doherty goes on to quote a 2011 op-ed in *The Boston Globe* by director of American Studies at Boston College Carlo Rotella, who claims that *The Wire*'s favor in the college classroom stems from its presentation of the "complex problems involving cities, crime, class, race, and our badly damaged political system" (para 14). Many teach with *The Wire* precisely because it illustrates more effectively for students than traditional academic texts the intersections of those complex problems by subverting their conventional treatments in pop culture. In "Learning Who We (and They) Are: Popular Culture as Pedagogy," Talmadge C. Guy argues that "popular culture teaches us about race, class, gender, and other forms of socially significant difference and can reify these differences into social relationships that take on the aura of normalcy" (16). For classes that engage *The Wire* to teach students about contemporary issues of poverty, the economy of drugs and judicial response, the challenges of education in the midst of urban crisis, or the limitations of individual choice in the face of institutional failure, *The Wire* presents a different "normal" for students, one that often challenges their pre-conceived understanding of meritocracy and the institutions that they inhabit.

As evidenced by the various works cited in this book, much recent scholarly attention underscores *The Wire*'s new place in academia's canons. Though there are far too many examples to catalogue here, the most recent and notable book-length projects on *The Wire* are Tiffany Potter and C.W. Marshall's (also contributors to this book) edited volume *The Wire: Urban Decay and American Television* (2009), which brings together scholarship about the show's representation of urban life from the streets to the halls of justice and education; Peter Beilenson's *Tapping into* The Wire*: The Real Urban Crisis* (2012) and *Crime and Justice as Seen Through* The Wire (2013), edited by Peter Collins and David Brody, both of which read *The Wire* as a sociological text through which to explore the contemporary ills of urban poverty, drug crime and violence, and the criminal justice system; and *Corners in the City of God: Theology, Philosophy, and* The Wire (2013), edited by Jonathan Tran and Myles Werntz (to which such esteemed scholars as Frederic Jameson and Slavoj Žižek are contributors), which posits itself as a "theological companion" to *The Wire* that explores the moral/ethical complexities presented in the narrative of a city riddled with corruption, crime, and poverty.

With the increasing volume of college courses and scholarly work about

The Wire, surprisingly little has focused on how it has been taught. Andrew Moore of St. Thomas University outlined his pedagogical approach to the show in a 2011 article in *Transformative Dialogues: Teaching & Learning Journal*. In *Contexts*, a publication of the American Sociological Association, Sarah Lageson et al. published "*The Wire* Goes to College," an article highlighting professors' pedagogical uses of *The Wire*, including Todd M. Sodano's (a contributor here) course "Inside HBO's America: A Case Study of *The Wire*" at Syracuse, William Julius Wilson's course "Urban Inequality and *The Wire*" at Harvard, Peter Beilenson's course "Baltimore and *The Wire*: A Focus on Major Urban Issues" at Johns Hopkins, and Marc Levine's course "The Crisis of the American City—Viewed through HBO's *The Wire*" at the University of Wisconsin–Milwaukee. This book expands Lageson et al.'s project by bringing together the ways in which we are making use of *The Wire* in our classrooms, how we teach it and to what ends.

As a quintessentially interdisciplinary text, *The Wire* in its five seasons proffers numerous subjects for academic study: televisual media, narrative, rhetoric, criminal justice, education, labor and industry, poverty, the economy of drugs and drug violence, urban studies, race and class studies, philosophy and ethics, and so on. Therefore, it is difficult, and perhaps counterproductive, to categorize *The Wire* and its place in the classroom. Nonetheless, it is helpful to understand specific disciplinary uses of the show, and so essays in this book are organized according to four broad categories of academic discipline: Media; Writing and Narrative; Ethics and Rhetoric; and Education and Literacy. Though the book is sectioned by discipline, many essays demonstrate the intertextuality and interdisciplinary nature of the show. For example, Nathan P. Gilmour's essay, which explains how season four of *The Wire* may converse with Friedrich Nietzsche's *Genealogy of Morals* and Alasdair MacIntyre's *After Virtue* to teach undergraduates modes of deliberation and analysis in an ethical context, could just have easily been placed in a section on education, for it is equally invested in reimagining how ethics, as part of a core general education liberal arts curriculum, can be taught. Organizing the pieces by discipline also showcases how teachers in different fields approach specific moments in *The Wire* with different pedagogical goals. Using the much taught scene from season one's episode "The Pager" in which D'Angelo dines out with his girlfriend (1.5), Paul D. Reich's essay explains how economic and racial divisions in the scene may be thought of alongside classic literary texts such as Richard Wright's *Native Son*. Daniel Listoe, whose piece focuses on literacy and discourse in the context of education, teaches the scene to illustrate for students the multiple discourses at work. Finally, Matt Applegate leverages this same scene to discuss the discursive construction of power in a distance-learning course titled "Television Culture."

In the opening part on "Media," essays discuss the necessity of and challenges to teaching *The Wire* as a specifically televisual text. Todd M. Sodano in "It *Was* TV: Teaching HBO's *The Wire* as a Television Series" explains how *The Wire* makes an excellent case study for upper-class and graduate students heading into media production careers because of its unique pastiche, production and promotion, and critical reception. Alex M. Kupfer's "The Angriest Auteur on Television: Teaching Media Authorship Through David Simon" examines the complexities of authorial identity by thinking about *The Wire* through its primary creator. From the perspective of Bourdieu's conception of cultural capital, Michael L. Wayne looks at *The Wire* through the discourses of taste, as well as its place in the history of television, in "Post–Network Era Television, Cultural Hierarchies and Sociological Uses of *The Wire* Beyond Urban Inequality."

The second part, "Writing and Narrative," features essays on using *The Wire* in writing and literature courses. In "'Dope on the damn table': Narrative Discourse in *The Wire* and African American Literature," Paul D. Reich narrates his experience teaching *The Wire* in an African American literature course that juxtaposed the show alongside classic works of fiction such as Zora Neale Hurston's *Their Eyes Were Watching God* and James Weldon Johnson's *The Autobiography of an Ex-Coloured Man*. Our essay "'They're not learning for our world; they're learning for theirs': Changing the First Year Writing Experience" takes readers through the genesis, execution, and assessment of teaching season four of the show as their primary text in a first year writing course, ultimately demonstrating through three years of data how *The Wire* positively affected student persistence and performance in the class. Michael Ennis in "Exercises in Revision and Form" explains his use of *The Wire*, itself a revision of the creators' previous work, to teach the process of revision as fundamental to a text's meaning. The final piece in this section, C.W. Marshall and Tiffany Potter's "Closure in the Classroom: 'Final Grades,'" looks exclusively at the final episode in season four as the means to teach closure theory.

In the part on "Ethics and Rhetoric," James W. McCarty III's essay "'The gods will not save you': On Teaching Ethics with *The Wire*" explains how students in an introductory philosophical ethics course applied foundational concepts of ethical reasoning to the show. Nathan P. Gilmour's "Good Lives in Tragic Worlds" imagines a general education ethics course in which season four of *The Wire*, alongside philosophical texts by

Friedrich Nietzshe and Alasdair MacIntyre, facilitates the practice of reasoned deliberation to introduce entry-level students to philosophical worldviews. Tom Nurmi's essay "Wallace's Choice" discusses *The Wire* as part of a law and literature course, focusing primarily on the visual rhetoric of surveillance in the show's theme and structure, which creates a dialogue between the visual narrative and viewers as they watch the ethics of choice unfold through a character like season one's Wallace.

In the final part, "Education and Literacy," Daniel Listoe's essay "Reading the Scene: Discourse, Literacy and Pedagogy Through *The Wire*" highlights key scenes of reading in the show to demonstrate literacy as enacted through usage and context. Matt Applegate's "*The Wire* at a Distance: The Socio-Cultural Determination of Meaning and the Challenges of Online Learning" discusses the difficulties of teaching a multi-layered text like *The Wire* in an online learning environment, which he finds paralleled in the show's institutional critique. Lastly, Tia Sherèe Gaynor studies 20 college syllabi across disciplines that feature *The Wire* as the primary text in order to demonstrate the show's richness for teaching cultural competency, ending with specific ideas for teaching the show in various college courses.

All of the contributors here speak as teachers who use *The Wire* to expand understandings of and approaches to their respective disciplines. Our sincere hope as editors is that teachers find this book genuinely useful for their own pedagogical endeavors.

Works Cited

Aper, Jeffrey. Letter to the author. 27 July 2012. TS.
Bennett, Drake. "This Will Be on the Midterm. You Feel Me? Why So Many Colleges Are Teaching *The Wire*." *Slate*. The Washington Post Company, 24 March 2010. Web.
Doherty, Thomas. "Storied TV: Cable Is the New Novel." *The Chronicle Review*. *The Chronicle of Higher Education*. 12 September 2012. Web.
Guy, Talmadge C. "Learning Who We (and They) Are: Popular Culture as Pedagogy." *New Directions for Adult and Continuing Education* 115 (Fall 2007): 15–23.
Lageson, Sarah, Kyle Green, and Sinan Erensu. "*The Wire* Goes to College." *Contexts 10.3* (August 2011): 12–15. American Sociological Association.
Moore, Andrew. "Teaching HBO's *The Wire*." *Transformative Dialogues: Teaching & Learning Journal 5.1* (July 2011): 1–14.

PART I

Media

It *Was* TV

Teaching HBO's The Wire *as a Television Series*

Todd M. Sodano

Described as a "somewhat angry show" by its creator David Simon (qtd. in Penfold-Mounce et al. 154), *The Wire* examines what happens when social institutions fail the individuals they are supposed to protect. According to critic J.M. Tyree, "The show's implicit argument condemns a criminally negligent and culturally pervasive *failure to notice*" (38). This failure, represented by the characters who work in law enforcement, politics, education, and media, is a leitmotif in the series, as each season tackles a different institution in the city of Baltimore, Maryland.

Similarly, the discourses surrounding *The Wire* have spotlighted pressing sociological and cultural issues in lieu of unpacking it as a television show. Through its slogan "It's Not TV, It's HBO," the premium cable network that aired Simon's series repudiated any notions of having its programming be associated with "TV" and any inherent pejorative connotations. Simon boasted that his series was a visual novel, a notion that supplants the medium in which he was working in favor of a more respected one. Journalistic television critics, whose praise sustained the low-rated series during its five-season run, often lauded his work by drawing similarities to Charles Dickens novels. Moreover, like some TV dramas before and after it, *The Wire* was considered a work of art. In sum, according to film scholar Linda Williams, "much of this praise borrows a literary prestige that corresponds to the series' excellence but not closely enough to its actual serial television cultural form" ("*The Wire*: Realistic").

Like most of the research written about *The Wire,* more attention has been paid to themes and problems inspired by the series and less to how it represents a television text.[1]

Renowned sociologist William Julius Wilson, whose own work inspired the second season's theme of the death of work in America, said of his Harvard class on the series, "To be clear, this course was not intended to teach students *about* the show, per se. Instead, the course integrated academic research *with* the series to develop a rigorous examination of urban inequality" (qtd. in Lageson, Green, & Erensu, 11). Former Baltimore City Health commissioner Peter Beilenson said his Johns Hopkins University class was "based loosely on the [show's] five seasons" (Lageson et al. 13). Marc Levine, a history professor at University of Wisconsin-Milwaukee, makes sure his students "get an interdisciplinary, social science handle on the complex layers of the urban crisis," and resists "the temptation to get caught up in the brilliant drama, the humor, and the inherently interesting, multi-faceted nature of the characters" (qtd. in Lageson et al. 14).

These courses represent the prevailing approach to teaching *The Wire,* which consciously ignores it as a television series, disregards any stylistic choices made by the show's creators (by urging that we do not "get caught up in the brilliant drama"), minimizes the medium's power, and prevents students interested in TV production and filmmaking from learning about writing, dramatic storytelling, cinematography, production design, and so on.

My course, however, was intentionally different, as it appeared in a television-radio-film program, where learning objectives for my students who were pursuing careers in these media industries were different from those in classes taught in the liberal arts and social sciences. These objectives included learning how social issues are mediated through a cable television series, examining HBO's influences on American culture, discussing important issues surrounding the current landscape of television, engaging in meaningful dialogues (written and oral) with classmates, and writing effectively and persuasively about *The Wire,* HBO, and television.

Pedagogy

In the spring of 2008, when HBO was airing the show's fifth and final season, I taught "Inside HBO's America: A Case Study of *The Wire*" at Syracuse University, a class that positions the series primarily as "a serial television cultural form" (Williams, "Mega-melodrama"). As Simon looked at the American city through the microcosm of Baltimore, my course took a similar "inside-out" approach by examining the then-current state of the U.S. television industry through an in-depth look at *The Wire*'s production, distribution, and reception, a template I also used for my doctoral dissertation on the series ("All the Pieces").

My 500-level course was offered to upperclassmen and graduate students, most of whom were television-radio-film majors with some journalism and Pan African Studies majors. Twenty-seven students registered for the three-hour seminar that met once a week. The structure was uniform each week: I opened with a 20- to 30-minute lecture, the topics of which were inspired by the show's production (e.g., how it was written, shot, produced, and edited), distribution (HBO's role in greenlighting, renewing, and promoting it), reception (professional television critics' influence over the show's improbable survival and the TV Academy never bestowing it with any Emmy Awards), and some of the social issues (e.g., the war on drugs, sexual orientation, language and violence on television) inscribed in it. For instance, from the famous scene in which homicide detectives Jimmy McNulty and "Bunk" Moreland investigate a murder by communicating to each other using different expressions of the word "fuck," we examined broadcasting indecency and freedoms afforded by premium cable outlets like HBO (1.4). From another episode that provides insight into the character development of lesbian narcotics detective Kima Greggs, we examined televisual representations of sexual orientation (1.10).

Lectures were followed by—and not always connected to—a screening of the next episode of the season. One of the most common pedagogical struggles for today's instructors of modern television is deciding which moment(s) or episode(s) to screen for their students. This difficulty becomes more pronounced when teaching serialized television because of the amount of exposition it takes to bring uninitiated students up to speed. While it might be instructive and entertaining to show the humorous courtroom scene in which stick-up man Omar Little accuses a drug organization defense attorney of being exploitative just like him—"I got the shotgun; you got the briefcase" (1.6)—these scenes mean little, as it were, outside of the context of the series. The student would have a fuller understanding of the scene if she or he knew better the characters of Omar and Maurice Levy. Moreover, by the time the instructor supplies the exhaustive background information, interest in watching the scene has waned. I consistently face this struggle in a television history class, in which I can devote only one week of the semester to *The Wire;* by watching the first episode in class, students do not even see Omar, who makes his first appearance in the third episode.

As I wrote in my syllabus, "An examination of *The Wire* necessitates an in-depth, semester-long, full-season commitment" ("TRF"). The show's sheer size and scope make it almost impossible to examine the entire corpus in one semester; accordingly, I focused only on the first season. Furthermore, because my class situated the series as a work of television and was not topical (i.e., rooted in urban inequality, state power, heteronormativity, etc.), I required us to watch all thirteen episodes together. The shared viewing experience represents a critical component of teaching visual media. Akin to watching a film in a movie theater, emotions can be magnified when viewers are surrounded by others, as my class learned when we all viewed the murder of teenaged boy Wallace (1.12). One student, who had already seen the show, grew upset and ran out of the classroom before Wallace's friends pulled the trigger and killed him. In a dark classroom where texting and second-screen devices were prohibited, distractions were minimized and students offered more detailed and precise descriptions of particular moments. I also did not have to jog their memories about what they might have watched in the week leading up to class. Unfortunately, though, watching the episodes together meant we lost approximately 60 valuable minutes per session that we could have devoted to in-class discussions. In fairness as well, watching television this way—in the dark, on a large screen, with 26 other people—does not necessarily mirror the traditional TV-viewing experience that we enjoy at home.

We capitalized on the nearly equivalent 14-week semester and 13-episode seasons that many HBO (and cable dramas) employ, and watched in order one episode each week, which created gaps between episodes that mimic the traditional broadcasting schedule. In his article on HBO's *Deadwood* and serial fiction, Sean O'Sullivan writes, "[I]t is in that between-state that we as readers or viewers do most of our interpreting—speculating about plot developments or resolutions, wondering about characters and their choices, luxuriating in the details of the story's construction" (123). Despite the ability (through DVDs and HBO On Demand) to binge-watch more of *The Wire,* our class viewed the first season weekly, akin to how HBO had aired them. We treated each episode as an individual installment and tried to limit our discussions to what took place in that particular episode (and what preceded it). Students who so desired were more than encouraged to "read ahead" and watch as many episodes as they wanted. In fact, numerous students had already seen the first four seasons and watched the final one as it aired concurrently with our class that spring, and at least one newcomer binged the entire series in less than two months.

Following a short break after each week's screening, two or three students individually delivered 10- to 15-minute oral presentations on topics (chosen by the students) that either advanced what we discussed in class, such as how and why the Emmy Award eluded *The Wire* or representations of homosexuality on television, or on material that we could not fit into this class, such as public education in Baltimore or the science behind police interrogations. These presentations supplemented one of the two 5-page essays that students had written on these same topics. Since my class appeared in a communications school, I assessed students' oral presentation skills along with the content they included.

The final 30 to 40 minutes of each class were reserved for discussions that (re)visited issues related to the lectures, episodes, presentations, and reading questions posed by students. Prior to each week's meeting, two to three students took turns composing questions to guide their classmates through the readings for that unit, which served as prompts for our class-wide discussions. For example, one student asked, "How does acceptance of Kima's and [her partner] Cheryl's sexuality differ from acceptance of Omar's? Would you argue that class is a more important factor than race in measuring their acceptance?" Another student, in preparation for our discussion about the influence of TV critics, asked, "How much cultural production can occur if critics are writing about the show, but the viewing audience remains comparatively small?" We were able to incorporate social issues into our dialogues while remaining rooted in our examination of a television series and the surrounding industry. At the conclusion of the semester, students recommended that more time be allocated to our discussions and less time for their presentations.

Students were not permitted to reveal spoilers—or plot points from upcoming episodes or seasons—for their classmates who had not seen the show. This became particularly challenging when discussing the execution of certain writing techniques. We could not discuss the irony of drug lord Avon Barksdale's defiant proclamation in his first scene to his naïve nephew D'Angelo that he doesn't "know shit about jail," only to end up there by the first season's end (1.1). We could not discuss how Avon's right-hand man Stringer Bell's murder in season three (3.11) or Omar's in season five (5.8) might have been foreshadowed. We could not discuss the eventual murders of the three low-level dealers who appeared in the popular scene in which D'Angelo explains to his uncle's low-ranking dealers Bodie and Wallace how to play chess through a metaphor for their standing in the world (1.3).

I carefully chose where I, the instructor, adhered to this rule, though. After Detective McNulty in the first episode tells his partner that he was the one to disclose to a judge how powerful Avon's crew is, which forces the narcotics and homicide departments to investigate, he confesses to his supervising sergeant how he would prefer not to be demoted to the Marine Unit. Twelve episodes later, in the season finale, after the Barksdale case is closed, McNulty ends up on the boat. Discussing this narrative plant as soon as we watched it in class allowed us to explicate it across numerous contexts. More specifically, in addition to the scene showing us that McNulty's well-intentioned actions were met with indignation by his colleagues, we discussed how Simon blurs the line between good and evil by having two superior law enforcement officials castigate a detective for doing the right thing, i.e., by eradicating a successful, violent drug ring. Moreover, what might appear to be a throwaway scene actually pays off at the season's other end, evincing the expansive structure of *The Wire*. Having watched all thirteen hours of the first season in a few days, a binge-watcher could certainly recall what McNulty said to his sergeant. However, the attentive viewer, who remembered that moment from twelve weeks earlier, might enjoy that payoff considerably more: Simon and his writers intended for their show to be viewed weekly, since they were working within the traditional scheduling paradigm of one episode airing per week and not all of them at once, à la HBO rival Netflix's full-season releases of *House of Cards* and *Orange Is the New Black*. The students who knew of McNulty's fate could then discern other signposts throughout the season that foreshadowed his demotion and make meaningful contributions to our dialogues.

The Most Important of the Five W's

When an instructor teaches television—especially an individual series—is just as important as *what* he or she covers. Ranging from the increase in programming options to the advances in distribution platforms, the television landscape of early 2008 is drastically different from today, changes that can shed light on how a particular series was created, delivered, and consumed in the contexts of when we examine it along with when the series aired. When my class commenced in January 2008, HBO and television were at a crossroads, which was an important context for my TV and film students, who were merely months away from moving to New York City and Los Angeles to pursue careers in entertainment. Our class began flush in the middle of the writers' strike, which began the prior November and ended three months later, a work stoppage that shut down productions on scripted programming (and films) while writers sought an increase in financial compensation from their work that was being distributed through new media such as DVDs and online platforms. The strike afforded my students an additional, unforeseen backdrop from which they could examine *The Wire*.

Simon's series, which had begun its final season a mere ten days before our first class, premiered at a pivotal moment in the channel's history: *The Sopranos*, HBO's signature show, had completed its six-season run just seven months earlier, and the network decided not to continue its popular western drama *Deadwood;* worse for the network, a month before the highly anticipated *Sopranos* finale, then–CEO and Chairman Chris Albrecht, who had developed HBO's groundbreaking original programming, resigned after he was arrested for physically assaulting his girlfriend in a Las Vegas parking lot outside of a boxing match that his network had broadcast; and HBO began to face stiffer competition from other cable outlets such as AMC's *Mad Men*, Showtime's *Dexter* and *Weeds*, and FX's *The Shield*, *Nip/Tuck*, and *Rescue Me*.

Throughout the run of *The Sopranos*, *The Wire*, *Six Feet Under*, *Oz*, *Sex and the City*, and *Deadwood*, "It's Not TV, It's HBO" was seared into the psyches of TV watchers. In examining the medium's evolution in the current post-network era through the success of *The Sopranos*, television studies pioneer Horace Newcomb challenges the catchphrase's meaning: "[W]hat once was known as 'television' is no longer 'TV.' HBO's slogan is, in effect, dependent on a set of assumptions about the medium that no longer hold, a retro activation—and implicit denigration—of older general meanings and attitudes" (574). He also acknowledges the "aesthetic conventions" of today's programs that have supplanted what once was "television" (574). My media students have examined these conventions—from television's past and present—as well as their implications.

Recognizing this backdrop reveals more layers of context from the moment when our class examined *The Wire*, which undoubtedly would be different had the course been offered today with the benefits of hindsight and the outburst of scholarly articles that have been written since the series concluded. Furthermore, HBO might not have green-lighted or renewed *The Wire* at a different time in the company's history.

Distribution

In order to teach *The Wire* as a piece of television, it is essential to understand not just what took place on the screen but also the impact of the series' distribution mechanism, HBO. Without the network's "remarkable sustained support of the program" (Hanson 67) and despite the critical adoration the show received, *The Wire*'s continuously low ratings and inability to earn any Emmy recognition might have been enough to interrupt Simon's vision for a five-season series (Sodano, "All the Pieces"). In their analysis of *The Sopranos* as "brand equity," Mark C. Rogers, Michael Epstein, and Jimmie L. Reeves examined the series' "overlapping economic, technological, regulatory, and corporate *contexts*" that "constitute the enabling conditions that make possible the production" of HBO's original series (43). A common (mis)perception from students is that writers flock to premium cable outlets merely because they are permitted to include foul language and nudity in their scripts. Fleshing out writers' freedoms and challenges allows students to understand the differences between television's various economic models and their influences over narratives.

HBO is neither advertiser-supported nor regulated for indecent content by the Federal Communications Commission. Thus, the channel can tell stories in a cutting-edge way that provides value to the viewer but that would make the conservative, ratings-driven broadcast networks nervous. According to media scholar Deborah Jaramillo, "This pay cable chauvinism not only holds broadcast TV to a different standard but also implies that pay cable consumers can handle graphic language, sex, and violence in a more thoughtful and productive way than broadcast viewers" (66). In other words, those elements need not appear carelessly and gratuitously—though, of course, they often do. Furthermore, because HBO is commercial-free, its stories need not ramp up to a climactic break every six to eight minutes with a cliffhanger to keep viewers tuned in during the advertisements, an economic model, according to Simon, that limits the possibilities of complex storytelling and "has kept television a juvenile medium" (qtd. in Egner).

Cable outlets such as HBO that offer original programming call for far fewer episodes than their broadcast network competitors. Jaramillo adds, "Fewer episodes ordered means more money to spend and more production time in which to spend it" (63). This discrepancy explains how *The Sopranos* produced only 86 one-hour episodes in eight-plus years and *The Wire* 60 episodes in six years, compared to broadcast series that tend to eclipse the 60-episode mark by the end of their third season. This fundamental difference between broadcast and cable (and streaming) television as well as HBO's cultivation of its auteurs (discussed later in this section) allow for the 21-month breaks between *The Sopranos'* fifth and sixth seasons and *The Wire*'s third and fourth seasons, compared to the traditional four-month summer break for network shows.

HBO and its premium cable counterparts Showtime, Starz, and Cinemax endure challenges and freedoms that these "enabling conditions" provide. For instance, subscriber-based channels regularly battle "churn," or the turnover rate at which customers discontinue their monthly subscriptions. Because ratings do not translate into advertising revenue, pay cable channels instead must continuously provide incentive to their subscribers, which might take the form of original programming, on-demand or streaming services, the manufacturing of "buzz,"[2] or the development of a "strong brand identity" (Rogers et al. 47).

In 2001, HBO introduced HBO On Demand, a video on-demand (VOD) service, and HBO GO, a streaming service for online and mobile devices, in 2010. Both services offer subscribers access to original series, movies, comedy specials, sports, and documentaries. Aside from borrowing a friend's username and password to access HBO GO, nonsubscribers may watch through DVDs,[3] the preferred binge-consumption practice in the early 2000s before streaming video became more desirable.[4]

A common practice today is for studios to release the most recently completed seasons of their series just before the premieres of upcoming ones in order to allow new viewers to catch up. However, the seemingly infallible HBO made crucial errors while *The Wire* was on the air by releasing the first season DVD set in October 2004, when season three was still airing, and the second season set in January 2005, after the third season had finished ("*The Wire*"). This unusual blunder marks an exception that proves the rule with respect to HBO's meticulous crafting of its brand and content. As the next section describes, the series builds as a novel would—by expanding slowly and focusing on character, story, and setting—which makes it difficult for new viewers to start watching without having seen the first season(s). For students pursuing careers in entertainment, understanding how a leading television brand distributes its properties and promotes its work is critical.

Media historian Christopher Anderson has elevated HBO's programming, namely its dramas, by aligning it with more highly regarded art forms in the hierarchical scale of American culture, in which television is traditionally at the bottom. More specifically, the network has required its viewers to adopt "an aesthetic disposition [that] brings to television the cultivated expectation that watching certain television series requires and rewards, the temperament, knowledge, and protocols normally considered appropriate for encounters with museum-worthy works of art" (24). Invoking cultural theorist Pierre Bourdieu, Anderson claims that HBO has "cultivat[ed] an aura of aesthetic distinction" (29). Inherent in this distinction is how the channel positions itself—and is recognized by cultural critics—more as art and less as broadcast entertainment. Anderson acknowledges HBO's public relations for "promot[ing] a television culture in which it is possible to think of a television series as a work of art. This is a crucial step in the creation of HBO's distinctive cultural value" (35). Referring to creators on his network, HBO co-president Richard Plepler said, "Great artists want to be with a gallery owner who gets them, and with whom they have a shared vision" (qtd. in Aspden). Tyree, in his review of *The Wire*'s fourth season, which earned the series its highest praise and a renewal for a final season, says to "[c]redit the Medici-like largesse of HBO; there was something decidedly Florentine about how the funding kept coming through for such a ratings dog" (32). Enjoying the subscriber-based economic model, where low ratings do not translate into lower advertising revenue and higher cancellation rates, HBO looks elsewhere to decide a series' fate, often to the intangible buzz that the network craves.

According to Anderson, HBO's public relations has "masterfully pulled the strings of a credulous press," adding how the network "feeds the press coverage of its programs back through the public relations machinery, so that people begin to speak about the positive press coverage" (38). Leading up to *The Wire*'s fourth season premiere in the summer of 2006, Albrecht and Simon took their puppet show to the biannual Television Critics Association (TCA) Press Tour in Los Angeles, where at the show's presentation they baited many critics into heaping hyperbole and superlatives into their reviews in hopes of persuading more viewers to watch the new season and thus avoid what seemed to be an imminent cancellation. By dangling this threat—as well as Simon's to write the last season as a novel if HBO did not renew (Zurawik, "David Simon")—over the heads of the press and the show's cult following, Albrecht and Simon successfully galvanized many critics from the TCA, in large part by giving them the full season of screeners in advance rather than just a few episodes as HBO had done with the first season. This brilliant maneuver yielded the following reviews from critics who binged on the fourth season: "Thirteen hours ago, I was a different person" (Buckman, "Re-*Wired*"); "This season of *The Wire* will knock the breath out of you" (Heffernan); "[*The Wire* is] surely the best TV show ever broadcast in America" (Weisberg).

Before the premiere, Simon suggested that the show's ratings, its DVD sales, and critical responses would contribute to whether or not HBO would renew one last time ("Exclusive David Simon Q&A"). Considering the series' meager 1.53 million viewers who tuned in on September 10 (Martin) as well as the undisclosed DVD sales figures, the renewal seemed to hinge on the journalists to reach their readers and persuade them to watch. Or did it? After the show was renewed 48 hours after the fourth season premiered, Simon said, "As ridiculous and wonderful as the reviews were, they gave me a lot more confidence than I had.... But I really think we won the battle with HBO before we aired" (qtd. in Martin). Despite HBO's exceptionalism, though, it is usually impossible to isolate one particular criterion for any of its renewals or cancellations.

Coincidentally, another drama in the "greatest TV show ever" conversation aired its first season on the same Sunday nights that *The Wire* aired its last: AMC's *Breaking Bad* (2008–2013). Creator Vince Gilligan's basic cable series, which also initially struggled to produce high viewership, enjoyed a freakish ratings increase of 442 percent over its final two seasons due to Netflix's ability to attract new viewers who could catch up in advance of the bifurcated fifth season (Hibberd, "*Breaking Bad*"). To ensure my students can understand this type of growth, my television history and *The Wire* classes always include a brief introduction to ratings and shares.[5] Students who enter careers in broadcasting, advertising, public relations, sales, or media research must know the distinctions between these two figures and how complicated calculating television viewership has become in an era of fragmentation and multi-platform viewing.

Comparing the histories of two of the most critically acclaimed dramas of all time may be an enjoyable conversation on its face (see Koo), but since *The Wire* and *Breaking Bad* were contemporaries of each for just a few months, it is crucial for students to note how the technological landscape that developed alongside Gilligan's series revolutionized the medium just as its precursor was concluding. Gilligan said, "I don't think our show would have even lasted beyond season two if it wasn't for streaming video on demand.... It's a new era and we've been very fortunate to reap the benefits" (qtd. in Koo). Compare this to Simon's reliance upon the show's ratings, DVD sales, and pre–Twitter TV critic conversations for survival, and *The Wire* creator sounds as if his era featured VHS tapes, television set knobs, and newspapers, not one that still enjoyed its own technological advantages such as HBO On Demand and repeat airings on HBO's multiplex channels (e.g., HBO2, HBO Signature, HBO Zone).

Television as Visual Novel

In a self-referential newsroom scene from the show's final season, *The Baltimore Sun* staff gathers around a table to hear their executive editor declare the topic for one of their next series (5.2). Thinly developed as a straw villain, James Whiting proudly uses the word "Dickensian," an unsubtle nod to the critics and journalists who used a similar adjective in describing *The Wire*.[6] More controversially, however, is how Simon positioned his series as a visual novel, a notion we debated in my class. He said, "If you give me 13 hours of a visual medium, I should be able to give you a story as detailed as a 400-page novel, in terms of its use of characters" (personal interview). Referencing *Moby Dick*, Simon noted how we do not see the whale in the first chapters of Herman Melville's book. Not coincidentally, the first season of *The Wire* is more than halfway completed by the time the Baltimore Police Department's investigative detail actually sees their mysterious target Avon Barksdale, which builds suspense and anticipation, and the eponymous surveillance device that gives the series its name is not implemented on the payphones in the Western Baltimore projects until the sixth episode.

The controversy of the visual novel claim has rested not necessarily in placing one's work next to one of the greatest American novels but, rather, in situating it alongside the printed text. As media scholar Jason Mittell wrote in his exploration of *The Wire* as more an interactive video game and less a novel, "[T]elevision at its best shouldn't be understood simply as emulating another older and more culturally valued medium. *The Wire* is a masterpiece of television, not a novel that happens to be televised, and thus should be understood, analyzed, and celebrated on its own medium's terms" ("All in the Game"). Over the course of the five seasons, the exploration of how the social institutions have failed the people of Baltimore grows richer as the story expands and the number of characters increases.

In my class, I introduced "television as literature" as our second-week topic as a way to discuss the structure of the series, not knowing how heated discussions would grow surrounding this notion. Mittell echoed my students' aversion to this characterization: "By asserting *The Wire* as a televised novel, Simon and critics are attempting to legitimize and validate the demeaned television medium by linking it to the highbrow cultural sphere of literature" ("All in the Game"). Once again, despite the advances that television and television studies have made over the last decade and a half, the medium is still maligned, leading its most notable writers to defend it (and themselves) and modify the conversation about how it is legitimized.

The viewer can experience this deliberate, novelistic story development symbolically. In my class, I performed what I call the Kima Greggs Finger

Analysis, in which I explore the symbolism surrounding the detective's near-fatal shooting. In her first scene in the pilot, after she and narcotics detectives Thomas "Herc" Hauk and Ellis Carver make a street arrest, Greggs admonishes her careless colleagues for not finding the second gun in the backseat of a car (1.1). She flashes her index and middle fingers to remind them that there were two guns that they should have retrieved during the bust. Nine episodes later, Greggs again is in the backseat of a car—this time, as an undercover detective—in a botched drug-dealing sting (1.10). The driver, a nightclub manager who was a police informant, ends up dead and Greggs is critically wounded. Unlike the first episode, though, this time she cannot reach the gun taped unsuccessfully under the front seat of the old vehicle, and thus her fingers cannot reach the weapon to protect herself. In the last scene of the next episode, Greggs lies in a coma in a hospital bed with machines beeping around her (1.11). A close-up of her still left hand is shown, perhaps to suggest the finger-twitch that assures the familiar TV viewer that she will be fine. However, *The Wire* resists predictability and cuts back to the long shot of a motionless Greggs in the bed as the episode fades to black.

In the season finale two episodes later, Greggs, awake and talking, is asked to identify the two men who shot her.[7] Homicide detective Moreland shows her photo arrays of men whom he and Greggs know were responsible and subtly suggests (with what he later calls his "fat finger") that Avon's henchman "Wee-Bey" Brice was the second shooter. Moreland says Greggs' ability to identify the two shooters would "play a whole lot easier" in court, but she cannot—nay, *will* not—finger (i.e., identify) him because she did not see Wee-Bey through the dark that night. She concedes, "Sometimes things just gotta play hard" (1.13).

Whether one envisions *The Wire* as a book, a video game, or a television show, these four moments that all symbolically involve Detective Greggs' fingers both literally and figuratively illustrate its expansiveness, its subversion of television drama conventions, and the complex construction of its characters. From a pedagogical perspective, this scaffold analysis requires students to recall what they learned throughout the semester and apply it across numerous contexts, including the series specifically and television generally. For the many students who proclaim to be visual learners, seeing these contexts in action can be much more illuminating than the instructor merely lecturing about them. Nevertheless, as Mittell advises, "the best insights about the show can be found not by looking at it as either a novel or a game but in terms of what it truly is: a masterful example of television storytelling" ("All in the Game").

Production

Students often characterize *The Wire* as "realistic" and "authentic," two controversial yet nebulous terms in media storytelling. It is important to tease out these words, and on what students base these characterizations. The instructor who teaches *The Wire* as television, in turn, ought to impart to the class how it was produced, a vital education for students who seek work in the field.

Before creating *The Wire,* Simon adapted *The Corner: A Year in the Life of an Inner-City Neighborhood,* a nonfiction book he co-wrote with Ed Burns in 1997, into an Emmy-winning HBO miniseries in 2000. Simon also wrote *Homicide: A Year on the Killing Streets* in 1991, which NBC turned into a fictional drama series called *Homicide: Life on the Street* in 1993.[8] He wrote this book after taking a leave of absence from *The Baltimore Sun,* where he ultimately worked for 13 years as a crime reporter, to spend a year with the Baltimore Police Department's Homicide Unit.

His background in journalism and ethnographic writing informs our understanding of him as a television storyteller, as evidenced by his complicated characters who erase the proverbial line between good and evil. The characters' complexity differs from the narrative complexity that many of today's popular dramas employ. The latter refers to a shift towards serialized programs whose story lines traverse episodes and seasons. Stand-alone episodes, which do not require the viewer to have a prior understanding of the characters and events, have largely disappeared in programs from this genre. In addition, according to Mittell, who has written extensively about this form, "narratively complex programs invite temporary disorientation and confusion, allowing viewers to build up their comprehension skills through long-term viewing and active engagement" ("Narrative Complexity" 37). Fans who struggle to summarize *The Wire* in one sentence also likely warn the new viewer to pay close attention when watching it for the first time. They also rewatch episodes not only to revisit a favorite moment but also to catch what they might have missed, be it an unclear line of dialogue, a meaningful glance, or a subtle plot development. Through this "productive confusion," Mittell adds, "Simon and the writers have always assumed that viewers should have to work to understand their fictional vision of Baltimore" ("*The Wire* in").

Simon's journalistic pedigree explains his series' quest for authenticity. Episodes are layered with insider jargon, nuanced characters (ranging from law enforcement officials, politicians, and school officials to drug dealers, longshoremen, and newspapermen), and a lack of expository dialogue written by journalists and novelists. On numerous occasions, Simon has declared he does not care if the viewer can follow his series, an approach that he modified from his time at *The Sun*. "I was always told to write for the average reader in my newspaper life," he said. "He knows nothing and he needs everything explained to him right away, so that exposition becomes this incredible story-killing burden. Fuck him. Fuck him to hell" (qtd. in Hornby 76–7). Simon's quest for authenticity undoubtedly caught the attention of the journalism majors in my class.

Students often mischaracterize *The Wire* as an improvised show because of the raw, unfiltered language and street jargon that its actors deliver so naturally. Simon and his writers quickly note that mostly all of them stay "on book" and deliver their lines as written. Nevertheless, that these lines are so poetic, memorable, and believable speaks, as it were, to the ears for dialogue that the writing staff possesses. In striving for authenticity and realism, Simon's goal through his show is for "a homicide detective, or a drug slinger, or a longshoreman, or a politician anywhere in America to sit up and say, 'Whoa, that's how my day is'" (qtd. in Hornby 77).

The incorporation—and purposeful exclusion—of sound is also an important element in the show's production. Unless it explicitly appears in a class dedicated to audio production, how television programs and films record, manipulate, and incorporate sound is largely ignored in the college classroom. In my class, we examined how the series used music and sound to contribute to the stories. For example, save for each season's closing montage, *The Wire* does not include nondiegetic music. Rather, the only music that plays in each episode, in addition to the opening and closing credits' theme songs, comes from the characters playing it—for instance, in their cars, at work, or in a club. Furthermore, no musical score guides the viewer's emotions. One of the series' most suspenseful moments is achieved without the aid of music. When Detective Greggs is shot in the above-mentioned buy-and-bust operation, the subsequent moments when her fellow officers struggle to find her car is riddled with palpable confusion, tension, and anxiety, all of which were created by a carefully constructed montage of sound effects (approaching cars, wailing sirens, screaming officers, a hovering helicopter) and facial expressions of dread and concern. In class, we identified each of these elements and discussed how they were edited together to produce these emotions.

Simon's "standard for verisimilitude" (qtd. in Hornby 76) applies to visual codes as well. In calling *The Wire* "social science-fiction," Ruth Penfold-Mounce, David Beer, and Roger Burrows suggest "a sense of the authentic is achieved ... [through] lighting, sound, setting and scenery, language, props"

(158). The series was filmed in and around Baltimore. Despite building the soundstage and offices for the last two seasons in Columbia, a wealthy nearby suburb, keeping the show on location supported the claim that Baltimore was a major character and the appropriate backdrop for this gritty series.[9] Simon said, "People ask me who I loved writing for the most and I always tell them, the city of Baltimore. And that's totally true. I've never said anything more honest about the show" (qtd. in Egner).

To match Simon's writing approach with a visual aesthetic that depicts the "city as character," the show employed an "unusual emphasis on wide shots, in which groups of human figures merge with their environment" (Tyree 36). Furthermore, with most of their master shots in motion, via tracks or dollies, *The Wire* used long lenses and moving shots to match one of the show's overarching themes and produce what one of its directors, Joe Chappelle, called "that sense of constant surveillance, of eavesdropping" (qtd. in Griffin).

The authenticity of the mise en scène for which Simon and his cast and crew strived is also achieved through the show's scenery and props. For instance, when the show moved its season-long focus to the media, the art and construction departments recreated the *Baltimore Sun*'s newsroom on the soundstage by using the same carpeting from rooms the actual newspaper no longer used. When I visited the set during filming of the fourth season, producer Laura Schweigman, who was Simon's assistant at the time, pointed out how the trash cans in the police department were lined with items that actual Baltimore police would use (e.g., certain brand-name products) and how the vending machines (not functional, though) featured snacks that would be found in the Baltimore Police Department. In addition, the cubicles from the Homicide Unit's office would be dressed to match the holiday season in the show's diegesis. No matter if they ever intended to shoot inside the trash can or offer a close-up of the desk, the set designers filled those receptacles with crumpled coffee cups and filled out Christmas cards that a homicide detective *would* hang up at his cubicle (Schweigman, personal interview). Despite this meticulous attention from story and dialogue to scenery and props, *The Wire*'s aesthetics tend to be "conventional," at least according to Mittell, who notes the show's "objective narration" (i.e., no voice-overs) and refusal to incorporate "flashbacks, voice-overs, fantasy sequences" ("*The Wire*"; "All in the Game"). The only flashback in the series' sixty hours appears at the end of the first episode, when the viewer is reminded that the murder victim was seen earlier testifying against D'Angelo Barksdale, who was on trial for murder. After Detective Moreland rolls over William Gant, the viewer sees the victim's face and hears the officer identify him, followed by the flashback to Gant nervously testifying (1.1).

In every class in which I have used *The Wire,* ranging from the dedicated class on the series to a topical HBO course to a television history survey course, after we watch the first episode together, I ask students if they needed the flashback to remind them who the murder victim was. Invariably, about half of them raise their hands, prompting a discussion about the various codes that inform the viewer that the victim was, in fact, the man who had testified at D'Angelo's trial, all of which could (and, to some students, *should*) have obviated the need for the flashback: a police officer informing the homicide detective of the victim's name and age, the nametag on his work uniform that reads "W. Gant," and Gant's distinguishable facial hair.

HBO executives insisted Simon include this flashback to jog viewers' memories of what took place fifty-five minutes prior. Simon joked that he should have said to HBO, "Brother, if you think you need a flashback here, you're gonna need 17 flashbacks an episode, 'cuz nobody's gonna follow this fuckin' show." He called the flashback a "visual affront" and "an interesting artifact of somebody seeking an old TV remedy to try to fix something that they thought was wrong with a new TV show" (Simon, personal interview). Simon listened to his executive producer Robert Colesberry, a film veteran, who advised him to concede this battle.

Through such examples, students in television and film programs learn about the contentious relationships between creators and network/studio executives, the histories of these visual artifacts, and how to produce meaningful content within them. Regardless of whether a student pursues a career in pre-production, production, or post-production, filmmaking classes serve as critical foundations for understanding better how these works are made. Learning how a show like *The Wire* was written, shot, produced, and edited in the context of its distribution provides an important backdrop for a student.

Reception

In addition to production and distribution, the third prong I deemed essential for my class to achieve a fundamental understanding of *The Wire* as a work of television looked at how the series was consumed (received *and* interpreted)—by the medium's arbiters of taste, the industry, and its fans. The disconnect among these pockets of viewers epitomizes today's niche programming in which critical consensus is impossible to reach.

Television criticism represents more than employing a zero- to four-star rating system for a program, offering its highlights, or telling a reader or viewer (not) to watch it; critics cover industrial trends and patterns as well. Television scholar Amanda Lotz, who has written extensively on the field, adds, "Understanding how critics and audiences talk about television informs our perspective of what 'television' is, which is particularly important during periods of profound institutional change" ("Seventeen" 23). We are in the midst of such change, as streaming straight-to-series programs (Rose), "zero TV" homes and "cord-cutters" (Nakashima), and second-screen viewing (Bauder) have become common practices well after *The Wire* concluded. When I taught my class, though, the industry was experiencing its own changes: a writers' strike, a proliferation of new programming outlets, and the emergence of the dilemma of how to monetize social media. During both of these transformative times, TV critics have been especially needed to help viewers navigate the landscape and keep them apprised of technological, industrial, regulatory, and cultural developments.

In cultivating its premium status, HBO for years has used popular criticism as a way to reach its fans, validate its offerings, and increase its "cultural value." Anderson writes, "By drawing attention to the aesthetic claims of TV critics, HBO has contributed a measure of legitimacy and cultural authority to those who would speak about television series as works of art" (38). As mentioned earlier, this legitimacy better serves HBO's economic model than merely airing a show that earns high ratings.

The Wire earned much critical praise while it was on the air; in its afterlife, though, more academics and scholars have taken to teaching and researching it. However, the volume of praise the show received overall belies the critical responses to its first and last seasons. The *New York Post*'s Adam Buckman, who "was a different person" before binging through the fourth season, wrote in 2002 that the first season "looks and feels like an ordinary show from some other network that snuck on to the air while the HBO execs' backs were turned" (para 14). David Bianculli, then of the *New York Daily News,* wrote the show "seems to take the real-time aspect of [FOX's] *24* and reduce it to slow motion." He continued, "When it comes down to *The Wire,* this show falls short" (para 10).

Some of my students had similar reactions, finding the series' pacing slow. My task as instructor was not to correct them, agree with them, or mitigate their concerns, but rather to give them an outlet to express their views. One particular pedagogical challenge I found was tempering the fanaticism that many students exhibited: ranging from effusively praising the series and wearing to class a t-shirt featuring Omar's face to offering perspectives of why they did not like the show. In the latter, at least two students regularly apologized to me—privately and aloud in class—for disliking *The Wire*, citing its slow pace and its perpetuation of African American stereotypes. I enjoyed these contrarian views and cultivated a classroom environment that encouraged students to feel comfortable disagreeing with each other without resorting to ad hominem attacks or taking offense to criticisms of a show with which some were obsessed. Nevertheless, it was a challenge for both my students and me to include those perspectives.

Simon's relationship with fans and television critics, another topic we examined in class, has often been contentious. Perceptions of the first season were less than favorable, in large part due to its pacing coupled with critics—having received only a few screener episodes from HBO—who might have been unfamiliar and/or not in favor of Simon's novelistic approach. Bianculli gave the show a 2.5-star (out of 4) rating and found that the show improved over the course of the season. In reference to the plot line in which Greggs was shot, he wrote, "It took until just a few episodes ago, in fact, when one of the officers was unexpectedly ambushed and shot, that it really took hold" ("Home Box"). Of the many critics whose opinions changed, Simon said, "I would think to myself, 'It's going at the same speed.... You're now getting the rewards of the accumulation of plot and detail and character'" (Simon, personal interview).

Critics lambasted the show's final season, which examined how the media have ignored the issues that have plagued Baltimore. *USA Today*'s Robert Bianco, who previously championed *The Wire*, called the stories of *The Sun* "the series' weakest and worst-acted subplot" and concluded that the show "simply went on too long." David Zurawik, the actual *Sun*'s TV critic, characterized the newsroom scenes as the season's "Achilles' heel" ("*The Wire* Loses"). One week after the show ran its last episode, Simon posted an essay, or what one critic called "an ill-advised kiss-off" (Goodman), in which he castigated critics for their misinterpretations of the final season. He wrote, "[E]veryone stayed dead-center and literal, oblivious to the big-ass elephant in our mythical newsroom" (Simon, "*The Wire*'s Final"). Simon wondered how they could "studiously avoid any sustained discussion about whether the depicted newspaper is, in all respects, capturing the meaningful narrative of the depicted city" ("*The Wire*'s Final").[10] Having journalism students in our classroom—two of whom created their own blog about television—enabled us to have a more informed discussion about this disagreement between TV critics and a former reporter.

A few years later, Simon found himself at loggerheads with critics and fans. After being asked about a bracket posted on a popular culture and sports blog that resembled the annual college basketball tournament, in which characters from the show squared off against each other as fans determined who was the greatest, he again criticized viewer interpretations and expressed his dissatisfaction with latecomers to the show who were only admiring characters' coolness. Simon added, "That this stuff singularly crowds out any continued discussion of our real problems and the show's interest in arguing those problems is the disappointing part" (qtd. in Sepinwall).

He also criticized the popular recaps that professional and amateur TV critics write after each episode, finding their criticisms to be premature and incomplete. Simon advised, "Nobody knows what anyone's building until it's built" (qtd. in Egner). He expressed his desire to see an episode's merits and faults be dissected after the season concludes so that the viewer has a complete picture of what the show tried to achieve, adding, "You would never see anyone review a novel in similar fashion. No one would read three chapters of a novel and go, 'What so and so's trying to say here'" (qtd. in Sepinwall). A course on *The Wire* offered today, i.e., after its conclusion, would have to incorporate Simon's relationship with critics, as it sheds light on an important component of the show's history as well as the distance between fans and creators, and fans and critics, that social media has enabled to shrink. Studying audience reception need not target only the average viewer; professional and amateur (re)viewers, i.e., television critics, deserve scholastic attention as well, something to which we invested a full week in my class.

Despite the lavish, sometimes excessive, critical praise piled on *The Wire*, which often bolsters students' own fervor, the series never managed to win any Emmys, the industry's most recognizable award for television excellence. Having earned only two writing nominations, *The Wire* represents one of, what I call, today's "critic-adored, award-ignored" series, which puzzles many students who cite a show's successful Emmy record to validate their passion for their favorites and who in class then learn how to explain the evident disconnect between cultural arbiters and industry insiders.

Many reasons might explain why *The Wire* was consistently shut out by the Academy of Television Arts & Sciences. First, its enormous ensemble cast, featuring more than 80 regular and recurring characters across all five seasons, comprised mostly actors of color ("HBO: *The Wire*"). Despite his claim that the show has "precious little to do with race," Simon suggested that race could have been a reason for the show's low ratings; that is, viewers—including Emmy voters—were not used to seeing that many faces of color on their TV screens and therefore changed the channel when *The Wire* came on ("Exclusive David

Simon Q&A3"; "Talking with"). Another reason is the "geographic bias," wrote Emmy historian Tom O'Neil, in which the show, filmed and set in Baltimore, might have been penalized for being produced outside of entertainment capitals New York City and Los Angeles (qtd. in Zurawik, "From HBO").

Third, a paucity of entry points into the expansive "visual novel" might explain why it was continuously snubbed. Emmy voters who missed the first season might not have understood stories from subsequent seasons in spite of the cast's powerful performances. Ultimately, the simplest explanation might be *The Wire*'s low viewership numbers. Ratings continued to decrease over its five seasons; a larger audience might have increased buzz as well as the Academy's awareness. In his article on surveillance and spectacle in the show, media scholar Joseph Christopher Schaub writes, "This inverse relationship between *The Wire*'s stellar reviews and marginal audience was just one of many contradictions that made the series unique" (122). Simon responded to the Emmy oversight defiantly: "I don't give a fuck if we ever win one of their little trinkets.... Secretly, we all know we get more ink for being shut out. So at this point, we *wanna* be shut out" (qtd. in Gordon). His antipathy towards awards was made clear in the show's fifth season, when he developed Pulitzer Prize-hungry characters at *The Sun*.

The Wire was not completely ignored by industry tastemakers, however, winning a prestigious Peabody Award in 2004, which annually recognizes excellence in television and radio broadcasting. The show won a Writers Guild of America Award for Dramatic Series in 2007 and appeared on the American Film Institute's list of top TV programs of 2006. Furthermore, in 2008, it earned the Television Critics Association's Heritage Award, which recognizes a "long-standing program that has had a lasting cultural or social impact" ("AMC Scores"). The paradox, of course, is that the series made little impact while it was on the air.

Conclusion

The Wire is being studied inside and outside the classroom more now than when it was on the air. Such is the life—or, afterlife—of a niche series in today's fragmented television culture. Not surprisingly, considering the substantial space that has been devoted to the social and political implications of Simon's fictional world, a conspicuous gap in the classroom conversations surrounding *The Wire* has emerged. The "enabling conditions" (Rogers et al. 43) along with the "industrial, technological, and aesthetic contexts" (Mittell "*The*

Wire in") that made the show possible and that have contributed to its popular and critical acclaim have been largely ignored in favor of examining questions of social inequality that the series has provoked. This does not mean, though, that those social issues do not deserve that level of attention or that foregrounding *The Wire* "as television" would minimize the show's relevance or cultural impact. If today's students and tomorrow's storytellers—filmmakers, TV producers, journalists—wish to illuminate other pressing areas of social inequality by emulating "surely the greatest TV show ever broadcast in America," they will need to have a strong grasp of how this exemplar was written, designed, shot, acted, recorded, edited, distributed, consumed, and interpreted.

Mittell suggests, "[W]e should view *The Wire* using the lens of its actual medium of television to best understand and appreciate its achievements and importance" ("All in the Game"). It would not bode well for the future of television if we judge its best work only thematically; we would be resigned to share Baltimore Police Major "Bunny" Colvin's incredulity after learning that his collaboration with a local sociology professor might culminate in something that only other academics would find interesting: "What, they gonna study your study? When do this shit change ..." (4.13).

Notes

1. Jason Mittell has "outline[d] the specific industrial, technological, and aesthetic contexts of television that helped shape *The Wire*, and enabled it to make it to commercial television in the first place" ("Narrative"); Linda Williams ("Mega-melodrama"; "*The Wire*") has redefined the term melodrama through *The Wire*; Marsha Kinder has examined how the seriality of *The Wire* enabled its "systemic analysis of urban corruption" (50); and Joseph Christopher Schaub has positioned the show as a "dramatic alternative to reality TV" (129).

2. "Buzz," according to television scholar Amanda Lotz, is "discussion, excitement, or interest in the network" ("Promotional" 7).

3. See Derek Kompare's article that examines how DVDs "reconceived" the relationship between television series and its viewers.

4. In the spring of 2014, HBO joined forces with Amazon Prime to stream its older and recent content to Prime members at no additional cost (Hibberd, "HBO Makes").

5. Ratings are percentages of households with television, for instance, watching a particular program, and shares are percentages of households using television during that time tuned to a particular program.

6. Simon made it clear, though, that his show wasn't taking a leaf out of Dickens's novels, despite how both used bleak stories to examine social inequalities and poor work conditions. Instead, he and his writers borrowed from Greek tragedians such as Euripides, Aeschylus, and Sophocles. See Mark Chou's analysis of *The Wire* as a contemporary Greek tragedy.

7. See Rabia Belt's article on disability in *The Wire*, which addresses the implications of how the show mostly ignores Greggs's suffering, recovery, rehabilitation, and caretaking.

8. The network subtly substituted "life" for "killing" because it sounded more positive.

9. *The Wire* was not the first HBO series whose location served as a character: *Sex and*

the City (1998–2004), *The Sopranos* (1999–2007), and *Six Feet Under* (2001–2005) had already done so.

10. *Time*'s TV critic James Poniewozik's response featured the humorously alliterative meta-headline: "David Simon Criticizes Critics' Critique of *The Wire*'s Critique."

Works Cited

"All Prologue." *The Wire*. HBO. 6 July 2003. Television.
"AMC Scores First-ever TCA Awards with Top Honors." TVCriticsAssociation.com. Television Critics Association, 19 July 2008. Web.
Anderson, Christopher. "Producing an Aristocracy of Culture in American Television." *The Essential HBO Reader*. Eds. Gary R. Edgerton and Jeffrey P. Jones. Lexington: University Press of Kentucky, 2008, 23–41. Print.
Aspden, Peter. "It's TV, But Not as We Knew It." *Financial Times*. 23 Sept. 2011. Web.
Bauder, David. "Study Shows Growth in Second Screen Users." *Associated Press*. 12 Dec. 2012. Web.
Belt, Rabia. "'And Then Comes Life': The Intersection of Race, Poverty, and Disability in HBO's *The Wire*." *Rutgers Race & the Law Review* 13 (2011): 1–28. Print.
Bianco, Robert. "Too Few Were Plugged In, But HBO's *The Wire* Was Electric." *USA Today*. 5 March 2008. Web.
Bianculli, David. "HBO Show Arrives Under *The Wire*—Baltimore Crime Drama Suffers by Comparison." *New York Daily News*. 29 May 2002. Web.
———. "Home Box Score for 3 Series." *New York Daily News*. 5 Sept. 2002. Web.
Buckman, Adam. "No Way to Treat a Town." *New York Post*. 31 May 2002. Web.
———. "Re-*Wired*." *New York Post*. 25 Aug. 2006. Web.
Chou, Mark. "'We Like Them Bitches on the Chessboard': Tragedy, Politics, and *The Wire*." *CTheory*, 20 Jan. 2011. Web.
Egner, Jeremy. "The Game Never Ends: David Simon on Wearying *Wire* Love and the Surprising Usefulness of Twitter." *New York Times*. 5 April 2012. Web.
"Exclusive David Simon Q&A." Borderline-productions.com. Borderline Productions, 2006. Web. 9 Nov. 2008.
"Exclusive David Simon Q&A3." Borderline-productions.com. Borderline Productions, 2006. Web. 9 Nov. 2008.
"Final Grades." *The Wire*. HBO. 10 Sept. 2006. Television.
Goodman, Tim. "*The Wire*." *San Francisco Chronicle*. 26 March 2008. Web.
Gordon, Devin. "Good Mourning, Baltimore." Newsweek.com. 5 Jan. 2008. Web.
Hanson, Christopher. "Some Last Words on *The Wire*." *Film Quarterly* 62.2 (Winter 2008–09): 66–7. Print.
"HBO: *The Wire*: Cast and Crew." HBO.com, n.d. Web. 24 March 2014.
Heffernan, Virginia. "Higher Learning in the Drug Trade for Four Baltimore Students." *New York Times*. 9 Sept. 2006. Web.
Hibberd, James. "*Breaking Bad* Series Finale Ratings Smash All Records." *Entertainment Weekly*. 30 Sept. 2013. Web.
———. "HBO Makes Huge Amazon Prime Deal: See Which Shows Are Going Online." *Entertainment Weekly*. 23 April 2014. Web.
Hornby, Nick. "David Simon (Interview)." *The Believer* 5.6 (August 2007): 70–8. Print.
Jaramillo, Deborah. "The Family Racket: AOL Time Warner, HBO, *The Sopranos*, and the Construction of a Quality Brand." *Journal of Communication Inquiry* 26.1 (2002): 59–75. Print.
Kelly, Lisa W. "Casting *The Wire*: Complicating Notions of Performance, Authenticity, and 'Otherness.'" *darkmatter* (May 2009). Web.

Kinder, Marsha. "Re-wiring Baltimore: The Emotive Power of Systemics, Seriality, and the City." *Film Quarterly* 62.2 (Winter 2008–09): 50–7. Print.

Kompare, Derek. "Publishing Flow: DVD Box Sets and the Reconception of Television." *Television and New Media* 7.4 (2006): 335–60. Print.

Koo, Ben. "*The Wire* Never Got to Thrive Like *Breaking Bad*." *Bloguin.com*. 18 Dec. 2013. Web. 23 June 2014.

Lageson, Sarah, Kyle Green, and Sinan Erensu. "*The Wire* Goes to College." *Contexts*, 19.3 (Summer 2011): 12–5. Print.

Lotz, Amanda. "The Promotional Role of the Network Upfront Presentations on the Production of Culture." *Television & New Media* 8.1 (2007): 3–24. Print.

_____. "Seventeen Days in July at Hollywood and Highland: Examining the Television Critics Association Tour." *Journal of Popular Film & Television*, 33.1 (Spring 2005): 22–8. Print.

Martin, Denise. "HBO's Down with *Wire*." *Variety*. 17 Sept. 2006. Web.

Mittell, Jason. "All in the Game: *The Wire*, Serial Storytelling, and Procedural Logic." *Electronic Book Review*, 18 March 2011. Web.

_____."Narrative Complexity in Contemporary American Television." *The Velvet Light Trap* 58 (Fall 2006): 29–40. Print.

_____. "*The Wire* in the Context of American Television." *MediaCommons*. 9 Feb. 2010. Web.

Nakashima, Ryan. "Broadcasters Worry about 'Zero TV' Homes." *Associated Press*. 7 April 2013. Web.

Newcomb, Horace. "'This Is Not Al Dente': *The Sopranos* and the New Meaning of 'Television.'" *Television: The Critical View (7th Edition)*. Ed. Horace Newcomb. New York: Oxford University Press, 2007, 561–78. Print.

O'Neil, Tom. "Mystery Solved: Why So Much Emmy Hate?" LATimes.com 29 Aug. 2006. Web.

O'Sullivan, Sean. "Old, New, Borrowed, Blue: *Deadwood* and Serial Fiction." *Reading Deadwood: A Western to Swear By*. Ed. David Lavery. London: I.B. Tauris, 2006, 115–29. Print.

Penfold-Mounce, Ruth, David Beer, and Roger Burrows. "*The Wire* as Social Science-Fiction?" *Sociology* 45 (2011): 152–67. Print.

Poniewozik, Jamie. David Simon Criticizes Critics' Critique of *The Wire*'s Critique. Time.com. 18 March 2008. Web.

Rogers, Mark C., Michael Epstein, and Jimmie L. Reeves. "*The Sopranos* as HBO Brand Equity: The Art of Commerce in the Age of Digital Reproduction." *This Thing of Ours: Investigating* The Sopranos. Ed. David Lavery. New York: Columbia University Press, 2002, 42–57. Print.

Rose, Lacey. "Pilot Season: 4 Hot Trends for 2014." *The Hollywood Reporter*. 28 Feb. 2014, 91. Print.

Schaub, Joseph Christopher. "*The Wire:* Big Brother Is Not Watching You in Body-More, Murdaland." *Journal of Popular Film & Television*, 38.3 (2010), 122–32. Print.

Schweigman, Laura. Personal interview. 20 Oct. 2005.

"Sentencing." *The Wire*. HBO. 8 Sept. 2002. Television.

Sepinwall, Alan. "Interview: David Simon Doesn't Want to Tell You How to Watch *The Wire*." Hitfix.com. 6 Apr. 2012. Web.

Simon, David. Personal interview. 20 Oct. 2005.

_____. "*The Wire*'s Final Season and the Story Everyone Missed." *The Huffington Post*. 17 March 2008. Web.

Sodano, Todd. "All the Pieces Matter: A Critical Analysis of HBO's *The Wire*." Diss. Syracuse University, 2008. Web.

_____. "TRF 530.3 Inside HBO's America: A Case Study of *The Wire* Course Syllabus." Syracuse: Syracuse University. Slate.com. 31 March 2010. Web.

"Talking with the Creator of One of the TV's Best and Smartest Shows." *Rolling Stone*. 25 Sept. 2006. Web.

"The Target." *The Wire.* HBO. 2 June 2002. Television.
Tyree, J.M. "*The Wire:* The Complete Fourth Season." *Film Quarterly* 62.2 (Winter 2008–09), 32–8. Print.
"Unconfirmed Reports." *The Wire.* HBO. 13 Jan. 2008. Television.
Weisberg, Jacob. "*The Wire* on Fire." Slate.com. 13 Sept. 2006. Web.
Williams, Linda. "Mega-melodrama! Vertical and Horizontal Suspensions of the 'Classical.'" *Modern Drama* 55.4 (Winter 2012): 523–43. Print.
_____. "*The Wire:* Realistic, Modern Social Melodrama." *Débordements.* 8 March 2014. Web.
"*The Wire.*" Wikipedia.com. n.d. Web. 1 April 2014.
Zurawik, David. "David Simon Has Novel Ideas about *Wire.*" BaltimoreSun.com. 10 Sept. 2006. Web.
_____. "From HBO to AMC, Cable TV Is Mobbed with Emmy Nods." BaltimoreSun.com. 20 July 2007. Web.
_____. "*The Wire* Loses Spark in Newsroom Storyline." BaltimoreSun.com. 30 Dec. 2007. Web.

The Angriest Auteur on Television
Teaching Media Authorship Through David Simon

Alex M. Kupfer

The characterization that contemporary television is in the midst of (yet another) "Golden Age" has been a prevalent trope among critics, academics, and fans for a number of years now. Discussions of "quality" shows such as *The Sopranos, Mad Men, Breaking Bad, Friday Night Lights,* and *The Wire* often celebrate their narrative and aesthetic achievements through hailing the unique creative vision of their creators which permeates every aspect of the production and guides the interpretation of the text. The interest in these creators, however, is not a recent phenomenon, and stems from what Derek Johnson and Jonathan Gray characterize as an enduring cultural fascination with the author and the super powers ascribed to them. As they explain, "The author is thus imagined to stand at the gateway and threshold between creativity, innovation, wonder, and magic, and us" (2). Within media studies, this romantic conception of the singular genius writer/ producer formed the basis for auteur theory. Focusing on the Hollywood studio system and European art cinemas, advocates of the theory distinguished the auteur from ordinary directors. Critics contended that even though commercial movie-making was an industrial process, motion pictures could still serve as a vehicle for artistic expression and a way to articulate a specific worldview. Authorial identity continues to be a central means through which we interpret movies and television shows. For instance, authors help audiences and critics establish a set of expectations about what a film or show will be like even before it is released. Authors are used for commercial purposes as well, and are often highlighted in print and television advertisements to bring in people familiar with their previous work. Critics and fans of the recent wave of "quality" television dramas continue to evoke this type of authorial figure to legitimate the genre and the medium as a whole.

In this new "Golden Age" no show has been as critically praised or received as much attention from academics as HBO's *The Wire*. The admiration for the show has both benefitted from and led to an increased focus on David Simon, one of the show's co-creators (along with Ed Burns), its head writer, and show runner for all five seasons. Through being elevated to the status of "auteur" Simon has been discursively framed as the authority which grants legitimacy and distinction to *The Wire* while also guiding readers in interpreting meaning from the text. In other words, across hundreds of characters, sixty episodes, and five seasons, viewers relied on Simon's authorial identity to make sense of the show's narrative, complex characterizations, and its specific socio-political argument. Simon (or as I will discuss later, the discursive construction "David Simon") accomplishes this by trying to limit the possible meanings viewers can take away from the show through articulating and rearticulating *The Wire*'s critique of neoliberalism and the damage it has caused to a wide range of civic institutions and the citizens they are supposed to serve. Using a course on *The Wire* that I taught in the Cinema Studies department at New York University in Fall 2012 as a case study, this essay explores how David Simon and the show can be used in undergraduate media studies classrooms to examine and problematize theories of authorship in film and television studies to interrogate how cultural production is conceptualized and invested with meaning. *The Wire* serves as an ideal vehicle to examine this topic because Simon represents the complexities in trying to assign title of "author" to an individual working in a collaborative medium like television.

Throughout my course on *The Wire*, students engaged with the ways that discourses of professional authority and notions of authenticity stemming from Simon's background were critical in legitimating the show's socio-economic arguments. Specifically, his portrait of the criminal justice system and the devastation caused by Baltimore's drug trade is based on his experiences working as a reporter for *The Baltimore Sun* from 1982 to 1995 and writing the nonfiction books *Homicide: Life on the Streets* (1991) and *The Corner: A Year in the Life of an Inner-City Neighborhood* (1997, co-written with Ed Burns). *The Wire* adapted numerous events and characters from Simon's writing days, giving a sense of authenticity to the show's narrative. For example, we watched the first episode of season five, "More With Less," in which Bunk, Detective Norris (played by former Baltimore Police Commissioner Ed Norris) and Jay Landsman interrogate a murder suspect by pretending a photocopier is actually a polygraph machine and pre-loading pieces with the words "true," "true," and "false" printed on them. The tactic is taken directly from the pages of Simon's book *Homicide*. For Baltimore detectives, "polygraph by copier was an old trick; it had been attempted on more than one occasion in the sixth-floor Xerox room" (204). And just as in the book, in *The Wire* after asking the suspect his name and address and having the copier "respond" with the word "true," when the suspect's denial is met with the "false" response, he confesses to the murder.

Homicide opened the door for Simon to leave his newspaper career and move into television when it was adapted into a weekly police drama for NBC by noted film director and Baltimore native Barry Levinson. Simon served as a producer and writer for the show which ran from 1993 to 1999. However, unhappy with the way that NBC handled *Homicide*—particularly the network's insistence on neat endings at the conclusion of episodes—Simon and David Mills turned *The Corner* into a six-part miniseries on HBO in 2000. Many cast and crew members who appeared in *The Corner* would also later work on *The Wire*, including producers Robert F. Colesberry and Nina Kostroff Noble as well as actors like Clarke Peters, Lance Reddick, Corey Parker Robinson, and Reg Cathay. To examine stylistic and thematic consistency in Simon's television projects, the class watched the first two episodes of *The Corner*. Selections from the *Homicide* book as well as newspaper articles written by Simon were assigned to give students a background for a discussion of authorship.

Students should be cautioned that authorship of media texts can be attributed to a wide range of individuals and groups who contribute to the creative work involved in the production of movies and television. Just in the context of the classic Hollywood studio system, the term auteur has been used to describe the work of writers, composers, stars, cinematographers, and studio moguls. However, the author concept has been most frequently associated with directors. I discussed in lectures how in the 1950s and 1960s French critics associated with the journal *Cahiers du Cinéma* (including André Bazin, François Truffaut, Jean-Luc Godard, and Claude Chabrol) and American critics such as Andrew Sarris and Peter Bogdanovich argued that the director was the central source of a film's meaning and the individual responsible for its artistic content. The politique des auteurs, or auteur theory, posited that select filmmakers, whether working in international art cinemas or the Hollywood studio system, expressed a unique personal vision or worldview through a film's mise en scène in the same manner that the most highly regarded artists do. Despite efforts to attribute authorship in a manner that more accurately reflects how movies and television are collaboratively produced, the assigning of auteur status to the director continues to remain the norm.

To further historicize the development of auteur theory, course readings and lectures emphasized how the exaltation of the director as author was also closely linked to notions of art and quality. Auteurism served a more practical disciplinary function, legitimizing film studies as the study of art and meaning, not just popular (or "lowbrow") culture. As Gilles Deleuze declared, "The great auteurs of the cinema may be compared, in our view, not merely with painters, architects, and musicians, but also with thinkers. They think with movement-images and time-images instead of concepts" (xiv). Television scholars have similarly relied on the figure of the auteur—applied though to show creators (or showrunners) rather than directors—to legitimate specific shows or even the medium as a whole as a subject worthy of scholarly consideration by comparing notable figures to highly regarded artists. As students saw in a number of readings across the semester, in the case of *The Wire*, David Simon is frequently likened to great novelists or esteemed movie directors. For instance, Garry Watson compares David Simon to writers T.S. Eliot and D.H. Lawrence and filmmaker Jean-Luc Godard. Watson places them together based on the similar effect their work has on the reader/spectator, explaining that they belong "to a select band of artists whose work changes one's sense of what is possible.... After full exposure to the work of artists like these, the world looks and in some sense *is* different" (34).

A key component of Simon's authorial person has been his "outsider" status in the newspaper and later the television industries. This conception of Simon recalls how directors elevated to the status of auteurs were often romanticized as lone individuals fighting the corporate Hollywood Studio system. As Dana Polan explains, traditional auteurist premises frequently adhere to "dialectics of freedom and constraint in the Hollywood system" ("Auteur Desire"). Students read a chapter from *The Genius of the System: Hollywood Filmmaking in the Studio Era* in which film historian Thomas Schatz similarly celebrates the individual artist's ability to produce expressive works despite institutional control, with the authorial voice coming out of this dialectic. Schatz explains that the author-artists were those individuals "whose personal style emerged from a certain antagonism toward the studio system at large-the dehumanizing, formulaic, profit-hungry machinery of Hollywood's studio-factories" (91). In other words, auteurs were able to flourish in spite of the constraints imposed by the commercial imperatives of the studio system because they were able to integrate their personal style into each film despite the industrialized mode of production.

Class discussions of Simon's authorial status were used to examine the extent to which this dialectic of freedom and constraint continues to define the relationship between individuals and media companies. Students were assigned multiple readings on *The Wire* from both popular and academic sources which highlighted this dialectic in action. Simon was often characterized as "the angriest man on television" (to borrow the title of a profile from *The Atlantic*) who took on the media industries to deliver his critique of neoliberalism and nuanced analysis of institutions and individuals not found anywhere else on television. Efforts to define Simon's "worldview" often highlight his reporting career to examine how Simon mined his articles from the *Baltimore Sun* for *The Wire* as well as how the dialectics of freedom and constraint at the newspaper shaped his later work. The most notable article students read was his 1995 piece "The Metal Men." The article is a detailed portrait of metal salvagers and the effect of their illicit vocation on already depressed parts of the city. Students recognized many similarities between Simon's article and the show. *The Sun* piece paints a bleak picture of Baltimore and those struggling within it: "Now, a good afternoon's work can be dragging a pair of 250-pound radiators for 12 blocks in the hot summer sun. But still, that's $10. And $10 will get you a vial of heroin and a cap of cocaine to go on top. The ants are here; the picnic is us" (Simon "The Metal Men"). The salvaging (or stealing) of scrap metal becomes a vital source of income to purchase drugs for Bubbles—albeit one which despite its illegality involves an incredible amount of labor. Readers will also recognize a similar structure between the article and *The Wire*. Both utilize a complex narrative involving numerous institutions and stakeholders who cannot be neatly placed into a good/evil binary and address systemic urban problems lacking easy solutions. In "The Metal Men" Simon addresses the concerns of the metal men Tyrone and Kenny as well as Gary (who was one of the protagonists of *The Corner*), nonprofit workers, housing authority engineers, scrap yard owners and executives, and Baltimore detectives.

Students were asked to think about the role "The Metal Men" played in shaping Simon's relationship to the press and his understanding of the media as an institution—a topic which would become the central concern of *The Wire*'s fifth season. Students read an article by film scholar Linda Williams, who argues that "The Metal Men" is a "late and decisive" work in Simon's career since it led to a fight with his editors which resulted in him quitting journalism and moving into television (220). One of Simon's editors at *The Sun*, John Carroll, was concerned that the piece was too similar to his work on *The Corner*, particularly since the figure of Gary appears in both. Another editor, Bill Marimow, felt that the story glorified thieves who were destroying the infrastructure of the city. Simon not surprisingly disagreed with their assessment and interpreted their concerns as deriving from the indifferent logic of Wall Street and the award culture that had taken over newsrooms like *The Sun*. He viewed the approach of Carroll and Marimow at *The Sun* as a formula for winning Pulitzer Prizes. As Simon explained, they would "[s]urround a simple outrage, overreport it, claim credit for breaking it, make sure you find a villain, then claim you effected change as a result of your coverage. Do it in a five-part series, and make sure you get 'the Baltimore Sun has learned' in the second graph" (qtd. in Lanahan 26). Ultimately, Simon found the constraints of the newspaper industry to be too much of an impediment to the stories he wanted to tell and decided to continue his work in a new industry and new media platform.

Simon's anger and frustration with his beloved newspaper industry also provided a means of examining in class how the emotions and opinions of authors are inscribed into film and television narratives. We screened a number of episodes from season five which were set in a fictionalized *Baltimore Sun* newsroom. Discussions focused on the relationship between the themes of that season stemming from Simon's own experiences and his concerns about the shortcomings of outlets like *The Sun*. These included the failure of the newspaper to report on news of consequence such as Omar's death and ignoring events like the discovery of bodies in the row houses unless it could be reported on from a sensationalized and sexualized angle. The season also critiqued the paper's overriding interest in winning prizes through the character of Scott Templeton, an ambitious general assignments reporter who begins falsifying information for stories which will impress the ranking editors. Despite concerns raised about his work by his colleague Alma Gutierrez and City Desk Editor Gus Haynes, since Templeton has the support of Executive Editor James Whiting and Managing Editor Thomas Klebanow he is able to continue writing in the way that he sees fit. Perhaps evoking a sense of fatalism that Simon felt about his own newspaper career, ultimately, both Gutierrez and Haynes are demoted for challenging Templeton's claims. Templeton even wins a Pulitzer Prize for his flawed reporting on the homeless in Baltimore—with Whiting and Klebanow standing right next to him on stage as he proudly accepts his award.

The narratives involving the fictionalized *Sun* were linked to Simon's own experiences and frustrations with his editors and the current state of the newspaper industry. The cast of season five was partially a reflection of his time at the newspaper, as twenty former employees were cast in small parts in the newsroom, with many such as Bill Zorzi "playing" themselves. Yet, many critics (and students) felt that this season was too heavily determined by Simon's "excessive" authorial presence. They contended that his anger negatively affected the way the season unfolded as too many character were portrayed as wholly virtuous (Alma, Gus, Mike Fletcher) or villainous (Templeton, Klebanow, and Whiting), a departure from the nuanced characterizations of previous seasons. Students read articles by Lawrence Lanahan in *Columbia Journalism Review* and Mark Bowden in *The Atlantic* that framed Simon as a vengeful figure who used television as a platform to openly attack the former editors at the *Baltimore Sun* who he felt wronged him and helped bring down one of the great icons of American journalism. For these critics, Simon's excessive authority over the text becomes a distraction and hampers the qualities of the series which made it so exceptional in the first place.

Lanahan and Bowden each reference the minor character Lieutenant Marimow (played by Boris McGver), who appears in six episodes in season four. The fictional Marimow, who was named after one of Simon's former editors at *The Sun*, is installed as the commander of the Major Crimes Unit by Bill Rawls to punish the detectives and prevent them from making waves after Lester Freamon issued a series of subpoenas. Befitting his nickname "the unit killer," Marimow shuts down the wiretaps on Marlo Stanfield and forces them to focus on the unproductive (albeit stat-accumulating) work of going after low-level drug dealers. One of the most disliked commanders in the Baltimore police department, Marimow is portrayed with having the singular goal of looking good to his superiors, not performing actual police work. Evoking the way that Simon was driven from *The Sun*, the fictional Marimow drives Kima Greggs and Lester away from Major Crimes. His tactics even lead Jay Landsman, as loyal to the departmental hierarchy as anyone, to remark that "Marimow does not cast off talent lightly. He heaves it away with great force" (4.4).

To more fully consider how authorship can be ascribed to the proper sources, other events from the world of journalism were discussed in lectures to compel students to consider how crediting Simon as the source of these narratives is problematic. As we discussed in class in conjunction with the screening of season five episodes, Templeton's fabrications also appear to be based on the well-known cases of reporters at esteemed outlets who falsified stories or sources. Discussions included well-known cases like Jayson Blair at the *New York Times*, Stephen Glass at *The New Republic*, and even Jim Haner at the *Baltimore Sun*. These types of narratives—which can potentially derive from multiple sources and authors—make attributing authorship to a single figure problematic and exemplify some of the challenges of theorizing authorship in television texts.

Due to the inherently collaborative nature of commercial media production, *The Wire* provides a rich topic for media studies courses for undergraduates to illustrate the particular challenge motion pictures and television shows present to theories of authorship. As numerous scholars and critics have pointed out, elevating the director or showrunner to the status of auteur overlooks the contributions of screenwriters, actors, cinematographers, composers, and other creative workers involved in the production process. This problematic has been present since the emergence of auteur theory in film studies. James Naremore notes, "the film director emerged as a creative type at the very moment when authorship in general was becoming an embattled concept" (6). This is not to suggest that auteurs always elide the contributions of others. We watched interviews with Simon where he praised others who worked on the show and highlighted their contributions. Most notably, he has repeatedly credited Executive Producer Robert Colesberry with developing the visual look of the show. Simon's acknowledgement that the show's distinctive visuals were created by others represents an important departure from conventional claims of authorial influence since auteurist critics focused specially on directors' treatment of the mise en scène. The visual elements were the component of the production over which directors in the system typically had control in the rigidly defined division of labor of the Hollywood studio system. By crediting Colesberry with this aspect of *The Wire*, Simon is not only locating his perceived authorial influence elsewhere in the text, but also opening space for consideration of additional authors of the show.

Students were assigned a scholarly essay and interviews with cast and crew of the show on the topic of production cultures in the television industry and the complex processes by which numerous parties contribute to a program like *The Wire*. Scholarship in this area often highlights the contributions of below-the-line workers (individuals who are not the director, producer, screenwriter, or actors) to the authoring of a text. John Caldwell for instance examines a number of practices which exemplify the cooperative and collaborative creation of television including writing by committee, mentoring, and note giving. These industrial practices certainly run counter to the romantic notion of the individual genius and greatly expand our conception of who can be considered an author of a text. While this type of ethnographic research is typically not possible for students interested in *The Wire*, the study of production cultures can open up new avenues of research into how conceptions of control and value have resulted in the contributions of these individuals being elided in the press and popular imagination.

In the case of *The Wire*, there have been a few publications which discuss the below-the-line workers who contributed to the show's look and message. For instance, students read selections from the show's companion book *The Wire: Truth Be Told*, including an interview with Vince Peranio and Pat Moran, the show's art director and on-location casting director. They also read a short piece from the same book describing the work done by Jen Ralston, the supervising sound editor for all five seasons. The relationship of the cast and crew to Baltimore further complicates the task of determining authorship by facilitating new and unexpected contributors. One notable instance occurred when Michael K. Williams, who played Omar, temporarily became a casting director after he met Felicia "Snoop" Pearson in a local Baltimore bar and arranged a screen test for her. Upon landing a part on the show, Snoop too helped "author" her memorable character. As students read about in her autobiography, she recalled that *The Wire*'s producers "wanted me to keep my walk and my talk and even my name. They wanted me to be Snoop.... Snoop is real-life me and Snoop is a pretend character on TV" (223–24). While cast and crew were not explicitly presented as "authors," the work of Peranio, Moran, Ralston, Williams, and Snoop certainly shaped the relationship between the viewers and the text.

The elevation of the author as the solitary font of meaning has been met with criticism from those calling attention to the role of the reader, textual systems, and institutional forces and discourses in authoring texts. Even prior to the emergence of auteur theory in film studies, the romantic conception of the author had already come under attack in literary studies. Most notably, W.K. Wimsatt and Monroe Beardsley in their influential article "The Intentional Fallacy" argued against romanticizing the author: "the design or intention of the author is neither available nor desirable as a standard for judging the success of a work" (3). Trying to ascertain meaning based on the author's intentions serves as a distraction as the text should serve as the exclusive source of meaning. Theorists argued too that interpretive privilege should not rest with the individual author. Roland Barthes famously asserted that we should kill off the author entirely, arguing in "The Death of the Author" that readers need to separate a text from its creator as "a text's unity lies not in its origins, but in its destination" (148). Praising author-less works where meaning is reinscribed with each reader, Barthes contended that ascribing an author to a text means imposing limits on that text. Others contended that meaning did not lie with the author, but rather with the texts that came before it. Julia Kristeva for instance, argued that meaning was constructed outside of the text itself from its intertextual predecessors.

Despite efforts to foreground a readerly approach, the author endured as a central figure in textual studies. Students were introduced to Michel Foucault's contention that authors were useful since they indicated a conceptual coherence. He posited that we should think of individuals like Simon as fulfilling the "author function." Instead of meaning being ascribed to a single author, Simon represents a particular discursive formation into which the work of all the contributors of *The Wire* can be grouped. Foucault also emphasized that the author function always exists in relation to its culture. As Henry Jenkins explains, since only certain texts are read as authored, the author function serves as a sign of value. It "allows fans to distinguish it from the bulk of commercial television which they see as faceless and formulaic, lacking aesthetic and ideological integrity" (188). The concept of the "author function" therefore drew students' attention to the way the figure of the author provides coherence to the text. "David Simon" helped them determine the values, themes, and aesthetics of *The Wire* even when it was felt that it is impossible to disentangle the individual contributions in an inherently collaborative medium like television.

To account for the collaborative nature of commercial media production practices, course readings introduced students to frameworks for analyzing the corporate structures which provided the means of production and distribution for both the motion picture and television industries. Jerome Christensen argues that movie studios should be regarded as the author of Hollywood movies—not the director, screenwriter or producer. Christensen also highlights the importance of corporate art to the reception of motion pictures by the public. He defines corporate art as a tool of corporate strategy which is coordinated and implemented by executives and a set of actions taken to attain competitive advantage that will advance its particular interests—whether financial, social, cultural or political. Christensen explains that the corporate organization provides the social condition for art and that this "social institution organizing human efforts to a common end" plays a significant role in the production and reception of these films (2, 14). Combined with the difficulty of distinguishing between the individual authorial contributions to the final text, Christensen argues that it is more productive to replace a conception of the individual as author with the corporation as author.

The author function also served as means of evaluating how television networks like HBO can utilize corporate art and "author" a text. Specifically, students read about how networks have utilized the linkages between authorial identity and high-art ideologies to brand themselves as exceptional within the crowded media landscape. Not only does *The Wire* become a "quality" television show in part through the elevation of an authorial presence, but HBO itself is branded as a network of distinction as well. Catherine Johnson explains that networks can employ various strategies to "create an experience over and above watching an individual program that can be attributed back to the channel itself" (275–76). Throughout the semester we discussed how *The Wire* was used by HBO to define its authorial function through strategies like the use of interstitials and logos, promotion and branding, and the scheduling of programs.

In the case of HBO, the network sought to connect its original programs like *The Wire* to discourses of taste and quality in order to differentiate its products from other channels and justify its cost to customers paying for the channel. In the late 1990s and early 2000s, HBO began producing original dramas and comedies, often described as "quality television," as part of a corporate strategy of product differentiation to distinguish its product from reality shows like *Survivor, Fear Factor,* and *American Idol* which were dominating the Nielsen ratings at the time. The network introduced shows that achieved critical and popular success, including *Oz* (premiered in 1997), *Sex and the City* (1998), *The Sopranos* (1999), *Curb Your Enthusiasm* (2000), *Six Feet Under* (2001), and *The Wire* (2002).

These original programs helped HBO define itself as a niche channel with a unique authorial voice and brand identity. Dana Polan explains that HBO aimed its quality programming at urban, sophisticated audiences who have been raised on televisual codes; are interested in seeing sex, violence, and graphic language; could follow complex narratives; and can understand references to other texts. Complex and challenging programs were aimed at audiences trained to understand cultural work as hermeneutic and who were willing to find meaningfulness in cultural products ("Cable Watching"). In conjunction with reading the Polan essay, early in the semester we watched the fourth episode of season one, "The Detail," which included the famous scene where Bunk and McNulty only use the word "fuck" as they retrace a murder scene. This type of language would only be found on HBO or other pay-channels. By positioning itself as the corporate home of quality programming, HBO developed a unique brand identity which positioned the network as the author, or at least one of a number of authors, of the viewing experience. Audiences watching *The Wire* then were prepped to interpret it not only as a detective or police procedural, but also actively look for its meaningfulness—as an HBO show and as a "quality" text.

In his essay "When Is the Author?" Jonathan Gray calls attention to the failure of theories of authorship to account for the importance of temporality, as "texts are erroneously imagined to *be*, rather than imagined to be *becoming*" (88–89). Emphasizing the idea of authorial flux, Gray explains that authorship is not only constructed in particular discursive moments, but it is also continuously being built and rebuilt. David Simon's efforts to shape the reception of *The Wire*, particularly after its HBO run finished in 2008 (though it continued to find new audiences), exemplify how authority and authorship of a text are in flux as both the author and reader help shape the meanings of a text.

Foucault noted that the presence of an imagined author works to regulate the reception of texts, influencing how texts should and should not be interpreted. What makes Simon unusual compared to his fellow television auteurs is his continuing willingness to publicly engage with fans and critics who interpret or reinterpret the show in ways that he did not perhaps originally intend. *The Wire* thus provides an excellent opportunity for students to investigate how authors define themselves, particularly as extratextual forms like blogs, podcasts, and online fan sites make this engagement easier and put it in the public sphere. Building on Foucault's theorization of the "author function," Derek Johnson identifies a complimentary "audience function" which accounts for co-creative participation or collaboration and its influence on authorship. Johnson explains, "If the imagined author governs how audiences make meaning and grant legitimacy to cultural works, a similarly imagined audience—understood in this case as participatory—might govern how producers position themselves as authors and lay claim to the cultural legitimacy of their work" (137). Johnson here calls attention to the ways new media technology can bring fans and creators together and how audiences can shape the way that authorship is positioned.

Students looked at examples of how Simon angrily contested interpretations of *The Wire* which did not align with his conception of the show's broader socio-political contexts. Simon at times overtly functioned as an author trying to limit a text's possible meanings by imposing a particular interpretive strategy which emphasized the serious, structural issues of neoliberalism and the drug war rather than the "bad" televisual objects of narrative and character. Thinking about contemporary authorship through this lens thus allowed students to consider how authorship is constantly changing as meaning is expanded, limited, and even negotiated.

One notable instance of this "audience function" occurred in April 2012, four years after *The Wire*'s run on HBO was completed, when in an interview with the *New York Times* Simon complained about bloggers and people who did not watch the show until it was released on DVD or online via HBO Go. "If you want television to be a serious storytelling medium, you're up against a lot of human dynamic that is arrayed against you. Not the least of which are people who arrived to 'The Wire' late.... You got led there at the end and generally speaking, you're asserting for the wrong things" (qtd. in Enger). Simon explained in a follow-up interview that the "wrong thing" he was criticizing was a bracket-style tournament, patterned after the elimination brackets used in conjunction with the NCAA basketball tournament. This was a reference to a series of twelve short articles and two podcasts entitled "Smacketology" (named after ESPN's bracketology segments which predicts the NCAA tournament participants and seeding each year) from the sports and pop culture website Grantland.com in early March 2012, which sought to select *The Wire*'s "best" character. As a case study, students read and listened to all of the Grantland pieces, talked with two guest speakers (Chuck Klosterman and Andy Greenwald) who contributed to the Grantland tournament, and read a couple of interviews where he criticized the ideas behind the tournament.

Notably, the creators of the Grantland bracket acknowledged in their opening piece on the site that these types of articles would not sit well with Simon, and that the tournament was "probably also going to make David Simon mad" (Pappademas). They got the reaction they wanted. Emphasizing the coherence of *The Wire* as a singular text, Simon analogized the bracket to someone breaking down a deck of cards and arguing whether the jack of spades or jack of hearts is better. As he explained, "'The Wire' wasn't about whether Stringer was better than Omar, or this scene better than that scene, or season 2 versus season 3. That's what we were trying not to build. I was expressing distaste for that" (Sepinwall). Despite Simon's frustrations, the tournament proceeded as planned. Over the course of seven articles and two podcasts, the Grantland writers pitted 32 characters from all five seasons, and as the students predicted, stick-up artist Omar Little was selected as the show's greatest character.

The Wire is in many ways an ideal vehicle for teaching media authorship, including how it has been traditionally theorized as well as how new media platforms have impacted the way that fans think about it. As detailed in this essay, *The Wire* illustrates how discourses of authority and authenticity, often linked to our outside knowledge of an author's background and persona, help legitimate a show as a "quality" text and one in which meaning can be found. *The Wire* can be used effectively to teach undergraduates how media authorship can be productively attributed to the range of individuals, groups, and even corporate institutions which help determine a show's production and reception. Studying *The Wire* also demonstrates how, despite the efforts of creators like Simon to condemn things like the Grantland bracket, the meaning of a particular text is not necessarily determined by authorial intent. While we may continue to use authorial identity as a guide to finding meaning in a movie or television show, the author does not have to limit the interpretive possibilities for fans or critics. Ultimately, the study of *The Wire* and authorship can instill in students a more nuanced awareness of a media landscape characterized by changes to televisual aesthetics and narrative paradigms and help make them more media literate.

Works Cited

Alvarez, Rafael. "The Legend of the Orange Sofa and the Unlikely Hollywood Careers of Vince Peranio and Pat Moran." *The Wire: Truth Be Told*. New York: Grove Press, 2010. 175–195.

_____. "Omar's Whistle: Jen Ralston and the Sound of *The Wire*." *The Wire: Truth Be Told*. New York: Grove Press, 2010. 293–298.

Barthes, Roland. "The Death of the Author." *Image/ Music/ Text*. Trans. Stephen Heath. New York: Hill and Wang, 1977. 142–148.

Bowden, Mark. "The Angriest Man on Television." *The Atlantic* (Jan./ Feb. 2008). Web. 5 May 2012.

Caldwell, John. *Production Culture: Industrial Reflexivity and Critical Practice in Film and Television*. Durham: Duke University Press, 2008.

Christensen, Jerome. *America's Corporate Art: The Studio Authorship of Hollywood Motion Pictures*. Stanford: Stanford University Press, 2012.

Deleuze, Gilles. *Cinema 1: The Movement-Image*. Trans. Hugh Tomlinson and Barbara Habberjam. Minneapolis: University of Minnesota Press, 1988.

Enger, Jeremy. "The Game Never Ends: David Simon on Wearying 'Wire' Love and the Surprising Usefulness of Twitter." *New York Times*, 5 Apr. 2012. Web. 6 Apr. 2012.

Foucault, Michel. "What is an Author?" Trans. Donald F. Bouchard and Sherry Simon. *Language, Counter-Memory, Practice: Selected Essays and Interviews by Michel Foucault*. Ed. Donald F. Bouchard. Ithaca: Cornell University Press, 1977. 113–138.

Gray, Jonathan. "When Is the Author?" *A Companion to Media Authorship*. Eds. Jonathan Gray and Derek Johnson. Malden, MA: Wiley-Blackwell, 2013. 88–111.

Jenkins, Henry. "'Infinite Diversity in Infinite Combinations': Genre and Authorship in Star Trek." *Science Fiction Audiences: Watching Doctor Who and Star Trek*. John Tulloch and Henry Jenkins. New York: Routledge, 1995. 175–195.

Johnson, Catherine. "The Authorial Function of the Television Channel: Augmentation and Identity." *A Companion to Media Authorship*. Eds. Jonathan Gray and Derek Johnson. Malden, MA: Wiley-Blackwell, 2013. 275–295.

Johnson, Derek. "Participation is Magic." *A Companion to Media Authorship*. Eds. Jonathan Gray and Derek Johnson. Malden, MA: Wiley-Blackwell, 2013. 135–157.

Johnson, Derek, and Jonathan Gray. "Introduction: The Problem of Media Authorship." *A*

Companion to Media Authorship. Eds. Jonathan Gray and Derek Johnson. Malden, MA: Wiley-Blackwell, 2013. 1–19.

Kristeva, Julia. "Word, Dialogue, Novel." *The Kristeva Reader.* Ed. Toril Moi. New York: Columbia University Press, 1986. 34–61.

Lanahan, Lawrence. "Secrets of the City: What the Wire Reveals About Urban Journalism." *Columbia Journalism Review* 46.5 (Jan./ Feb. 2008): 23–31.

Naremore, James. "Authorship." *A Companion to Film Theory.* Eds. Toby Miller and Robert Stam. Malden, MA: Blackwell, 1999. 9–24.

Pappademas, Alex. "Smacketology: A Tournament to Determine The Wire's Greatest Character." *Grantland*, 6 Mar. 2012. Web. 7 Mar. 2012.

Pearson, Felicia "Snoop," and David Ritz. *Grace After Midnight: A Memoir.* New York: Grand Central, 2007.

Polan, Dana. "Auteur Desire." *Screening the Past* 12 (March 2001). Web. 15 Jan. 2010. http://www.latrobe.edu.au/screeningthepast/firstrelease/fr0301/dpfr12a.rtf.

_____. "Cable Watching: HBO, The Sopranos, and Discourses of Distinction." *Cable Visions: Television Beyond Broadcasting.* Eds. Sara Banet-Weiser, Cynthia Chris and Anthony Freitas. New York: New York University Press, 2007. 261–283.

Schatz, Thomas. *The Genius of the System: Hollywood Filmmaking in the Studio Era.* New York: Henry Holt, 1996.

Sepinwall, Alan. "Interview: David Simon Doesn't Want to Tell You How to Watch 'The Wire." *Hitfix,* 6 Apr. 2012. Web. 1 May 2012.

Simon, David. *Homicide: A Year on the Killing Streets.* Boston: Houghton Mifflin, 1991.

_____. "The Metal Men." *Baltimore Sun,* 3 Sep. 1995. Web. 1 May 2011. http://articles.baltimoresun.com/1995-09-03/features/1995246139_1_metal-carts-copper-shopping-cart.

Watson, Garry. "The Literary Critic, the Nineteenth Century Novel and *The Wire.*" *Cineaction* 84 (2011): 32–40.

Williams, Linda. "Ethnographic Imaginary: The Genesis and Genius of *The Wire.*" *Critical Inquiry* 38 (Autumn 2011): 208–226.

Wimsatt, W.K., and Monroe Beardsley. "The Intentional Fallacy." W.K. Wimsatt. *The Verbal Icon: Studies in the Meaning of Poetry.* Lexington: University of Kentucky Press, 1954. 3–21.

Post–Network Era Television, Cultural Hierarchies and Sociological Uses of *The Wire* Beyond Urban Inequality

MICHAEL L. WAYNE

Although David Simon has cited a work of sociology as his inspiration for the second season of HBO's *The Wire* (Bennett), sociology's pedagogical use of *The Wire* is largely confined to structural issues. A sociology/criminology capstone course at the University of West Virginia, for example, addresses topics such as poverty, inequality, segregation, violence, and education as they relate to urban populations (WVU Today). Lest students be confused about the nature of a Northeastern University sociology course titled "*The Wire* and the Study of Urban Inequalities," the professor states on the first page of the syllabus, "Please note that it is structured as a sociology course, not a media or screen studies course. Thus, the primary focus is not the show per se, but rather what the show reveals about aspects of racial and class inequality that have been the concern of urban sociologists for decades" (Kimelberg). Most notably, in an op-ed piece for *The Washington Post*, Harvard's William Julius Wilson justifies building a course around the show that addresses urban inequality by noting, "*The Wire* is fiction, but it forces us to confront social realities more effectively than any other media production in the era of so-called reality TV. It does not tie things up neatly; as in real life, the problems remain unsolved, and the cycle repeats itself as disadvantages become more deeply entrenched" (Chaddha and Wilson).

For all of its usefulness in illustrating the myriad factors that shape structural inequality, I have found *The Wire* has just as much pedagogical value regarding the social forces associated with cultural inequality. My undergraduate course, "Mass Media & Society," which has taught both seasons one and four of *The Wire*, is scheduled as a two hour and forty minute block divided between lecture, screening, and discussion, allowing a full season of *The Wire* to be shown over the course of the fourteen week semester. The first half of the course uses urban ethnography, including Anderson's *Code of the Street: Decency, Violence, and the Moral Life of the Inner-City* (2000) and Moskos's *Cop in the Hood: My Year Policing Baltimore's Eastern District* (2009), to address structural inequality. The second half of the syllabus approaches cultural inequality by considering cultural capital and status hierarchies. "Cultural inequality" refers to differential access to the knowledge and behaviors most valued by the dominant structural system and is closely related to French sociologist Pierre Bourdieu's notion of "cultural capital."

I begin this essay by discussing the ways in which I have used scenes from *The Wire* to illustrate Bourdieu's (1984) conception of "cultural capital" and Sennett and Cobb's (1973) ideas regarding the "hidden injuries of class." In the next section, I position *The Wire* alongside other culturally legitimated prime-time cable serials. In particular, I focus on the relationship between such texts and the broader post-network discourses of legitimation which necessitate "the construction of divergent conceptions of television texts, technologies, and audiences" (Newman and Levine 7). In using *The Wire* to address a range of sociological issues including those related to the creation and maintenance of cultural inequality, it is necessary to walk a fine line between explaining the social processes that result in status hierarchies and unthinkingly reinforcing them by positioning the show to be the outcome of a chronological progression in which the "good," "complicated," "intelligent" TV of the present is an improvement upon the medium's past. In the third section, I explain how I have walked such a line by emphasizing the inherent tension between popularity and status, explaining the social mechanisms by which the opinions of some come to systematically matter more than the opinions of others, and describing the ways in which the importance of status hierarchies varies with social location.

Cultural Capital and the Hidden Injuries of Class in The Wire

Although first used to describe the non-monetary assets associated with social and intellectual knowledge, Bourdieu later argues that to possess cultural capital is to demonstrate competence in any socially valued practice. In a practical sense, cultural capital is a collection of habits and tastes that can be used to acquire economic and non-economic advantages in particular social contexts when others grant such habits and tastes symbolic importance. Like economic capital (money or resources) and social capital (access to money or resources through one's social network), cultural capital is closely related to structural inequality. In the context of the educational system, cultural capital reproduces inequality by conferring advantages to children with high cultural capital. Cultural capital is also central for Boudieu's concept of "habitus." As a set of dispositions structured by one's social position, habitus is reflected in a range of individual behavior from one's likes and dislikes to the way in which a person carries themselves through social space (body language, posture, etc.).

To explain cultural capital during lecture, I show a restaurant scene from *The Wire*'s fourth season episode "Know Your Place" (4.9). I set up the scene by explaining that, as a result of winning a teamwork contest, Bunny Colvin (a former high-ranking police officer) takes three "at-risk" students—Namond, Zenobia, and Darnell—to dinner at an upscale steak house. In the car on the way to the restaurant the mood is cheerful and upbeat. Once inside, however, the students' positive attitude begins to fade. Namond and Darnell give the hostess looks of distrust as they refuse to let her take their jackets. At the table, Darnell asks a question that seems to presume the hostess will be joining them for the meal. Of the three students, Zenobia has the best grasp of appropriate behavior, as evidenced by mocking Namond for his conflation of restaurant specials with retail discounts and chiding Darnell for failing to appropriately put his napkin in his lap. Nonetheless, by the time the server describes the evening's specials, which include "king salmon with sweet corn, chanterelles, and basil ravioli," all three have shut down completely. The tension only subsides when the group returns to Colvin's car, a neutral space where the corner kids can institute a familiar set of social norms.

After asking students for their interpretations of the scene, I propose the increasing discomfort is a reflection of shame. I explain that unlike guilt, which is produced through the transgression of moral values, shame is the sense of failure resulting from being seen as lacking in the eyes of others. Shame, as Rita Felski observes, "has less to do with infractions of morality than with infractions of social codes and a consequent fear of exposure, embarrassment, and humiliation" (39). In relation to cultural capital, shame is particularly significant because individuals tend to understand society's social arrangements as legitimate. On one hand, status, privilege, and similar social rewards allegedly are "earned" by individuals; that is, they are perceived as resulting from intelligence, talent, effort, and other strategically displayed skills. On the other hand, the absence of status and privilege is perceived to be the result of individual failure. I conclude my discussion of cultural capital by restating Bourdieu's position that an individual's social position is not based on merit but rather that privilege reproduces itself.

To address other components of cultural inequality, Sennett and Cobb's canonical book *The Hidden Injuries of Class* is particularly valuable. In this qualitative study of working-class families in Boston, the authors find that, despite achieving material success, individuals who began life in poor, ethnic enclaves often struggle with feelings of inadequacy. To illustrate this titular concept, I use a different restaurant scene from season one, which includes several exchanges between D'Angelo Barksdale and Donette, the mother of his child (1.5). Although the hidden injuries of class are related to cultural capital, they are not identical. I explain that if cultural capital is the habits, tastes, and behaviors through which inequality is reproduced, then hidden injuries are the toll that the reproduction of inequality takes on those disadvantaged by the class system. I ask students to read Sennett and Cobb's discussion of their interview with third generation Italian-American Frank Rissaro and then compare the hidden injuries of class with the ideas D'Angelo expresses during his date with Donette.

In the scene, after asking Donette if she thinks the other diners can tell that he is in the drug trade, D'Angelo continues, "Come on, you know, it's like we get all dressed up, right? Come all the way across town. Fancy place like this. After we finished, we gonna go down to the harbor. Walk around a little bit, you know? Acting like we belong down here, know what I'm saying?" Donette responds, " So? Your money good, right? Dee, we ain't the only black people in here." Yet, the issue is not racial and D'Angelo replies, "It ain't what I'm talking about ... I'm just saying, you know, I feel like some shit just stay with you, you know what I'm saying, like, hard as you try you still can't go nowhere, you know what I'm saying?" Failing to see the cultural impact of class, Donette invokes a version of the American dream, asserting, "Boy, don't nobody give a damn about you and your story. You got money, you get to be whatever you say you are. That's the way it is."

I argue this scene depicts the hidden injuries of class in three ways. First, by characterizing getting "dressed up" and eating at a "fancy place" as "acting like we belong," D'Angelo is evaluating himself on middle-class terms. According to Sennett and Cobb, Rissarro similarly believes that "people of a higher class have a power to judge him because they seem internally more developed human beings; and he is afraid, because they are better armed, that they will not respect him" (25). Second, in having achieved a measure of material success ("Your money good, right?") yet still feeling "like some shit just stay with you ... hard as you try you still can't go nowhere," D'Angelo understands this unhappiness as proof of his own inadequacy. Like Rissarro, D'Angelo has "played by the rules, he has gained the outward signs of material respectability" while also internalizing the belief that if "he still feels defenseless, something must be wrong with him" (25). Third, the contrast between D'Angelo's feelings and Donette's claim about "the way it is" points to the difficulty of becoming culturally middle-class. As Sennett and Cobb observe, this "tangle of feelings" is common among individuals who "have been successful in making the sort of material gains that are supposed to 'melt' people into the American middle class" (26). As *The Wire* makes clear, however, such melting is often impossible and, when possible, fraught with anxiety.

Cultural Legitimation in the Post-Network Era

Beyond depicting the importance of cultural capital, *The Wire* itself illustrates the social process of legitimation—the way in which a text, genre, or form comes to have value as cultural capital. This is particularly significant because, for most of its history, television could not have been considered cultural capital. From Minow's "vast wasteland" to the anti–TV activist groups of the 1990s who believed the medium to be a public health concern akin to illegal drug use (Mittell), television was largely considered a low-status cultural form. In reference to this history, the only way in which a show like *The Wire* could become culturally legitimated is through broader transformations in the medium itself.

In the context of a convergence culture, television is now another form of new media characterized by an increasingly diverse array of forms and contents. Technological innovation (digital video recorders, video on demand, the internet, etc.) and industrial shifts including conglomeration produce an environment in which choice has increased to such a degree that producers like advertiser-supported-cable networks can afford to create programming that will only be seen by very small portions of the available audience. In addition, increasing efforts to pursue diverse audiences led to the creation of niche content for premium networks, allowing culturally elite understandings to gain legitimacy. This economic and cultural context, as Amanda Lotz explains, creates the possibilities for "phenomenal television" as "programming affirmed by *hierarchies of artistic value and social importance*," and no network has capitalized on these opportunities for status acquisition like the subscriber-based cable channel HBO (40).

Home Box Office (HBO), which began broadcasting in 1972 as a subsidiary of New York City's Sterling Manhattan Cable, which was itself partially owned by Time, Inc. (Mullen 108), initially distinguished itself from other cable networks with uncensored movies and sports programming. By the late 1990s, however, the network had become "the TV equivalent of a designer label" (Edgerton 9). Both the expectations of viewers and the network's brand image are frequently associated with the introduction of the marketing slogan "It's Not TV" in 1996. Yet, as a host of scholars have noted, HBO's marketing strategy relies upon the long-standing marginalization of television and its audiences. Regarding television as a cultural form, Horace Newcomb observes, "HBO's slogan is, in effect, dependent on a set of assumptions about the medium that no longer hold, a retro activation—and implicit denigration—of older general meanings and attitudes" (574). According to Newman and Levine, however, HBO's efforts to distinguish itself from the medium more broadly are part of a larger social process.

While the cultural legitimation of television has been an ongoing effort since the 1940s, it is only during the first decade of the post-network era that television becomes bifurcated with the support of "cultural elites (including journalists, popular critics, TV creators and executives, and media scholars)" who invest "the medium with aesthetic and other prized values, nudging it closer to more established arts and cultural forms" (Newman and Levine 7). In particular, the increasing status of some post-network content results from its association with the active viewing experiences of elite audiences while the devalued status of other content remains unchanged in connection with presumptions regarding the passive viewing experiences of mass audiences during the network era. As the most prestigious post-network content, long-form storytelling and serialized narratives of original premium cable series like HBO's *The Sopranos* and *The Wire* "are seen as more engaging, addressing a committed and passionate viewer" in relation to episodic narratives of network procedural dramas like CBS's *CSI: Crime Scene Investigation*; specifically, the use of "terms such as 'original,' 'edgy,' 'complex,' and 'sophisticated'" in the discourses surrounding premium cable texts "functions to privilege serialized storytelling above other kinds of TV narrative" (Newman and Levine 80–81).

Although anti–TV branding defines television by emphasizing what it is not, like the intellectualizing discourses surrounding film use of language associated with French art criticism in the 1960s (Baumann), other post-network discourses of legitimation explicitly attempt to bring the medium more closely in line with traditionally highbrow cultural forms. According to Newman and Levine, "auteurist notions" (41) regarding "showrunners" of culturally legitimated prime-time serialized drama, like Terrence Winter of HBO's *Boardwalk Empire* and Vince Gilligan of AMC's *Breaking Bad*, for example, connect post-network television to "cinema, literature, painting, and other forms of serious, highly respected culture" (57). While not an official title, using the term "showrunner" in reference to the head of television production for shows in a variety of genres provides ideological support for other discourses of legitimation by drawing attention to the artistic status of some programming both promoted and consumed as authored texts. Like 1960s film directors' self promotion as artists, showrunners employing this strategy and critics who repeat such assertions rely on tropes of authorship familiar from older, already legitimated and aestheticized cultural forms, including Romantic notions of the author as a guarantee of art supported by autobiographical narratives in which the connections between experience and expression further guarantee the artistry (Baumann 64–66).

Beyond legitimizing discourses associated with notions of showrunners as auteur, by the start of the show's fourth season, the critical discourse surrounding *The Wire* explicitly began aligning the show with traditionally legitimated cultural forms. In an article for *TV Guide* Matt Roush claims, "This is TV as great modern literature, a shattering and heartbreaking urban epic about a city (Baltimore) rotting from within." Similarly, *Time* magazine's television critic observes, "They have done what many well-intentioned socially minded writers have tried and failed at: written a story that is about social systems, in all their complexity, yet made it human, funny and most important of all, rivetingly entertaining" (Poniewozik). In addition, an increasing number of cultural elites had come to believe that *The Wire* was "surely the best TV show ever broadcast in America" (Weisberg).

Yet, as literary critic Laura Miller argues, it makes little sense to consider *The Wire* in reference to American popular culture more broadly. As she explains, "American culture is fundamentally Romantic, individualistic and Christian; when it's not exhorting you to 'follow your dream' it's reassuring us that in the eleventh hour, we will be saved. American culture is a perpetual pep talk, trafficking in tales of personal redemption and the ultimate triumph of good over evil" (Miller and Traister). Despite, or perhaps because of, its distance from typical American popular culture, *The Wire* continues to be celebrated as the zenith of television's artistic and creative potential years after its conclusion (Zoller Seitz). Yet, as I have discovered, critical praise and HBO's anti–TV branding are more meaningful to some audiences than to others and it is precisely such issues that extend *The Wire*'s pedagogical value beyond the structural by providing opportunities to explore cultural inequality as a lived reality rather than as a product of shifting macro-level forces revealed with historical analysis.

Status, Taste and The Wire

At present, there is much scholarly debate regarding the best way to understand the relationship between social class and popular culture. On one hand, there is a significant amount of research demonstrating that cultural choices are diverging, which indicates the increasing importance of class and other categorical identities such as race and gender (Fischer and Mattson). On the other hand, research also demonstrates that cultural choices made by those in different socioeconomic locations are in fact converging, which indicates the decreasing importance of class (Peterson and Kern). Yet, as Herbert Gans notes, the boundaries separating the highbrow from the lowbrow have weakened and individuals, particularly the young, are no longer required to make cultural choices that have been deemed class-appropriate (12). Nonetheless, taste remains constitutive of the systems of classification that both shape and express social interaction while remaining linked to processes of identity formation and status-based exclusion. For educators addressing cultural inequality in the undergraduate classroom, the choice to use *The Wire* presents the opportunity to make explicit several uncomfortable, taken-for-granted realities for our students.

One such taken-for-granted reality is the tension between popularity and status. I refer to this as the "Hootie and the Blowfish paradox," which reveals the inverse relationship between quantitative popularity and cultural status. The band's debut album, *Cracked Rear View* (1994), was the best-selling album of 1995 (New York Times Staff), went on to be certified platinum sixteen times (Billboard News Staff), and remains the sixteenth best-selling U.S. album of all-time (David). Yet, when a cultural product is so widely embraced, questions of quality and substance are inevitable. Describing the band's follow-up effort *Fairweather Johnson* (1996) as "its predecessor's artistic equal" and "the musical equivalent of Mom's chocolate chip cookies and a big glass of milk ... paired with lyrics that reek of Hallmark-card sentimentality," music critic Jim DeRogatis concludes his scathing review by asking, "More than 8 million buyers can't be wrong. Or can they?" The crux of the paradox is the following: for something to be so massively popular, it must build an audience across a wide variety of demographic groups; yet, by appealing to a variety of demographic groups, including whomever constitutes the derisively labeled "lowest common denominator," a cultural text is no longer able to reward high status audiences' cultural capital.

In the context of contemporary American television, the tension between popularity and status is revealed in the inverse relationship between audience size and critical esteem, as the most popular shows have little cultural status while the highest status shows are significantly less popular. *The Wire*'s audience, which peaked at about four million viewers before dipping below one million during the show's final season (Bianco), was dwarfed by that of CBS's *CSI: Crime Scene Investigation*, which, over the same time period, consistently drew more than twenty million viewers (ABC Television Network). As one observer has recently noted, "More than other entertainment industries, TV seems to play by the rules of a peculiar Faustian bargain: *Be popular and scarcely acknowledged; or be praised and scarcely watched*" (Thompson). This tension also points to another essential truth of cultural inequality: all audiences are not equal. Put another way, the opinions of some matter more than the opinions of others. How, then, can we account for the cultural significance of *The Wire* in light of its minuscule audience?

As I explain to my students, part of the answer lies with the power of elite audiences like critics and academics. In the case of the former, many contemporary scholars follow Bourdieu and consider critics to be "cultural intermediaries" (325). As part of a broader category, the term refers to those sets of occupations and workers involved in the production and circulation of symbolic goods and services in the context of an expanding cultural economy in postwar Western societies. Specifically, critics writing for high status publications help create broader social views of what constitutes good or bad television. In addition, their approach to evaluating television frequently reflects the dominant cultural hierarchy and its views on mass and popular culture. Although there is a hierarchy of critics and criticism, as an occupational group, television critics can be understood as members of an increasingly college-educated middle-class.

Like critics, academics also play an important role in cultural consecration. Although Bourdieu argues that the composition of legitimate culture is a site of constant struggle and there can be little doubt that scholarly attitudes towards *The Wire* vary dramatically, among many academics the show's image is largely positive. This is particularly significant because, as Baumann explains regarding Hollywood film, "if an intellectual subject gets taken seriously by the academic community, it will likely get taken seriously by the rest of the public, particularly those who have post-secondary degrees, as well" (66).

Beyond the tension between popularity and status and the role of elite audiences like critics and academics, using *The Wire* in the undergraduate classroom creates an opportunity to discuss the ways in which the significance of cultural hierarchies vary with social location. As such, recognizing that the critical and academic adulation heaped upon *The Wire* is in fact the outcome of a social process is often difficult for many students. At the start of one lecture, for example, I asked the class if anyone recalled Bourdieu's position regarding the significance of cultural capital, "Why does taste matter?" A young man towards the back of the room turned to his female neighbor and, in a failed attempt to speak under his breath, said, "It doesn't!" After trying to deflect the sting of his comment with levity, I thanked the young man for his input as a reflection of what Janice Radway describes as "middlebrow personalism"—a mode of cultural engagement requiring and supporting a worldview where taste is a reflection of "individual, idiosyncratic selves" (283). As she observes and as this student reminded me, the middlebrow, the most common American taste culture, is frequently constructed in opposition to the highbrow cultural imperatives of academics and professionals.

Regarding *The Wire* itself, the importance of subjective assessment often comes to the forefront when addressing the show in a broader sociopolitical context. After reading the scholarly exchange between Chaddha, Wilson, and Venkatesh and Atlas and Dreier, I ask my students to complete a writing assignment weighing in on the debate as to whether or not *The Wire* is too cynical. Many students side-step the question by referencing the subjective nature of assessment. One student writes, for example, "One of the key ways to ascertain whether *The Wire* is too cynical would be to determine what should be viewed as 'too much' or deviating too far outside of the realm of what should be portrayed. The answers to these questions are relative in nature, contingent upon the thoughts and views of the person who is making the judgment." Nonetheless, for individuals concerned with social mobility, such middlebrow opposition to highbrow cultural imperatives can be self-defeating. In an effort to emphasize the ways in which the significance of status hierarchies varies with social location, I often discuss these issues using myself as an example. I admit that although I might study television academically and teach a course structured around *The Wire*, in fact, my favorite show is FX's *The Shield*. Only half kidding, I add that with sixty minutes to live, I would want to watch *The Shield*'s pilot episode one more time. I explain that in a middlebrow context dominated by an ethos of "different strokes for different folks," perhaps my feelings about *The Shield* would be interpreted as a reflection of my distinct personality. Yet, in higher status cultural contexts, interpretations would likely be quite different. I mention that it is unlikely the department head would have responded in a similarly positive manner if I had proposed structuring a course around *The Shield*.

In addition to struggling with *The Wire*'s cultural status, some students find the show's narrative unsatisfying and overly cynical. This hesitancy, I suspect, is related to dominant cultural attitudes. According to Gans, cultural products intended for the numerically dominant "lower-middle culture" are "user-oriented," meaning that they were produced with the intention of being entertaining for the audience rather than fulfilling for the creator (110–111). The importance of critical assessment associated with highbrow cultural forms is mirrored by the significance of individual, subjective assessment in the cultural world of many middle-class Americans.

In addition, Gans notes that a central characteristic of drama in lower-middle-culture is the tendency to "express and reinforce the culture's own ideas and feelings" (111). In such a cultural context, definitive moral conclusions are particularly important because they encourage the ideological belief that large-scale social problems can be addressed with individual-level resolutions. Of course, *The Wire* fails to provide its audience with this type of conclusion and, as a result, further distinguishes itself from typical television texts and increases its distance from middlebrow norms. Not surprisingly, among students who find the show to be overly cynical, the absence of narrative closure is particularly problematic. One young woman asserts, the show "offers no justice at the end of season one.... Instead of change, [D'Angelo] was sentenced to twenty years in jail and his hope for a better future has completely disappeared." Another similarly claims, "The show never promised a happy ending ... but that still does not take away from the fact that its viewpoint comes from quite a cynical and bleak place, leaving viewers with a message that in the inner-city, yes, things are sad and unfortunate, but that's just how they are and nothing can be done to change it."

Furthermore, in the context of such forms of cultural engagement, whether *The Wire* can or cannot be appropriately categorized as Dickensian frequently matters less than a given student's ability to identify with and relate to something in the text. For students who cannot find anything in the text with which they can identify, I encourage them to develop a variety of critiques that they can hopefully apply to other forms of popular culture in the future. For those who question the image of post-industrial Baltimore, I recommend Michael Johnson Jr's analysis of the show's authenticity. For those who find the depiction of poor women problematic, I suggest Elizabeth Ault's critique regarding African American motherhood. For those who find the social critique to be overly cynical, I suggest Erika Johnson-Lewis's treatment of the show's serial narrative. Using *The Wire* to help students develop a reflexive sense of themselves culturally is not always possible; therefore, I believe helping students strengthen their critical skills is an acceptable alternative.

In the broadest sense, the amount of academic attention paid to *The Wire* is nothing short of remarkable as the historically low status of television ensured its exclusion from established taste hierarchies. Regarding the discipline of sociology in particular, Penfold-Mounce, Beer, and Burrows claim that the show is "an uncommonly effective and deep exploration of contemporary socio-political themes" that can "best be approached as a form of *social science fiction*. As a work of fiction it certainly accomplishes the telling of a certain kind of 'truth'..." (154). As this essay indicates, however, the binary proposed by their assertion that "the kind of 'truth' being generated is less attuned to the aesthetics of the humanities and more aligned with the sensibilities necessary to stimulate the sociological imagination of the viewer" is a false one (154–155). Furthermore, in claiming *The Wire* for sociology, these sociologists rely upon established cultural hierarchies to assert, without irony, that the show is "a new take on reality TV" and offer the following semantic suggestion: "Using 'authentic television' rather than reality TV helps differentiate *The Wire* and its realism from reality shows such as Big Brother" (159). Even if one assumes these authors have more familiarity with the genre of reality TV than is implied by such a suggestion, their argument certainly indicates that taste both distinguishes oneself from others and reveals one's status. From the cultural legitimation of post-network era television to the critical and academic embrace of some texts but not others, it is clear that the social forces surrounding *The Wire* extend far beyond the structural inequality portrayed over the course of five seasons and sixty episodes. Indeed, it seems unreasonable to expect otherwise from a text created by a producer with enough disdain for the medium in which he works to proclaim, "Fuck the average viewer" (Burkeman).

Works Cited

ABC Television Network. *Season Program Rankings 2003–2009*. Print.

Anderson, Elijah. *Code of the Street: Decency, Violence, and the Moral Life of the Inner City*. New York: W.W. Norton, 2000. Print.

Atlas, John, and Peter Dreier. "Is The Wire Too Cynical?" *Dissent* 55.3 (2008): 79–82. Print.

Ault, Elizabeth. "'You Can Help Yourself/but Don't Take Too Much': African American Motherhood on The Wire." *Television & New Media* 14.5 (2013): 386–401. Print.

Barry, David. "Shania, Backstreet, Britney, Eminem, and Janet Top All-Time Sellers." *Music Industry News Network*. 18 Feb. 2003. Web. 18 July 2014. http://www.mi2n.com/press.php3?press_nb=47877.

Baumann, Shyon. *Hollywood Highbrow: From Entertainment to Art*. Princeton: Princeton University Press, 2007. Print.

Bennett, Drake. "Why Are Professors at Harvard, Duke, and Middlebury Teaching Courses on David Simon's The Wire?" *Slate Magazine*. Graham Holdings Company, 24 Mar. 2010. Web. 18 July 2014. http://www.slate.com/articles/arts/culturebox/2010/03/this_will_be_on_the_midterm_you_feel_me.html.

Bianco, Robert. "Too Few Were Plugged In, But HBO's 'The Wire' Was Electric." *USA Today*. Gannett Co., Inc., 5 Mar. 2008. Web. 23 July 2014. http://usatoday30.usatoday.com/life/television/news/2008-03-05-the-wire_N.htm.

Billboard News Staff. "Hootie & the Blowfish." *Billboard Magazine*. 22 Mar. 2003. Web. 18 July 2014. http://www.billboard.com/articles/news/71970/hootie-the-blowfish.

Bourdieu, Pierre. *Distinction: A Social Critique of the Judgement of Taste*. Cambridge: Harvard University Press, 1984. Print.

Burkeman, Oliver. "Arrogant? Moi?" *The Guardian*. Guardian News and Media, 28 Mar. 2009. Web. 18 July 2014. http://www.theguardian.com/media/2009/mar/28/david-simon-the-wire-interview.

Chaddha, Anmol, and William Julius Wilson. "Why We're Teaching 'The Wire' at Harvard." *The Washington Post*. 12 Sept. 2010. Web. 18 July 2014. http://www.washingtonpost.com/wp-dyn/content/article/2010/09/10/AR2010091002676.html.

Chaddha, Anmol, William Julius Wilson, and Sudhir Venkatesh. "In Defense of *The Wire*." *Dissent* 55.3 (2008): 83–88. Print.

DeRogatis, Jim. "A Good Blowfish Is Hard to Find." *Citypages*. Minneapolis News and Events, 19 June 1996. Web. 18 July 2014. http://www.citypages.com/1996-06-19/music/a-good-blowfish-is-hard-to-find/.

Edgerton, Gary R. "A Brief History of HBO." *The Essential HBO Reader*. Ed. Gary R. Edgerton and Jeffery P. Jones. Lexington: University of Kentucky Press, 2008. 1–22. Print.

Felski, Rita. "Nothing to Declare: Identity, Shame, and the Lower Middle Class." *PMLA* 115.1 (2000): 33–45. Print.

Fischer, Claude S., and Greggor Mattson. "Is America Fragmenting?" *Annual Review of Sociology* 35.1 (2009): 435–55. Print.

Gans, Herbert J. *Popular Culture and High Culture: An Analysis and Evaluation of Taste*, 2d ed. New York: Basic, 1999. Print.

Herod, Rebecca. "WVU Sociology Capstone Introduces Students to Sociology of 'The Wire' and Pittsburgh Neighborhoods." *WVUToday*. West Virginia University, 9 Feb. 2011. Web. 18 July 2014. http://wvutoday.wvu.edu/n/2011/02/09/wvu-sociology-capstone-introduces-students-to-sociology-of-the-wire-and-pittsburgh-neighborhoods.

Johnson, Michael, Jr. "White Authorship and the Counterfeit Politics of *The Wire*." *African Americans on Television: Race-ing for Ratings*. Ed. David J. Leonard and Lisa Guerrero. Santa Barbara: Praeger, 2013. 322–41. Print.

Johnson-Lewis, Erika. "The More Things Change, the More They Stay the Same: Serial Narrative on *The Wire*." *Darkmatter* 4 (2009). Web. http://www.darkmatter101.org/site/2009/05/29/the-more-things-change-the-more-they-stay-the-same-serial-narrative-on-the-wire/.

Kimelberg, Shelley. "The Wire and the Study of Urban Inequalities." Northeastern University, 2013. Web. 18 July 2014. http://www.northeastern.edu/socant/wp-content/uploads/The-Wire_Spring-2013_syllabus.pdf.

Lotz, Amanda D. *The Television Will Be Revolutionized*. New York: New York University Press, 2007. Print.

Miller, Laura, and Rebecca Traister. "The Best TV Show of All Time." *Salon*. Salon Media Group, 15 Sept. 2007. Web. 18 July 2014. http://www.salon.com/2007/09/15/best_show/.

Minow, Newton. "Television and the Public Interest." Delivered to the Convention of the National Association of Broadcasters. Washington, D.C. 9 May 1961. *American Rhetoric.* Web. 18 July 2014. http://www.americanrhetoric.com/speeches/newtonminow.htm.

Mittell, J. "The Cultural Power of an Anti-Television Metaphor: Questioning the 'Plug-In Drug' and a TV-Free America." *Television & New Media* 1.2 (2000): 215–38. Print.

Moskos, Peter. *Cop in the Hood: My Year Policing Baltimore's Eastern District.* Princeton: Princeton University Press, 2008. Print.

Mullen, Megan G. *Television in the Multichannel Age: A Brief History of Cable Television.* Malden, MA: Blackwell, 2008. Print.

New York Times Staff. "Hootie Leads '95 Album Sales." *The New York Times.* 4 Jan. 1996. Web. 18 July 2014. http://www.nytimes.com/1996/01/05/arts/hootie-leads-95-album-sales.html.

Newcomb, Horace. "'This Is Not Al Dente': *The Sopranos* and the New Meaning of 'Television.'" *Television: The Critical View*, 7th ed. Ed. Horace Newcomb. New York: Oxford University Press, 2006. 561–78. Print.

Newman, Michael Z., and Elana Levine. *Legitimating Television: Media Convergence and Cultural Status.* Oxon: Routledge, 2012. Print.

Penfold-Mounce, Ruth, David Beer, and Roger Burrows. "*The Wire* as Social Science-Fiction?" *Sociology* 45.1 (2011): 152–67. Print.

Peterson, Richard A., and Roger M. Kern. "Changing Highbrow Taste: From Snob to Omnivore." *American Sociological Review* 61.5 (1996): 900–07. Print.

Poniewozik, James. "'The Wire' Gives TV Drama a Good Schooling." *Time.* 8 Sept. 2006. Web. 18 July 2014. http://entertainment.time.com/2006/09/08/the_wire_gives_tv_drama_a_good/.

Radway, Janice A. *A Feeling for Books: The Book-of-the-Month Club, Literary Taste, and Middle-class Desire.* Chapel Hill: University of North Carolina Press, 1997. Print.

Roush, Matt. "Save the Children Wire Taps into a Broken School System." *TV Guide.* CBS Interactive, 6 Sept. 2006. Web. 18 July 2014. http://www.tvguide.com/roush/save-children-wire-26746.aspx.

Sennett, Richard, and Jonathan Cobb. *The Hidden Injuries of Class.* New York: Vintage, 1973. Print.

Thompson, Derek. "Why Nobody Writes About Popular TV Shows." *The Atlantic.* Atlantic Media Company, 7 May 2014. Web. 18 July 2014. http://www.theatlantic.com/business/archive/2014/05/why-nobody-writes-about-popular-tv-shows/361872/.

Weisberg, Jacob. "Why The Wire Is the Best Show on Television." *Slate Magazine.* Graham Holdings Company, 13 Sept. 2006. Web. 18 July 2014. http://www.slate.com/articles/news_and_politics/the_big_idea/2006/09/the_wire_on_fire.html.

Zoller Seitz, Matt. "The Greatest TV Drama of the Past 25 Years, the Finals: *The Wire* vs. *The Sopranos.*" *Vulture.* New York Media LLC, 26 Mar. 2012. Web. 18 July 2014. http://www.vulture.com/2012/03/drama-derby-finals-the-wire-vs-the-sopranos.html.

PART II

Writing and Narrative

"Dope on the damn table"
Narrative Discourse in The Wire *and African American Literature*[1]

Paul D. Reich

Once restricted to convenient and self-contained forms, contemporary television series like *Breaking Bad* and *Game of Thrones* now require an engaged and consistent viewership that allows for these programs to become "finely crafted, adult-minded serials built around arcs of interconnected action unfolding over the life span of the series" (Doherty). In a 2012 *Chronicle* essay entitled "Storied TV: Cable is the New Novel," Thomas Doherty argues that "long-form episodic television"—a genre he calls "Arc TV"—poses a serious challenge to the critical aspirations of feature films and novels. Like the novel, these shows focus on character development and back story; as viewers become immersed in the series, the emotional payoffs occur not only at the end of an episode but at the end of a season.

Doherty and others correctly point to two "foundational models" for this tele-revolution: HBO's *The Sopranos* and *The Wire*. While the former certainly enjoyed a wider popular appeal, the latter has received more consistent critical attention. In its five season run from 2002 to 2008, *The Wire* presents its viewers with an uncompromising look at the city of Baltimore and has become a darling of television critics and academics. Labeled by many as the best television series ever, *The Wire* has found its way into essay anthologies, special issues of journals, and academic conferences—including a special session at the 2008 Modern Language Association conference. The series has also found a place in the classroom as instructors across disciplines—from film and media studies to sociology—employ its narrative to help illustrate the vicious cycles of class conflict, poverty, and urban decay (Bennett).

At times, the show's appeal to educators is almost too obvious. In episode eight of *The Wire*'s first season, homicide detective Jimmy McNulty follows Stringer Bell—drug kingpin Avon Barksdale's second-in-command—to a Baltimore City Community College class, "Introduction to Macroeconomics." Our limited view into the classroom shows Bell to be an attentive and prepared student, easily answering his instructor's question about the elasticity of product demand. When we next see him, he's attempting to introduce these principles to the employees of his copy shop, a business serving mostly as a front for laundering drug money. Unfortunately—and this becomes a running theme in the series—Bell is unable to make palatable these ideas to a drug culture that privileges reputation over profit.

This episode, appropriately titled "Lessons" (1.8), is full of teachable moments, from McNulty and fellow detective Kima Greggs's conversation with a circuit court judge about the power of the judicial system to the study session between two detectives in preparation for a promotional examination. But unlike its televisual predecessors, *The Wire* doesn't abandon these moments when the episode ends; instead, they become elements of a much larger story arc. For the literature student, these scenes become opportunities for critical analysis of the show's thematic and narrative goals. As a *visual* narrative, *The Wire* can illustrate narrative devices in unique and engaging ways for our students; in the classroom, the series can—to quote Lieutenant Cedric Daniels in the episode "The Hunt"—put "dope on the damn table" (1.11).

Although we'd all like to have an attentive and committed student like Bell, his ability to relay plot points from William Faulkner's *The Sound and the Fury* is less useful than his analysis of the stylistic devices used to create the unique narrative voice of Faulkner's Benjy. In the literature classroom, knowledge transfer is typically less important than development of our students' critical thinking and writing skills. We want our students to show in class discussions and their written work that they are able to identify an author's intentions, to locate major themes and symbols, and to make connections to other works we have read in the course. We also want our students to see literature as an expression of the human experience. And in courses that feature writings of historically under-represented groups, we want students to connect that experience to the discriminatory practices that shaped it. Moreover, we need them to trace the development of those practices and come to understand their contemporary equivalents.

I have taught three courses focusing exclusively on African American narratives at the small liberal arts college where I work. While not intended to be survey courses, I do seek to provide students with a broad overview of the historical development of African American fiction; grounding texts in their historical moments allows us to review the context in which each narrative was written and understand how it speaks to issues engaging African Americans in one particular time and place. Viewed collectively, though, these narratives can form a picture of the African American experience and shed light on issues that continue to influence African American society.

My first course focused on six novels, ranging from James Weldon Johnson's *Autobiography of an Ex-Coloured Man* to Toni Morrison's *The Bluest Eye*. This sophomore-level class was intended for both English majors and non-majors—many of who would be taking it to satisfy a general education requirement—and included students from the college's evening degree program. As with most lower level courses, the focus of the class was on critical engagement with literary texts. In both their written and verbal work, I worked with students to develop skills of literary analysis while encouraging consideration of how this literature served as an expression of racial injustice and arbiter of social change.

Despite those fairly pedestrian goals, the majority of my students were unable to demonstrate consistent critical analyses in their written work. Both in their examinations and research papers, students could not form complete arguments or develop readings of a text in support of their claims.[2] Moreover, I was struck by my students' inability to connect the class differences, gender discrimination, and racism demonstrated in the texts we read contemporary society. Instead, they remained stuck in the historical moment. In our discussions of Ann Petry's *The Street*, for example, we could agree that the novel's protagonist Lutie Johnson drowned under the weight of the discriminatory forces of the 1940s, but I could not get students to see how those forces continued to work against the Luties of the 21st century. This, coupled with their inability to move beyond rather basic character analysis, left me feeling as though the course had failed them, that I had failed them.

As I prepared to teach the course again more than a year later that sense of failure was still fresh in my mind, and I made a number of revisions to both the course content and structure. While still serving as a lower-level elective for English majors and non-majors, this course moved away from a narrow focus on novels to a broad focus on African American narratives, particularly ones that would help students develop their close reading skills and encourage them to make connections across historical eras. In a first year composition course focused on race and gender the previous semester, I had successfully used David Simon and Ed Burns's HBO miniseries *The Corner* (2000) to guide class discussion and generate topic ideas for the course. Still, I had dismissed their dramatic series, *The Wire*, because it was too long and involved for my purposes. In a course on African American narratives, however, the first season of *The Wire* presented an interesting alternative to the more traditional texts studied in the course. *The Wire* could become a framing device for our study of black narratives and, most important, force students to accept discrimination not as a part of our historical past but as a dominant influence on our historical present and future.

With *The Wire* as a frame for the course, I selected complimentary texts from the 20th century that focus on urbanized settings, adding works like Gloria Naylor's *The Women of Brewster Place* and Richard Wright's *Native Son* to Petry's *The Street*. I also included August Wilson's *Fences* in the hopes students would draw parallels to the performed narratives of the play and television show. Because this was an entry-level course, I anticipated working with students to develop methods for literary analysis, and we spent a good part of the first few weeks developing a language with which to examine the texts. Based on my experience with *The Corner* and other television series in past courses, I also anticipated the need for us to develop a way to "read" *The Wire*. To that end, we watched the first episode of season one together. Students would then be responsible for watching the next eleven episodes outside of class. We would view the final episode of the season on our last day together. Structured in this way, *The Wire* would be unlike any other text in the course; each week we would discuss the evolution of Simon and Burns's narrative as we analyzed print narratives from our historical past.

For that first meeting, I wanted to convey to students that even though *The Wire* differed from our other narratives it should be viewed as a text, read and understood through a critical lens. That argument, as you can imagine, is much easier to make with traditional forms of literature, and my attempt to critically analyze a television show was initially met with some skepticism.[3] My students were accustomed to viewing television passively and were resistant to becoming active viewers; television, they argued, was for entertainment. Watching the first episode in class, then, became an integral step in transforming their understanding of the show and the role it played in the course.

As any one who has seen *The Wire* knows, keeping track of the series' protagonists is a monumental task, so I provided my students with a list of characters. A few of my more ambitious students immediately improved upon my work by printing out for the class color copies of character names and their pictures, all available on HBO.com. In addition to cast sheets, I also provided students with a bit of background on the genesis of the show, detailing David Simon's experience as a newspaper reporter and Ed Burns's stint as a homicide detective in Baltimore, and their previous collaborative productions (their book *The Corner* and its adaptation as an HBO miniseries). Most important, I explained to my students that, unlike traditional television shows that place a premium on exposition and an end-of-the-episode conclusion, *The Wire* should be "read" as what Simon has called a "visual novel" (25). The first few episodes of the show would be like the first few chapters of any novel: inevitably, you'll have more questions than answers.

Episode one, "The Target," begins with McNulty's interrogation of a witness to a homicide he is investigating, and the witness reveals that the victim was killed for robbing a craps game, something, the witness claims, he does every week. When McNulty asks why they continued to allow the victim in the game if he was only going to rob them at some point, the witness responds, "Got to. This America, man." This revelation immediately introduces viewers to a consistent theme in *The Wire*: the rules of the Baltimore city streets are the same rules that govern American society as a whole. As the show progressed, I reminded students to watch for instances where drug dealing and the street mirrored American capitalism, and they surprised me with their insights. When D'Angelo Barksdale murders a competitor in plain sight of a number of witnesses and forces his uncle (and soon to be target of a police investigation) to buy off those witnesses, my students identified his subsequent demotion to a less lucrative housing project as an appropriate punishment levied against a mid-level executive who makes a costly mistake. It would be akin, they argued, to an ad executive who is removed from a high profile portfolio because of a publicity faux pas.

A close reading of the language employed by this witness in McNulty's initial investigation also allowed the class to see how Simon crafted a discussion of the American experience through the speech patterns of a young Baltimorian. When asked how they would frame the same thought, their varied responses allowed opportunities for us to examine the ways in which geography and culture impacted our expression of ideas. McNulty's interrogation of the witness also established his role as interpreter for the viewer; after the witness gave context for the shooting, McNulty then restates the events in language more palatable for the network's viewership. This became an important moment in our initial discussion of *The Wire* and, as I explained to my students, not without literary precedent. Regionalist literature often employed characters whose experiences allowed them to serve as mediators between the subject world and reader. Such guides, though, have a subjective point of view, and the author may or may not make her character's subjectivity explicit. Readers, I explained, have an obligation to consider these biases as they are shown places unfamiliar to them. As we closed our discussion of this opening scene, I asked students how comfortable they were with a white detective directing our view into a predominantly African American world.

As the episode progressed, it became obvious that Simons and Burns were not going to filter the story completely through McNulty's often-blurred lens. As the show's creators begin introducing other characters, I shifted the conversation from point of view to other literary elements. After his release from jail, D'Angelo is driven home by Wee-Bey, another member of Barksdale's organization. As D'Angelo begins discussing the coercion employed by Barksdale's crew, Wee-Bey immediately stops the car and asks D'Angelo outside. We view their conversation through a long shot in which the characters are positioned under two neon restaurant signs—Wee-Bey under "Burgers," D'Angelo under "Chicken." In our discussion of the scene, students were initially concerned with content. Wee-Bey's admonishment of D'Angelo for discussing business in the car points to the sophistication of Barksdale's organization; D'Angelo is forced to recite the rule against conversations occurring in any place that could be monitored. With the scene still paused on the screen, I asked students to move beyond dialogue and consider the elements of the shot's composition. Why did the filmmakers choose a long shot?

While a close or medium shot would allow us to more clearly see facial expressions of the characters, a long shot enables viewers to also see the neon signs—objects further enhanced by the scene's evening setting. If Simon and Clark Johnson (the episode's director) were comfortable relying on body movement to help reinforce the characters' spoken language, then the signs—and their individual identification with each character—must convey an implicit message to the viewer. D'Angelo's placement under the "Chicken" sign, for example, can be read as a symbol to careful viewers of his inability to successfully navigate this world, foreshadowing much of his character development. Both the initial scene with McNulty and this one with D'Angelo suggest a more informed understanding of how the show requires careful and deliberate viewings. Part of the lesson, then, in watching "The Target" in class was to demonstrate how those viewings can occur and to encourage students to be open to moments of more considered analysis. Active viewing/reading, I argued, should be their default mode of interacting with any narrative—visual or print. In this way, our discussion of "The Target" functions both as a primer in viewing *The Wire* and, for the non-majors, in reading a text.

As we concluded our discussion of the first episode, we focused again on the show's interrogation of contemporary America and local government's inability to combat drug trafficking and the violence it produces. "The Target" does much to establish Simon's premise for the first season: "a dry, deliberate argument against the American drug prohibition—a Thirty Years' War that is among the most singular and profound failures to be found in the nation's domestic history" (Simon 12). Unimaginative thinking, bureaucracy, and competing political goals all work against solutions to a debilitating problem. *The Wire* suggests that these features of American society infect all the participants of this "game"—drug dealers, users, and police officers—with a sense of fatalism. When responding to a fellow officer's discussion of the war on drugs, one detective responds, "you can't even call this shit a war.... Wars end" (1.1). As the season continues to unfold, this pessimism gives way to a growing sense of environmental determinism that governs so many of these characters' actions. As I began to introduce other African American narratives alongside *The Wire*, the role environment plays in character development became much more apparent.

In each of the print narratives we read in the course,[4] environment is a controlling factor in their characters' lives. Each week, the class watched an episode of *The Wire* and read an assigned portion of a print narrative; as preparation for our discussion, students were required to submit response papers that would act as an impetus for class discussion and establish connections between the visual and written works. At times, this proved to be a fairly easy task, particularly with Petry, Wright, and Naylor, all of whose texts are set in large cities that mimic the Baltimore setting of *The Wire*. Wright's and Petry's—and to some extent, Naylor's—use of literary naturalism opened up the most avenues for comparison, as students identified the destructive environmental forces responsible for the protagonists' decline. For other texts, though, the weekly comparative assignments were more difficult for students to complete; our class discussions seemed forced and less organic. Looking back, I see now that my intent with the weekly writing was to legitimize our study of *The Wire*; these forced comparisons did not enhance our study of either text nor did they provide opportunities to improve students' analytical skills. Unfortunately, these assignments gave the show a special status in the course—I wasn't, for example, forcing students to make direct connections between other texts—and not the equal status for which I had argued.

When my students were able to draw explicit connections between an episode and their reading, the show functioned exactly as I had hoped: it enhanced and illustrated the printed text and led to a deeper understanding of the material. In our discussions of *Native Son*, for example, students were drawn to Bigger Thomas's reaction when he first arrives at the Dalton's home:

> Would they expect him to come in the front way or back? It was queer that he had not thought of that. Goddamn!...Suppose a police saw him wandering in a white neighborhood like this? It would be thought that he was trying to rob or rape somebody. He grew angry. Why had he come to take this goddamn job? He could have stayed among his own people and escaped feeling this fear and hate [44].

Thomas's uncertainty about the social customs are a direct result of the segregated world in which he lives; in a Chicago divided by strict racial geography, Thomas had rarely traveled beyond the largely African American South Side. Even as Thomas realizes his economic prosperity relies on his ability to navigate between these worlds, his fear and anger threaten his prospects: "This was not his world; he had been foolish in thinking he would have liked it" (44). Most students empathized with Thomas and even understood how his embarrassment led to the other emotions he experienced but had more trouble conceptualizing the divided world in which Thomas lived.

One of the most useful scenes in *The Wire* that highlights similar economic and racial divisions comes in episode five, "The Pager," when D'Angelo takes his girlfriend to dinner in an upscale Baltimore restaurant. This scene became a constant referent in our class discussions. It opens with D'Angelo and Donette entering the restaurant and requesting a table. When the maître d' asks if they have a reservation, D'Angelo's stumbling response clues readers into his feelings of embarrassment and uncertainty. Both reactions are atypical of the character; in his daily interactions with the subordinates in his drug crew, D'Angelo is assured and decisive. When they are seated and D'Angelo's request to be moved to a table farther away from the kitchen is denied—the maître d' replies, "those [tables] are for patrons who made reservations"—we see whatever power D'Angelo possesses on the streets of West Baltimore neutralized in this place. Donette's unhappiness over the table and her admonishment of him—"You should have pushed him, D"—merely exacerbate the situation and remind viewers of the shifted dynamics at play. At times, the episode's writer (Burns) allows for some humor in the scene; D'Angelo's surprised reaction to his server's crumb removal tool is a good example that played well to the class. But as we followed D'Angelo's gaze around the room, we also considered the Thomas-like concerns he voices to Donette:

> Do you think they know? ... You know, what I'm about? ... Come on, you know, it's like we getting all dressed up, right? Come all the way across town, fancy place like this. After we finish, we gonna go down to the harbor, walk around a

bit, you know, act like we belong down here ... I feel like some shit just stay with you.... Like, hard as you try, you still can't go nowhere.

I reminded students of Thomas's similar claims, his frustration and anger in his inability to bridge the racial and economic divisions in his world. I also asked students to consider Donette's response to D'Angelo's claims about social mobility: "So? Your money good, right?...You got money, you get to be whatever you say you are. That's the way it is" (1.5). As we debated both positions—and there was passion on both sides of the argument—I reminded students that Wright, and eventually Simon and Burns, had already shown us that their characters' early reactions to environmental determinism were correct. Donette's optimism, which in its belief in the economic power of the individual mirrored many of the students,' seemed misplaced in the worlds of Thomas and D'Angelo.

Even as these strong parallels between *The Wire* and the print narratives allowed for students to recognize the continued impact of discriminatory forces on African Americans, texts with less explicit connections to the show still served as engaging counterpoints when our conversations moved to the literary elements of a work, and I asked students specific, targeted questions that led them to see commonalities between the stylistic features of the two genres. After our discussion of the neon signs in "The Target," students were adept in identifying other symbols in both the print and visual narratives. Early in the semester, for example, the class focused its attention on the "blossoming pear tree" in Hurston's *Their Eyes Were Watching God* (10). A good part of our initial discussion of the text focused on the scene in which the novel's protagonist, Janie, spends a considerable amount of time beneath the tree:

> She stretched on her back beneath the pear tree soaking in the alto chant of the visiting bees, the gold of the sun and the panting breath of the breeze when the inaudible voice of it all came to her. She saw a dust-bearing bee sink into the sanctum of a bloom; the thousand sister-calyxes arch to meet the love embrace and the ecstatic shiver of the tree from root to tiniest branch creaming in every blossom and frothing with delight. So this was a marriage! She had been summoned to behold a revelation. Then Janie felt a pain remorseless sweet that left her limp and languid [11].

Between the confirmation of Janie's age—16—and the identification that she, too, "had glossy leaves and bursting buds" (11), Hurston leaves little doubt that this period was one of sexual awakening for Janie. Students focused on the sexually charged language and we discussed how Hurston's construction of this scene forces readers to investigate its significance. As we moved beyond the obvious signposts provided by Hurston, I asked students to consider how this moment defined Janie's expectations of marriage, and how each of her romantic relationships (and her three husbands) were measured against this experience. All of Janie's major decisions, Hurston implies, result from her pear tree "revelation"; just like D'Angelo, for Janie, "some shit just stay with you."

As the semester progressed, my students also identified and examined symbols in *The Wire*. One of our most memorable conversations occurred during discussion of the season's climatic episode, "The Cost" (1.10). This episode focuses most of its attention on the undercover assignment undertaken by Greggs. As the only female detective featured in this season, Greggs already occupies a privileged place in Simon and Burns's narrative, and she constantly must prove herself to male contemporaries. In "The Buys" when a drug suspect strikes another (male) police officer, Greggs joins her colleagues in beating the suspect as retaliation for his actions, a behavior that impressed one of the other officers enough for him to remark, "she beat him like a man" (1.3). In a police department where patriarchal power is absolute and women are viewed as weak and objects of desire, Greggs must adopt stereotypically male characteristics in order to be accepted. If she doesn't, she could find herself laboring under the same conditions that governed so many of the female protagonists in our print narratives and subject to the same limiting choices.

Greggs's struggle to prove herself in this first season engenders no small amount of sympathy from the show's audience, and our class was not exempt from those feelings: for many students, she was their favorite character on the show. A key part of the investigative unit's case against Barksdale's organization, the undercover operation in "The Cost" was also the most dangerous, and because it required an African American woman—she was to play the girlfriend of an informant who would attempt to purchase a large amount of drugs from a member of Barksdale's crew—Greggs's gender/race made her the only viable candidate for this operation. Simon and the show's director Brad Anderson leave little doubt to audiences of the situation's precariousness for Greggs. Both in their speech and non-verbal cues other characters express concern for their colleague. Like Hurston did with emotive language in the pear tree scene, Simon purposefully engages the audience with his placement of a favored character in this position.

As we follow Greggs through the initial part of the operation, the viewers' focus shifts back and forth between her and the rest of the unit that follows at a safe distance. Wearing a listening device, Greggs can communicate to her colleagues but they can't speak with her, and it is through this audio that we *hear* her being shot by two armed assailants. The search for her becomes particularly dramatic as Simon and Anderson direct a good part of our viewing through a police helicopter camera; it is through this camera that we and Greggs's colleagues locate the car in which she and the informant traveled to meet the dealer. As we shift to a more traditional camera focused on the car, our view is directed through the front windshield and onto the lifeless body of the informant. Hanging from the rear view mirror are two eight balls.

The other characters' sense of frustration and impotence as McNulty attempts to resuscitate Greggs mirrors our own. Simon and Anderson's use of the helicopter camera and police band broadcasts remind us that Greggs, while important to us, is merely part of a larger bureaucratic organization. In our investigation of the scene, though, the class kept returning to the two eight balls that appeared as the camera moved from the open passenger door to the informant's body behind the driver's wheel (Greggs is in the back seat). As we did with Hurston, we discussed how the writer and director constructed this scene, including their use of Greggs to emotionally charge the incident. The shot of those two objects, my students contended, was indicative of the position in which both the informant and Greggs found themselves. The informant had no choice but to work with the authorities, and the undercover work required an African American woman. Both characters were behind the eight ball.

These classroom moments reinforced my belief in the usefulness of *The Wire*, both in its ability to strengthen students' skills of literary analysis and as an illustration of the continued repercussions of discriminatory practices that shape the African American experience. While the students' evaluative comments indicated they appreciated the addition of the show to the course, student performance in the course was still below departmental average— albeit better than the first semester I taught the course. As mentioned earlier, the writing assignments that forced connections between the visual and print texts often led to less organic discussions, privileging the show in ways I hadn't intended. My examinations also forced students down analytical paths with which they may have been less comfortable; the essay section in particular failed to provide opportunities for the class to discuss the literary texts without also discussing *The Wire*. In future iterations of the course, I would have to consider more carefully how to assess my students' understanding of the course material.

As I prepared to teach another section of my African American narratives course, the ways in which *The Wire* was integrated into the course were modified based on student performance and my observations. The course itself would also be different. Taught as an upper-level English elective, this class wouldn't concern itself with introductions to analytical methodologies; as experienced majors/minors, these students would already be familiar with close readings and thematic development. I also adjusted the texts used in the course, moving away from those that focused mostly on the urban African American experience—Petry's *The Street* and Wright's *Native Son*—in favor of ones demonstrating a range of African American experiences in the 20th century.[5] In adding texts like Nella Larsen's *Passing*—set in 1920s Harlem—and Toni Morrison's *Home*—which chronicles the return of a Korean war veteran—I provided students with varied illustrations of black America and a broader range of writing styles.

As the course was also taught during my institution's accelerated summer term—we met twice a week for six weeks with each meeting lasting three hours—the elimination of Wright and Petry (and their 400+ page texts) made the reading load more palatable for the students. This altered format allowed for another modification to the course structure; we were able to watch eight of the thirteen episodes in class. As expected, the immediacy of the viewings led to fuller class discussions, and if the students from my last section used their viewings at home—despite my explicit instructions—as a "break" from their reading, then the students in this class became, by default, more directed, engaged viewers. While I still billed the show as a frame narrative for the course, I also modified both the written assignments and our class discussions in ways that removed the privileged position *The Wire* had in my previous course. In their weekly writing assignments, students could perform close readings of a selected passage from *either* the print or visual text. In class discussions, any comparisons between the show and the other course texts developed organically.

In our discussion of the show's narrative structure, for example, we examined how *The Wire*'s varied camera shots created a text with shifting points-of-view not unlike those found in Morrison's and Naylor's texts. We discussed the effect these shifts had on our readings. In *The Women of Brewster Place*, Naylor's decision to divide her narrative by providing the perspective of seven women complements Simon and Burns's method, and both texts are concerned with giving their readers as complete a picture as possible. Although *The Wire*'s inclusion of varied viewing angles certainly serves an aesthetic purpose, it also works to create a sense of distance from these subjects—felt most profoundly in the aforementioned scene in which Greggs is shot—while still providing an intimate look into their lives.

In their writing and the course as a whole, students performed significantly better than their predecessors. For the midterm assignment, I asked students to write a five-page analysis in answer to one of three prompts, which ranged from a discussion of social class to a close reading of an epigraph from a *Wire* episode to an evaluation of the final paragraph from Johnson's *Autobiography of an Ex-Coloured Man*. While students had a wide range of approaches for this assignment, their performance was consistently strong (the average was a B+), and a few of the best analyses focused on *The Wire*. One student, for example, used the social class prompt to examine the show through the lens of American literary naturalism. She used close readings of two scenes featuring D'Angelo and his subordinates—one an examination of the McDonald's chicken nugget, the other D'Angelo's attempt to teach his colleagues chess—to argue that "social conditions and environment determine the future for all these characters, and just as a game, all their actions are controlled" (Gutierrez). Another student successfully used the epigraphs from "The Target" ("all the pieces matter") to demonstrate how Simon and Burns used their multi-layered narrative to construct a subjective portrait of urban American life. This latter point led to a spirited class discussion on our willingness to accept Simon and Burns as appropriate creators of an African American narrative. As we considered the many contributors to the show—creators, writers, actors, and directors—we had a number of fruitful, passionate conversations about the responsibilities a creator has to her subject.

In their evaluations of this course, a number of students identified our "lively discussions" and the inclusion of both "visual and written media" as features that kept them engaged and interested. When used correctly, *The Wire* proved to be a useful addition to our class, and in literature courses that seek to develop critical thinking and writing skills, the inclusion of the show has a number of positive benefits. Through their "reading" of the show, students can develop the ability to identify major themes and symbols and make connections across genres and historical time periods. As we watched D'Angelo struggle in the final episode of the season between his obligations to himself and his family, students pointed out similar moments in the other texts we had read in the course, and I decided to include a question on those instances in their final examination. The conflict between the individual and her/his community was present in every text we read: Johnson's narrator chooses to pass and abandon his race in *The Autobiography of an Ex-Coloured Man* and Janie chooses love over class in *Their Eyes Were Watching God*. When D'Angelo's mother reminds him in "Sentencing" that if "you ain't got family in this world, what the hell you got?," D'Angelo—like Bigger and Lutie—surrenders to his environment and sacrifices any opportunity he has to be free (1.13). This was a sobering moment for my students, one that drove home the message found in so many of the works we read.

Characters in our historical present, D'Angelo and Greggs become examples of the continued impact of discriminatory practices in this country. In a course on African American narratives, *The Wire* serves as a valuable pedagogical tool by providing students with a perspective that encourages deeper examination of traditional texts, and it infuses discussions with contemporary examples of gender discrimination, class differences, and racism. As contemporary politics intersect with these issues, this kind of discourse is particularly relevant. The study of literature must, therefore, equip students with more than the ability to recognize theme and symbol: we must show them how a text fully engages with culture so that they might better understand the real-world applications of its lessons. In an America where many now claim discrimination is no longer a factor, *The Wire* reminds us that this game is far from over.

Notes

1. An earlier version of this essay appeared as "'All in the Game': Using *The Wire* in Teaching African American Narratives," *Teaching American Literature: A Journal of Theory and Practice* 3; no. 3/4 (2010): 1–9.
2. In their evaluations of the course, my students indicated a high level of engagement with the course material and their satisfaction with the course and the instructor was well above the college average, but the course grade point average was in the C range, more than a letter grade below the departmental average.
3. Considering Doherty's and other critics' arguments concerning television audiences' new appreciation for involved viewing, I imagine student skepticism would be more quickly defused in today's classroom.
4. James Weldon Johnson's *The Autobiography of an Ex-Coloured Man* (1912), Zora Neale Hurston's *Their Eyes Were Watching God* (1937), Ann Petry's *The Street*, Richard Wright's *Native Son* (1940), August Wilson's *Fences* (1986), and Gloria Naylor's *The Women of Brewster Place* (1980).
5. In their evaluations of my second class, a number of students complained about "feeling depressed and frustrated" with the course material, which they described as too "narrow" to be representative of this literary genre. In my desire to legitimatize *The Wire* with companion texts like *The Street* and *Native Son*, I may have gone too far; one text would have been sufficient in chronicling this experience.

Works Cited

Bennett, Drake. "This Will Be on the Midterm. You Feel Me? Why So Many Colleges Are Teaching *The Wire*." *Slate*. The Washington Post Company, 24 March 2010. Web. 10 May 2010.

Doherty, Thomas. "Storied TV: Cable is the New Novel." *The Chronicle Review. The Chronicle of Higher Education.* 12 September 2012. Web. 27 February 2014.

Gutierrez, Paola. "*The Wire* through a Naturalistic Lens." 31 May 2012. Student Essay. Rollins College. Print.
"The Hunt." *The Wire: The Complete First Season*. Dir. Steve Hill. 2002. Home Box Office, 2004. DVD.
Hurston, Zora Neale. *Their Eyes Were Watching God*. New York: Harper Perennial, 2006. Print.
"Lessons." *The Wire: The Complete First Season*. Dir. Gloria Muzio. 2002. Home Box Office, 2004. DVD.
"The Pager." *The Wire: The Complete First Season*. Dir. Clark Johnson. 2002. Home Box Office, 2004. DVD.
"Sentencing." *The Wire: The Complete First Season*. Dir. Tim Van Patten. 2002. Home Box Office, 2004. DVD.
Simon, David. Introduction. *The Wire: Truth Be Told*. By Rafael Alvarez. New York: Pocket Books, 2004. Print.
"The Target." *The Wire: The Complete First Season*. Dir. Clark Johnson. 2002. Home Box Office, 2004. DVD.
Wright, Richard. *Native Son*. New York: Perennial, 1998. Print.

"They're not learning for our world; they're learning for theirs"

Changing the First Year Writing Experience

Karen Dillon and Naomi Crummey

When we decided to use season four of *The Wire* as our primary text for the second semester of our first year writing sequence, the writing program and the campus community as a whole were ripe for change. The second semester course, WR 112, had for many years high failure and withdrawal rates, and the addition of a new faculty member (Karen) allowed for a fresh discussion about what the program needed to improve students' engagement and performance. Now with two full-time faculty members teaching in first year writing, where before there had been only Naomi and a handful of adjunct instructors, we decided drastic programmatic change was needed. Simultaneously, during a faculty mixer at the college president's house, we discovered our mutual passion for *The Wire* and decided it would be the perfect text to bring focus to WR 112 and to initiate a campus-wide dialogue about race and class that recent events had made evident was necessary. As a small, regional, and rural liberal arts college that draws students from the surrounding communities as well as from nearby urban centers, it is fair to say that our campus tends toward polarization—rural vs. urban, white vs. African American. This, coupled with a fairly conservative faculty and administration that would likely balk at the use of a television show (especially one with cops and drug dealers) in a writing course, made *The Wire* a controversial choice. However, despite knowing "heads might pop off" when presented with such a drastic change to the curriculum and a scathing indictment of the America most students had been raised to believe in, we knew first year writing and the campus as a whole needed *The Wire*.

After three years of teaching season four of *The Wire* in WR 112, assessment and survey data demonstrate that we made the right choice. Not only have failure and withdrawal rates dropped significantly over the three years, students' engagement with the issues presented in the show exceed that of the pre–*Wire* years in which students struggled to connect with similar ideas presented in more traditional academic texts such as scholarly essays and non-fiction narratives. Surely some of this results from our own increased engagement in the course, which gave us the opportunity to share with students a narrative we believe to be rich, compelling, and artfully told. In this essay we explain how the unique circumstances of our own campus and the not uncommon rut of first year writing curriculum necessitated a radical curriculum change. We provide the specific layout and execution of our course, as well as three years of assessment data that illustrates the impact of a complete reimagining of what texts first year writing can engage. Moreover, we share specific experiences that comment on the enriching quality of *The Wire* as an interdisciplinary academic text.

Background of Campus Culture and First Year Writing Program

Blackburn is a small liberal arts college in central Illinois, 40 miles south of Springfield and 60 miles north of St. Louis. Nearly half of our student population comes from small, rural, predominantly white communities. However, the college also draws significant numbers of students (12 percent) from nearby urban centers such as Springfield, St. Louis, and Chicago, which largely contributes to the population of students of color (13 percent). These stark differences in student background can create conflict, particularly when it comes to conversations about race and socio-economic class. A 2003–2004 study funded by the Lumina Foundation suggested that the college's work program helps mitigate some of these tensions by essentially forcing students to interact with and rely upon fellow students from different racial, ethnic, and/or socioeconomic backgrounds. However, students, faculty, and staff remain reluctant to engage in public conversation about race and class. It would not be a stretch to describe aspects of our campus culture as racially polarized; to illustrate, we offer an example. After Obama won the 2008 elections, a small group of African American men strode through their dorm shouting, "Yes we did," and a white student responded by hanging a Confederate flag out his dorm window. On a small and white majority campus, such occurrences are broadly felt, extensively whispered about, but rarely dealt with directly or in the classroom. Despite having to work alongside students of a different race and class, many (white) Blackburn students (and some faculty and staff) are reluctant to acknowledge, let alone discuss, the fact that racism still exists and that it results in very real, systemic consequences and outcomes for people of color.

In the fall of 2011, tired of seeing "rebel" belt buckles, hats, and bumper stickers, and prompted by a student complaint regarding a Confederate flag hung upon a door in a dorm hallway, the college's director of Intercultural Programs and Services asked the Student Life Committee to consider adopting a policy that would prohibit display of the flag. The ensuing discussions laid starkly bare just how far in the past many of our white students were. The student members of the committee argued that any such policy would infringe on students' freedom of expression and likened displaying the flag to wearing crosses or hijab. Similarly, one staff member likened banning the Confederate flag to banning the rainbow flag. The outspoken voices against the proposed policy failed to understand the strong historical rhetoric implicit in the flag and the negative response to it by many students, faculty, and staff regardless of color.

In light of this campus controversy, our biggest concern about teaching *The Wire* was that it might confirm for some of our students all the worst stereotypes supported by the myths of American meritocracy. Nevertheless, we both felt strongly that, particularly given the racial polarization and unabashed racism evidenced by campus discourse about the Confederate flag, the conversation needed to be had. Given that many first year writing courses attempt to introduce students to the rhetorical constructions of race, class, gender, and identity, *The Wire* seemed an appropriate text with which to challenge students.

Originally a patchwork of Peter Elbow style first year writing pedagogy from the 1970s and John Gardner style first year seminar content from the 1990s,[1] the first year writing program had been revised in 2006 to bring it in line with the Outcomes Statement for First Year Writing from the Council of Writing Program Administrators (WPA), which emphasizes genre conventions and drafting over self-reflection and authenticity of voice. The first semester course (WR111) focused on genres and the writing process, with particular emphasis on development and revision, as it worked through thematic units linked to identity. The second semester (WR112) narrowed its focus to conventions of analysis, argumentation and research, with particular emphasis on source evaluation and integration, with one unifying theme stemming from a core, source-based text. To put it simply: first year writing was a fairly conventional two-semester composition sequence.

Before *The Wire*, the first year writing curriculum attempted to engage themes relevant to larger campus concerns and programs: work, leadership, multiculturalism, and education. WR111 relied on theme and genre readers such as Andrea Lunsford's *The Presence of Others* and Jane Aaron's *The Compact Reader*; WR112 used multi-disciplinary, research-based books such as Howard Gardner's *Leading Minds*, *Freakonomics*, *The Tipping Point* (paired one semester with Alex Shakar's *The Savage Girl*), and *The Omnivore's Dilemma*. Program instructors hoped that the latter were broad enough to serve as an example of inquiry and research-based writing while allowing students to choose a topic either of personal interest or one relevant to their major. Written assignments in both semesters were conventional first year writing fare—summaries, analyses, and syntheses.

Despite these various well-intended efforts, by the second semester students were disengaged, evidenced by their frequent complaints of boredom and their high rates of withdrawal and failure in WR 112. In spring 2010, 15 percent of students withdrew from WR 112, and 21 percent of students who remained in the course failed it (at Blackburn "failure" of first year writing means receiving less than a C-). In spring 2011, the rate of withdrawal went up to 18 percent and 17 percent of students remaining failed. We knew we needed to boost student engagement and success, which required that we revise the curriculum while maintaining its alignment with WPA outcomes.

Content and theme were where we decided to make drastic programmatic change: *The Wire* would serve as the core text in 112. We chose season four because it situates the uncomfortable questions and conversations we wanted to have with our students in an engaging narrative. In particular, we knew students could and would identify with Michael, Dukie, Randy, and Namond, the four young men at the center of the season, which would humanize the show's challenging and sophisticated rhetoric surrounding race, class, and opportunity in America. In addition to the likability of its central characters, we knew that season four's highly sophisticated rhetoric would enable us to help our students meet the WPA outcomes for critical thinking, reading, and writing. Our hope was that *The Wire*'s interdisciplinary themes would allow students to identify and pursue inquiries based upon personal or academic relevance, thereby boosting their engagement and helping them make the leap from personal interest to academic analysis, argumentation, and source-utilization.

We both knew from our experiences teaching film and advertising in first year writing courses that students often responded more quickly and easily to visual texts. We didn't delude ourselves that this willingness and ease always yielded better, more insightful analysis, but we hoped that we could leverage students' familiarity and willingness to engage with visual media in the effort to help them read and respond to the ideas and texts of others. In other words, if we could get students to think critically and carefully about texts they thought they knew, to think about them in new and more sophisticated ways, perhaps they would be more willing and able to turn their analytical skills to extended print texts. In this way, our decision to use *The Wire* was similar to Mr. Pryzbylewski's lessons on probability and dice, which he characterizes to another teacher as "Trick 'em into thinking they aren't learning [in Prez's class, they're just playing dice; in ours, they're just watching TV] and they do" (4.7).

Finally, we knew we needed to surround our viewing with additional print texts for two reasons. First, we needed to challenge the stereotypes we were concerned would be cemented, and second, we needed to present models of prose in order to assist students in the reading, analysis/evaluation of, and writing in response to academic texts (again, in keeping with the sequence's and the WPA's outcomes for first year writing). In framing this print and visual partnership for our students, we encouraged them to think of visual texts as readable in similar ways as print texts: as systems of symbols, codes, and significations that create meaning at the intersection of text, creator, and reader/audience. We also frequently called attention to the similar and different ways print and visual text made and substantiated claims.

The New WR 112

In restructuring WR 112 around *The Wire*, we chose to focus only on season four. In a class serving first year students, the viewing schedule had to match expectations for a 100 level introductory course; viewing one season allowed us to immerse students in the show while leaving time for careful analysis of individual scenes at the pace of one episode per week. Season four works particularly well with first year students because as the four central boys enter the new school year at Edward Tilghman Middle, so have our students entered the new world of college. Furthermore, because these characters are new to the show, season four does not require too much knowledge of the first three seasons; one discussion at the beginning of the semester on the show's background effectively sets students up to begin viewing. Season four works particularly well as a core text in a claim-based research writing course because of its rhetorical complexity, and we were quite intentional in framing the course and the show in these terms. On the first day of class we share Simon's oft quoted remark that *The Wire* is about the ways in which individuals are ultimately compromised by the institutions they inhabit and identify with, which we identify as a claim central to the course. We then point out that all academic writing is, in a sense, claim-making, and that we will analyze Simon's claim in order to make claims in response. Lastly, season four, with the addition of the institution of education, expands opportunities for students to connect their own academic interests to the show's many arguments when selecting their final research topics.

As many first year students are still navigating the college's resources, viewing access was key for our classes. Therefore, to ensure they could watch without requiring them to purchase the season on DVD, we arranged twice weekly screenings on campus (Thursday and Sunday nights) and placed two copies of the season on reserve in the campus library. Attendance at the screenings tapered drastically each time we taught the course (spring 2012, 2013, and 2014) due to upgrades in the college's wireless, which allows students to stream episodes in their dorm rooms and on their phones, and also, as we discovered, to viewing parties held in dorm rooms each week. We discussed two episodes a week for the first two weeks of the semester, in part so that students had watched the entire season before going into their final research projects, but also to secure student immersion in the dense narrative, fearing that the overwhelming number of characters and intersecting storylines might alienate casual viewers. To further assist in this attachment process, we provided a character reference sheet (which students regularly referred to in class discussion throughout the semester) and brief episode summaries, both abridged from the HBO website. After immersing students the first two weeks, we then watched and discussed an episode a week.

Weekly episode discussions function in two ways. First, they provide opportunities for critical textual analysis. One particularly successful lesson focuses on Omar's first appearance in the season, in the episode "Home Rooms," in which he awakens in bed with boyfriend Renaldo and leaves their squatter's apartment in silk pajamas to purchase cereal at a corner store (4.3). First, we introduce the concept of close reading, of scrutinizing a text's elements for clues to its larger claim. Then, we ask students to perform a close reading of the episode's first three minutes, looking for details that help them form an impression about Omar. We play the scene in class and have students write down initial claims about who Omar is, which we share on the board. We then re-watch the scene, this time looking for detailed evidence to support the claims just made. Reading Omar's dress, his caution when leaving the apartment, and the shouts of "Omar comin'" that ring out as he walks down the street, students invariably are able to make insightful and accurate claims about Omar's status and the power he commands—even when unarmed and in his pajamas. After watching the scene twice and discussing the evidence, students refine their initial claims.

Second, weekly episode discussions serve as a common textual reference point for in-class activities in claim-making, information gathering, and source integration. We regularly draw material—clips, themes, characters—from the week's episode to illustrate abstract concepts, processes, or skills. For example, towards the middle of season four, Omar begins tracking Marlo Stanfield, staking out stash houses and courtyards in order to understand the machinations of post–Barksdale West Baltimore. At one point, he remarks to Renaldo, "on this caper, the more we learn, the less we know" (4.11). In class, we traced his information gathering process and likened this quote to claim-based writing and working theses, stressing that source-gathering isn't about finding random quotes that sound like they confirm pre-conceived conclusions. Rather, it is about following thoughts, ideas, and patterns to their sources, understanding the relationships between them, and then forming conclusions. One semester, this became a rallying point: research like Omar.

As students watch and discuss the season, they simultaneously read and discuss traditional scholarly print essays on race, class, and meritocracy. Paralleling these discussions is meant to familiarize students with different types of rhetoric while seamlessly transitioning between visual and print, "popular" and academic, in the hopes that students understand that all cultural texts are rhetorical in nature and that "reading" texts is the analytical goal of the class. Beverly Tatum's "Defining Racism" and Harlan Dalton's "Horatio Alger" allow us to present some basic assumptions upon which our conversations about race, racism, and meritocracy will be based. We follow these with Gregory Mantsios's "Class in America" and Paul Krugman's "The Sons Also Rise," which expand the conversation about systemic injustice and oppression to include class and family. Jonathan Kozol's "Still Separate, Still Unequal" provides, in the words of many of our students, a "real world" example of these systemic oppressions within the context of education, and Berry et al.'s "Race, Tragedy, and Outrage Collide After a Shot in Florida" provides more such real examples. Several chapters from Potter and Marshall's *The Wire: Urban Decay and American Television* serve as models for academic analysis: using a tool or perspective to interpret meaning from a text.

In addition to traditional scholarly essays on which students practice summary and synthesis and that they use as resources for their culminating argumentative research paper, we also assign a book length text each semester; for this we used Sandra Cisneros's *The House on Mango Street,* Daniel Woodrell's *Winter's Bone,* and Wes Moore's *The Other Wes Moore.* The purpose of the novel is to expand our discussion of the intersections of class, race, opportunity, and choice that were occurring about season four and in the scholarly essays beyond what, for students, became a black-white context. Cisneros's and Woodrell's novels were chosen deliberately to provide a female voice to the themes raised in season four but also for students to see those themes at work in contexts different from the show—a struggling Latino neighborhood in Chicago and a backwoods insular white community in the Ozarks. The third time we taught the course, we capitalized on the college's summer reading program selection and used Moore as a nonfiction account of the life of West Baltimore's corner boys.

In the new iteration of WR 112, we preserved the basic scaffolding of student work to emphasize analytical skill-building. Students write a summary of a scholarly essay, an analysis of how a character on the show is shaped by an institution of which they are a part, a synthesis of how an institution affects a character from the show and a character in the novel in similar and different ways, and a rhetorical analysis of a particular episode's argument, all of which leads to an argumentative research paper on a topic of the student's choice, drafted and revised in stages. All of this is to emphasize claim-driven writing, which we frame as an essential academic rhetorical move. We use the scope of the claims made in season four as a way to introduce disciplinary claims and analytical lenses; we pull various threads from the show—the critique of No Child Left Behind, the indictment of the war on drugs, the layers of political corruption, sexuality, parenthood, childhood emotional trauma—and offer them as opportunities to look at a claim and/or evidence used to support it from particular perspectives. We explain that this is a foundational mode of academic communication—written and oral; in this way, *The Wire* allows us to explore what the WPA outcomes statement describes as the "interactions among critical thinking, critical reading, and writing" and "the relationships among language, knowledge, and power in their fields" (http://wpacouncil.org).

To illustrate, the rhetorical analysis paper asks students to identify a single argument being made in one episode and delineate how the argument is made using details from specific scenes. The episode "Corner Boys" works well as an in-class example (4.8). After discussing the episode, we ask students to look for commonalities among the different narrative threads in the episode. We discuss Bunk's investigation into Omar's supposed robbery of "Old Face" Andre's corner market and Carcetti's ride-along with the police, during which a few teenagers are arrested for being high on pre-indicted corners and a man is arrested for unwittingly being caught up in a sting operation while riding his bike to work. Students are able to pinpoint the futility of such arrests and the injustice of Omar's, which we then connect to Prez's frustration with the meaningless "progress" of improved test scores. Thinking about Bunk's line that "this job ain't about the stories we like best," students work their way toward the episode's claim that justice and progress are empty words when they are equated with statistical improvement. Because we spend at least one class session a week engaging in these kinds of model analyses— breaking down individual episodes and mining them for claims—students are well-prepared to make their own written claims.

Assessment: Did *The Wire* Make a Difference?

Our sense during the first semester we taught *The Wire* was students were more engaged in both class discussions and their written work. They came to class prepared, discussions were animated, and students were, by and large, excited about their research projects. We were thrilled to have students not only doing the viewing required for each class period but also often working ahead. In the three years we taught season four, it was not unusual for a handful of students to watch ahead to the end of the season, and in some cases, the end of the series and go back to watch the first three seasons. Not only were they watching, they were coming to class with analytical questions for discussion: we often had to write questions on the board at the beginning of class to ensure we paced our discussion in order to answer them all. At such a small school, we were also able to see how students were connecting what they were learning from watching *The Wire* to the material in other courses. During the spring 2013 semester, four students were concurrently enrolled in WR 112 and an African American literature course, in which students were struggling with the difficult postmodern novel *Philadelphia Fire* by John Edgar Wideman. These four students leveraged their understanding of institutional critique in

The Wire to shed light on the novel, likening its representation of the urban crisis of poverty, limited employment opportunities, and systemic racism to the show as a means of interpreting for the other students. Phrases such as "It's institutions that..." and "It's like in *The Wire* when..." greatly enhanced the class discussion happening in the literature course and demonstrated that students were, indeed, making connections across texts, media, and disciplines.

Another measure of success came in the form of students finding topics or themes of personal or academic relevance for their own research projects: education majors often took on the critique of No Child Left Behind; criminal justice majors explored parallel examples of corruption; a political science major likened Carcetti and Clay Davis to Illinois governor Rod Blagojevich; a psychology major used *The Wire* to illustrate his analysis of the effects of misogynist hegemony on young men; an art major applied a framework for contemporary artistry she had learned in an art history class to Omar Little in order to claim he is a contemporary artist. A few more of our favorite final research paper topics include "Vigilantism in *Batman* and *The Wire*," "How Power Functions on *The Wire* and *Game of Thrones*," and "Representations of Gay Men on *The Wire* and *Modern Family*."

However, despite the fact that we knew as teachers that students' attitudes and performance had changed, we needed hard evidence. Were students remaining and achieving success in the sequence? Were we achieving our course objectives and meeting WPA outcomes? Were students' ideas about race, class, and social forces being challenged? We answered these questions in three ways: (1) we compared withdrawal rates and final course grades from before and after we used *The Wire*; (2) we analyzed data from the college's general education writing assessments; and (3) we administered questionnaires at the end of each semester. The results supported our anecdotal observations: students were remaining in the course, passing it, and developing their critical thinking and writing skills in significantly higher numbers.

Table 1 illustrates our first analysis (see Appendix A for the raw numbers upon which the table is based) of using *The Wire* with essentially the same assignments for three consecutive spring semesters against the two most recent pre-*Wire* 112 semesters (spring 2010 and 2011). We compared only spring sections of WR 112 because the two fall sections in those academic years consisted primarily of students who had been enrolled in the developmental writing course, which was eliminated in 2012. In the table below, Completion means the rate at which students did not withdraw from the course; Success means they completed the course with a grade of C- or better, which the college requires for a student to have completed the general education requirement

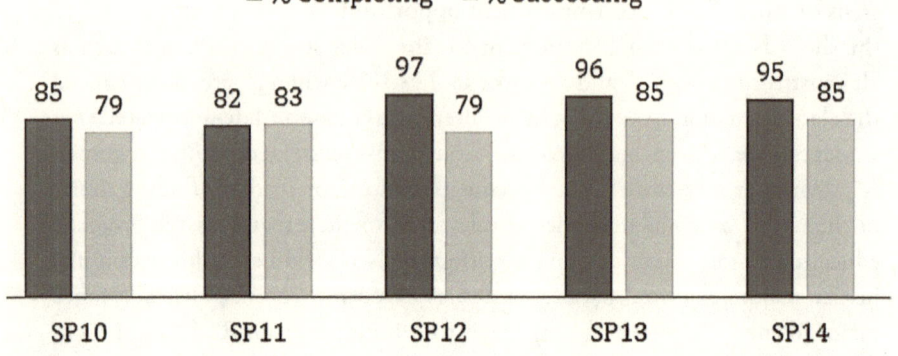

Table 1. WR 112 Completion and Success Rates.

towards graduation. In the first year we used *The Wire*, completion (or non-withdrawal) jumped 15 percent and has remained 10 percent above pre-*Wire* rates. Success declined in the first year, with a drop of 4 percent; however, we interpret this to mean that students who would have previously dropped were remaining in the course and doing better than they might have estimated in a previous semester. Success subsequently rose and has remained above pre-*Wire* rates, which is even more remarkable when one considers that in spring 2013, students who would have previously been enrolled in the developmental course are amongst those taking the spring sections. In other words, the success rate rises above pre-*Wire* levels despite the inclusion of less well-prepared students.

The data in Table 2 illustrates the findings of our comparative analysis of the college's general education writing assessment data. Blackburn uses a course-embedded approach to general education assessment. Instructors use faculty developed rubrics to assess how well students meet faculty determined goals and objectives on a faculty-selected assignment (see Appendix C for full details on the college's writing objectives and assessment scoring). The courses in which writing is consistently assessed include WR 112 and EN 140 and 161, the college's Introduction to Literature (required of all students) and Literary Analysis (an introductory course for literature majors) classes, respectively. We knew that both courses required analytical writing—thus, the kinds of assignments upon which the assessments were based were similar in nature. We also knew that at least one faculty member was scoring both 112 and 140 students, so we were confident in the inter-rater reliability and parallel nature of the assessments. To conduct our analysis, we sifted through four years of

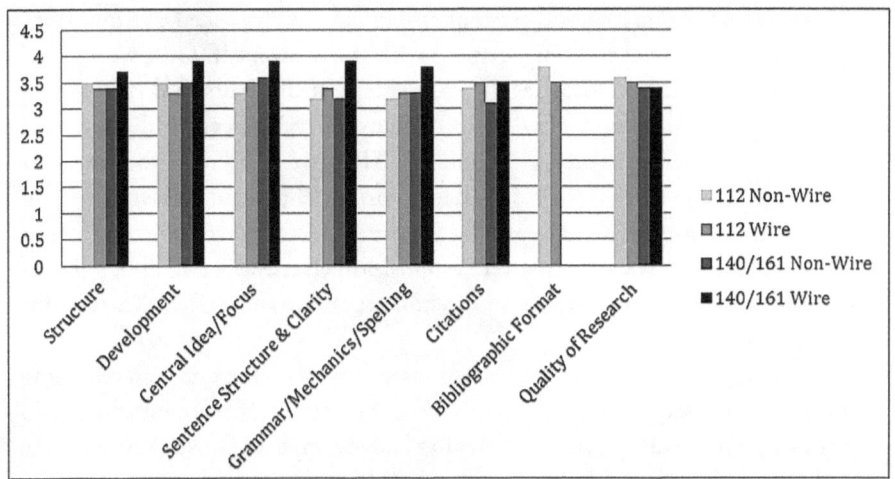

Table 2. Findings of Comparative Analysis.

data to identify students who had taken EN 140 subsequently to WR 112; then, we compared the 112 and 140 outcomes for those students, distinguishing between students who were enrolled in a 112 section that used *The Wire* (designated as *Wire* in the table) and those students who were not (designated as non-*Wire* in the table). Table 2 illustrates the comparative success in EN 140 for students who took *Wire* focused sections. Of particular note is that they outperform non-*Wire* students in the creation and support of claims (data points 1–4 in Table 2). We interpret this as evidence that our efforts to develop students' critical reading, writing, and thinking skills in *Wire*-focused sections have worked. Moreover, given the fact that students in EN 140/161 have far fewer opportunities to determine the parameters of their essay topics and claims, they are transferring analytical skills to more abstract, less personally relevant writing and thinking tasks. Our students are more successful in 112 than they have been historically and they are transferring those skills to other, subsequent courses—every composition teacher's (and the WPA's) goal.

Our final method of assessment was a questionnaire administered at the end of each semester on which we asked open-ended questions regarding the purpose of the course and what students felt they had learned from watching *The Wire*. Regarding the purpose of 112, 56 percent of respondents identified improved writing, 20 percent identified critical thinking and/or improvement of analysis skills, and 10 percent identified prepared for other courses; 8 percent made no comment and 6 percent identified the discussion of social issues. When asked if the course had met its objectives, 83 percent felt it had; 16 percent made no comment and 1 percent said it had not. We asked two questions to gauge students' level of engagement with the show itself. First, we asked if they would watch the show again; 50 percent of students said they would (one person responded by saying: "Of course!"), 33 percent indicated they might, and 17 percent said they would not. Then, we asked what they thought about the show: 68 percent responded favorably, 8 percent unfavorably, and 23 percent neutrally. We interpret an almost 70 percent favorable response to the core text of a second semester composition course as a triumph, particularly after the years we tried in vain to find accessible and theme rich texts for this course.

Some of the most interesting responses came from the question regarding what they learned from watching *The Wire*. Just over half of the students said they learned something about the reality and/or impact of institutions on the individual, including "the streets." Students were split on the nature of that impact, with 10 percent saying they learned that individuals could change or choose to reject that impact and 4 percent suggesting that, in the words of one student, "no matter what you do, you cannot make a difference." Some (7 percent) said they learned not to judge other people, and 2 percent reported learning that stereotypes are wrong. Only 4 percent reported learning something about socio-economic class, and only 1 person (.005 percent) directly addressed racism. While it's disappointing that only one person could explicitly connect the reality they reported having learned about to the continued prevalence of racism in the United States, perhaps given the open ended nature of the question, and our explicit efforts to situate race as one among many social factors that shape an individual's identity, we can take the various responses as evidence that students did learn to think more broadly and critically, that they learned, in the words of one student, that "life is neither black or white but shades of gray."

Ultimately, the data confirmed our observations and students' self-reported experiences: *The Wire* engaged our students in ways that improved their writing and thinking skills not just in our class but in subsequent writing-intensive courses. As asserted earlier, this may be in some part due to our own personal level of engagement; instructor enthusiasm goes a long way to engaging even the most reluctant students. However, given the extent of the positive and transferred outcomes across multiple sections and semesters, primary credit must be given elsewhere. Some may be given to the televisual nature of the text, and some may be given to the show itself. We believe credit also lies in the partnership of accessible, familiar texts and more challenging, less familiar texts. In other words, we think the course worked similarly to Colvin and

Parenti's: it allowed students to use what they know to engage with and better understand the value of less familiar, more abstract knowledge, which in our case was academic discourse. Finally, credit for the course's success needs to include the sense of community *The Wire* created in our classrooms and across campus. It was truly a shared learning experience.

Note

1. Elbow's approach to teaching writing focused almost exclusively on process and voice, and Gardner's emphasis on the first year addressed social transition rather than disciplinary concerns.

Works Cited

"Home Rooms." *The Wire*. Season 4, episode 3. HBO. September 24, 2006. Television.
"A New Day." *The Wire* Season 4, episode 11. HBO. November 26, 2006. Television.
"Unto Others." *The Wire*. Season 4, episode 7. HBO. October 29, 2006. Television.
"WPA Outcomes Statement for First Year Composition." Council of Writing Program Administrators. 2008. Web. July 26, 2014.

Appendix A: Raw Data for Table 1

Semester	N	Withdraw	Complete	A	B	C	Succeed	D	F
SP 2010	84	13	71	7	4	5	16	0	1
SP 2011	84	15	69	8	26	23	57	8	4
SP 2012	79	2	77	14	27	20	61	8	8
SP 2013	85	3	82	14	33	23	70	5	6
SP 2014	62	3	59	8	15	27	50	7	2

Appendix B: Raw Data for Table 2

Course	Structure and Coherence W1.1	Development W1.2	Central Idea/Focus W1.3	Sentence Structure & Clarity W2.1	Grammar/Mechanics/Spelling W2.2	Citations W3.1	Bibliographic Format W3.2	Quality of Research W4
112 Non-Wire	3.5	3.5	3.3	3.2	3.2	3.4	3.8	3.6
112 Wire	3.4	3.3	3.5	3.4	3.3	3.5	3.5	3.5
140/161 Non-Wire	3.4	3.5	3.6	3.2	3.3	3.1	NA	3.4
140/161 Wire	3.7	3.9	3.9	3.9	3.8	3.5	NA	3.4

Appendix C: Blackburn College's General Education Assessment Rubric

Writing Goal 1.1. Conceptualization and Thinking: Structure and Coherence/Organization

5 The central argument is fully developed and logically stated. All supporting points are relevant to the central idea and follow from each other in a logical sequence. Conclusion synthesizes central idea with supporting evidence.

4 Supporting points presented in body paragraphs mostly relate to and advance the central idea. Paragraphs focus on single ideas, building on each other logically. Some transitions may be unclear or illogical. The paper follows a plan, although one or two ideas out of order. Conclusion simply restates central idea with reference to supporting evidence.

3 Supporting points and/or transitions between them not clear or apparent. Individual body paragraphs contain multiple ideas. Follows general plan, but some ideas out of order. Conclusion simply restates central idea (introductory idea).

2 Paper attempts to follow a plan, but does not develop it. Individual body paragraphs contain multiple ideas. Supporting evidence not clearly related to central idea and/or is related to central idea but is not logical. Lack of obvious conclusion.

1 Arguments are unrelated to central idea. New and unrelated ideas randomly introduced but not developed. Supporting points not related to central idea and/or to each other.

Writing Goal 1.2. Conceptualization and Thinking: Development

5 Each point is fully explained and supported by appropriate evidence that advances the central idea.
4 Each point is supported by evidence, but the evidence is occasionally not conclusive or adequately explained.
3 Most points are supported with evidence and explanation, but some support is inadequate and/or inappropriate.
2 Points are occasionally supported by inappropriate or inadequate explanation, evidence, or logic.
1 No points are supported with appropriate evidence or logical explanation.

Writing Goal 1.3. Conceptualization and Thinking: Central Idea/Focus

5 The central idea or question is clearly stated or directly implied. The way in which points will be developed and supported is sufficiently previewed. The central idea or question can be supported with evidence or logical argument.
4 The central idea or question is apparent but lacks depth. The preview of supporting evidence needs development or further explanation. The logic of the argument in not complete or immediately apparent.
3 The central idea or question is present but vague, underdeveloped, or simplistic. The preview does not make clear how the central idea will be supported or developed.
2 The central idea is a vague or unclear general idea or question not logically developed. The preview of supporting evidence is missing, unclear and/or illogical.
1 There is no central idea or question stated. There is no indication of how the argument will be supported. Or, the central idea consists of assertions that cannot be supported with logic or evidence.

Writing Goal 2.1. Writing and Expression of Ideas: Sentence Structure and Clarity

5 Paper uses appropriate sentence patterns and language to express the relationship between ideas. Meaning of the sentences can be easily understood.
4 Paper occasionally includes an awkward sentence or confusing structure but generally reads well.
3 Sentences can usually be understood but must re-read more than once to do so. Some sentence variety is present but often the sentence structure is repetitious and/or awkward.
2 Awkward sentences and/or repetitious sentence structure interfere with meaning.
1 Paper generally uses simple sentences and expresses ideas with a listing of facts without explaining the relationships between them; or, the paper contains many awkward sentence structures; or, the meaning of sentences cannot be understood.

Writing Goal 2.2. Writing and Expression of Ideas: Grammar/Mechanics/Spelling

5 The paper contains no grammatical, mechanical, or spelling errors; demonstrates an understanding of grammar and syntax.
4 Paper has one-three errors but generally demonstrates control of grammar and syntax. (Note: Sometimes, a writer will make one error several times—spelling "their" as "there", for example; that would count as one error.)
3 The writer averages one spelling or common grammatical error per page.
2 The writer has several errors throughout the paper that do not interfere with meaning.
1 The writer makes many errors that sometimes interfere with meaning.

Writing Goal 3.1. Citations and Documentation: Citations
5   Paper effectively incorporates quotes, paraphrases, and summaries and always cites the source.
4   Paper sometimes clumsily incorporates borrowed material but always cites the source.
3   Paper has difficulty with anything other than direct quotes (i.e., paraphrases, summaries, etc.) but always cites the source. Or, the writer occasionally does not cite a summary or paraphrase when he/she should.
2   Paper only cites the source when using a direct quote and has difficulty with other forms of borrowing.
1   Paper does not appropriately incorporate sources into the text; writer clearly does not know when to document sources.

Writing Goal 3.2. Citations and Documentation: Bibliographic Format
5   Uses a standard bibliographical format accurately.
4   Uses a standard format but makes minor mistakes.
3   Provides most or all of the information needed but in an improper format.
2   Provides some of the essential bibliographical information.
1   Does not provide a bibliography even though sources used in the paper.

Writing Goal 4. Citations and Documentation: Quality of Research
5   Paper uses academic or otherwise appropriate sources that effectively support the argument in an unbiased manner. Other sources that may be appropriate include interviews, television documentaries or videos, or recent popular magazines and newspapers if dealing with a current topic.
4   Paper generally uses appropriate sources but, even though better sources are available, relies on popular magazines or newspapers to support its argument(s).
3   Paper uses a variety of sources but gives equal credibility to all of them. For example, the author might refute statements made in a scholarly journal using an obviously biased source. Or the author might cite an academic source and refute that source's assertion using a personal example or biased source.
2   Paper relies only on popular magazines, newspapers, encyclopedias, and/or biased and/or "author unknown" websites.
1   Paper does not use sufficient sources to adequately support its argument(s).

Exercises in Revision and Form

Michael Ennis

In 2009 and 2011, I used seasons one and four of *The Wire* as the central text for my first year writing courses in Duke University's Thompson Writing Program, and in 2014 I used seasons one through three for an upper-level writing course in the Program for Writing and Rhetoric at University of Colorado-Boulder. The series met my expectations of its ability to engage students with its gripping narrative of socially relevant themes, and it excelled in teaching three key skills that often elude students. Because *The Wire* draws on and revises so many different kinds of texts, it provides a compelling opportunity to think about source engagement and revision as processes that transform meaning. By comparing the rhetorical effectiveness of similar arguments made in various genres and media, students gain practice in analyzing and evaluating form in a broad and substantive way. Finally, because students engage in sociological topics relevant to them, they see themselves as writers with meaningful contributions to public discourses.

There are several challenges that confront the designer of a writing course. One of the most difficult decisions comes at the very beginning: how to introduce content into the course without distracting from the centrality of the writing process. Broadly speaking, there are two categories of introductory writing courses: inquiry-based classes that are centered on a topic or set of texts and skills-based courses that allow students to select topics through which to carry out writing exercises. Inquiry-based courses deliver cohesion, but run the risk of limiting students from exploring questions that are meaningful to them or distracting from the core purpose of the course—mastering writing skills. While students appreciate the freedom offered in skills-oriented courses, the lack of core content can sometimes undermine a sense of shared purpose in the classroom. On a day-to-day basis, shifting from topic to topic can undercut a sense of forward momentum, not to mention the students' belief that their work is building on their own previous writing and that earlier work in the semester can contribute directly to longer, more sophisticated papers. This is especially true when students must comment on each other's work. Small group workshops, for example, work much better when students have the confidence in their own expertise to comment meaningfully on their peers' work. As a central text for a writing course, especially for first year students, *The Wire* enables students to feel confident in their abilities to analyze the text because the form is familiar (a TV show), especially when compared to more unfamiliar academic topics. But the show's complexity and depth, range of sociological topics, and relevant themes also challenge students, fostering a genuine sense of inquiry and collaboration.

Having a semester-long inquiry into a text enables students to expand their notions of revision because their assignments can all contribute to longer projects. Students are often amenable to revision that involves editing, clarifying arguments, and tweaking organization. However, asking students to reconsider their work in more radical ways can be difficult because they are reluctant to make the broad changes sometimes necessary to effectively engage different audiences. Using *The Wire* as a central text facilitates students' reconceptualization of the role of revision as a process that sometimes involves wholesale changes in tone, style, and even genre and medium. Multi-staged writing assignments teach this process by specifically tasking students to revise their work into several different genres. For example, building a research paper from a proposal, then an annotated bibliography and review essay. Once the core argument has been articulated as a research essay, students must then revise it in other modes: presenting it using Prezi or PowerPoint, for example, and then translating it into writing that is appropriate for a digital forum such as a blog, a website, or podcast.

Writing assignments that ask students to write in different modes effectively teach them to attend to questions of form and the interrelations of purpose, genre, and audience; *The Wire* complements such activities in two key ways. First, early in the semester, students must come to terms with *The Wire* as the result of complex revision and synthesis of previous writing. The show draws on both David Simon's creative non-fiction *Homicide: A Year on the Killing Streets* and NBC's 1990s adaptation of this work. Moreover, he collaborated with Ed Burns for *The Corner: A Year in the Life of an Inner-City Neighborhood*, which was also adapted for television as an HBO miniseries that was filmed as a documentary (albeit scripted and performed by actors). All four of these projects took different approaches to documenting the War on Drugs and the decline of an industrial city. In creating *The Wire*, Simon and Burns fictionalized many of the stories and characters from their writing and combined that content with a synthesis of the visual styles of *Homicide: Life on the Streets* and *The Corner*. Of course, the multiple influences and sources of *The Wire* make it a rich text for students to analyze in terms of both content and style (and the relationship between the two). More importantly, the revision and synthesis of several texts carried out by Simon and Burns provides an authentic case study for students, thus transforming what could be an arid, out-of-context set of exercises into a meaningful inquiry with a model to emulate.

This essay will discuss detailed examples for using these texts in the hope that they provide ways of framing *The Wire* for students in inquiry-based writing courses. *The Wire* helps them gain skills in conducting interdisciplinary research, a conception of revision as a process that can transform meaning, and a metacognitive awareness of the relationship of form to meaning. I will ground these with concrete suggestions for pairings of texts that spark creative student work and examples of work students have carried out in these courses.

Course Structure

Before delving into examples of text pairings, some background on the course structure is necessary to get a sense of pacing and other practical issues that teaching *The Wire* raises. I have twice used all twenty-six episodes of seasons one and four (for the first year courses), and once all thirty-seven episodes from seasons one through three (for the upper-level course). In both courses, students gained skills in analyzing the television show through a sequence of short assignments that asked them to (1) discuss a scene in detail using multimedia; (2) compare representations in *The Wire* to selections from David Simon's and Ed Burns's non-fiction prose; and (3) discuss the role of a particular televisual element (character, plot, setting, cinematography, dialogue, etc.) in the overall "project" of the show. Students then revised and synthesized these short essays into a sustained critical evaluation of season one that engaged the work of other critics and evaluated the rhetorical success of *The Wire*.

The second half of the semester extended these central questions by requiring students to compare the limits and usefulness of *The Wire*'s arguments about a social issue (e.g., education reform, the war on drugs, political corruption, etc.) to similar arguments made in the academic literature. Again, scaffolding the assignments affords students the opportunity to build on their previous thinking and sustain an ongoing engagement with the show. When applying an academic reading to *The Wire*, students, in most cases, drew on a common text for this assignment. I used Jonathan Kozol's *Shame of the Nation*—a critique of education inequality in the United States—when discussing season four. I have also used selections from William Julius Wilson, Jr.'s *When Work Disappears* when using seasons one and two. After analyzing the formal differences between academic arguments and *The Wire*, students develop questions about one of the issues addressed by the show and the academic literature. Because Kozol's work speaks so directly to the issues addressed in the portions of season four set in a middle school—problems of school funding, managing standardized testing, institutional expectations for students—there was little variation from students wanting to use Kozol as a lens through which to read season four. The overlap between Wilson and season one is more implicit. By showing a longshoreman union struggling with deindustrialization, season two shows the process of joblessness that is already complete in season one, and links more directly to Wilson's ideas, although with different racial parameters as much of the union is white. Students often found Wilson more difficult than Kozol, and when I used Wilson as a common text, many students used other texts to analyze *The Wire*—in particular scholarly analyses of the War on Drugs and/or racial biases in the criminal justice system.

Based on their comparisons of these texts, student then developed more specific and detailed research questions about a topic that would help them explore a field relevant to their future studies. *The Wire* provides ample avenues for research in the humanities, social sciences, and even the natural sciences. The final project, then, put these different kinds of texts into conversation in order to both better understand the relative strengths of certain forms of writing and by extension to better understand the issue itself. When executed poorly, this kind of essay can end up as a tedious exercise in rhetorical analysis. However, because the show frames so many different issues in ways that speak directly to concerns of students—as students, as citizens, as media consumers, and as writers and scholars—students became genuinely invested in understanding the issues and the sites for public discourse about them. While I have some reservations that this kind of writing becomes somewhat detached from texts students will produce in other classes, not to mention their professions, I feel the benefit of critical awareness of the relationship between content and form these exercises generate outweighs that disadvantage. And when the papers were done well, which happened often, they ceased to be exercises for a writing class and became ambitious interventions into contemporary social issues. Finally, as a coda to project two, students brainstormed possible issues that might be represented in an imagined season six of the show.

The chapters in Joseph Harris's *Rewriting: How to Do Things with Texts* coincide with the stages of these assignments, and his general framework of all writing being "rewriting" helps students grasp how I ask them to conceptualize *The Wire*. In the book, Harris walks students through several of the "moves" that characterize academic writing as conversation. For example, his first chapter lays out several examples of how students can "come to terms" with texts by thinking about their "aims, materials, and methods" (19). The concepts and language in the chapter enable students to think about how Simon's drawing on real life stories combines with the show's realist/documentary style to produce a "purpose" to the show, which is imminent in the style, but certainly subject to some interpretation. Harris includes chapters on how to "forward" and "counter" the ideas of other writers, which provide practical advice for entering academic conversations in good faith. Finally, his chapter on "taking an approach," while abstract for some students, challenges students to think about the implications and methods of writing through the lenses of different philosophies and disciplines. *Rewriting* provides a readable companion for students and its structure can usefully guide students through scaffolded assignments.

In summary, after we discussed *The Wire* and its broad use of sources and prior "drafts," students researched the academic literature on one of the key issues in season four and compared its effectiveness to the show's narrative. Teaching research and information literacy in this way brings two key benefits. First, I found students entered the research project with a more robust sense of inquisitiveness than in other courses I had taught. Second, by assessing the effectiveness of the treatment of these issues, students gain a metacognitive awareness of argument, evidence, and form in academic writing. Class discussion revolved around the relative persuasiveness of texts. I encouraged students to decide for themselves which texts persuaded them most effectively and support their conclusions with textual evidence. I would ask them to compare, for example, the careful analysis in Wilson's treatment of the effects of joblessness with the more passionate polemics in Simon and Burns's *The Corner*. The resulting essays argued a broad range of positions about the roles of narrative, statistics, and data in the production of knowledge. Ironically, even though some students ultimately preferred the analytical approach of academic writing, their investment in the issues came from the powerful narrative *The Wire* provided.

Interdisciplinary Inquiry

It is worth starting with the end of the course—that is, outlining *The Wire*'s usefulness for instigating interdisciplinary research projects—because it often makes sense to reverse-design writing courses based on the final project. And while I build a good deal of flexibility into what my students research, a different, more targeted approach can yield other kinds of benefits in terms of enhanced understanding of a specific discipline or sub-discipline. This approach would work well in a "writing in the disciplines" course. Also, it can be useful to have a sense of what kind of archive students bring to the table.

Because *The Wire* draws on so many different kinds of texts and different kinds of writing, students who have different disciplinary interests can find research projects that speak directly to the course's use of the show as a common text. In other words, *The Wire* allows flexibility to student research while giving the writing seminar focus. For example, *The Wire* applies to many concerns in the humanities, from literary history to film and television studies. Many students are quick to pick up the deep thematic echoes from the literary canon. In particular, the realism of Dickens—an author students usually have encountered in high school—strikes a chord with students and they are able to make the leap from Dickens's attempts to document industrialization in the nineteenth century to *The Wire*'s documentation of deindustrialization in the twenty-first. Such comparisons are so rich they inspired a History course at Duke University that explored constructions of childhood and class in Victorian England and today's United States based on *The Wire* and Dickens. Even more commonly, students see resonances with *The Great Gatsby*. This happened even before the recent Baz Luhrmann film adaptation and even when students were not viewing season two, during which D'Angelo Barksdale discusses Gatsby in a prison reading group. Making these connections not only deepens student appreciation of *The Wire* as more than simply a TV show (although given the renaissance of television in the last fifteen years, that has become less of an issue), but more importantly it teaches the ability to historicize a contemporary text in a deeper tradition.

Of course, *The Wire* resonates with the history of genre fiction, as well as film and television crime dramas. I have had several students who independently chose to compare how *The Wire* constructs "ethnic" criminality compared to such landmarks as *The Godfather* and *The Sopranos* (Italian), *Gangs of New York* and *Boardwalk Empire* (Irish), and even *Once Upon a Time in America* (Jewish). Likewise, students with some background in cinematic portrayals of African American life find it interesting to situate *The Wire* against other films that they come to college familiar with. In particular, Spike Lee's *Do the Right Thing* (1989) and John Singleton's *Boyz n the Hood* (1991) have found a fairly broad base of viewers. Finally, many students come to the class familiar with other drug-trafficking narratives. Of course, *Breaking Bad* has recently shown up on the radar, but earlier representations of the drug trade have bubbled to the surface as well. Particularly, Fernando Meirelles's *City of God* (2002) has found an avid viewership among the current generation of college-aged students. These different genealogical connections enable student writers to explore profound thematic resonances and to analyze and problematize how different cultural media construct arguments about those themes. Beginning with short writings about *The Wire*, students used crime drama to explore the construction of race and ethnicity, questions of ethics and class, critiques of American capitalism, and even broader philosophical/theoretical questions surrounding power and the reproduction of society.

Finally, in the humanities, *The Wire* offers possibilities for introducing students to theoretical work, although including theory often has diminishing returns. When I used selections from Louis Althusser's RSA/ISA essay, the results were decidedly mixed. I invested a lot of time into contextualizing the essay, excerpting selections that were crucial to his argument, and working with students to get a grasp on a difficult argument because I thought it would give them a critical vocabulary for discussing some of the show's major themes. We even spent time in class applying the concepts to specific scenes, which helped clarify Althusser's ideas. For example, I explained how Althusser's concept of interpellation—the idea that ideology "calls" us to assume certain roles, even when we are never fully conscious that the calling comes prior to our identity—could productively explain the scene where Stringer Bell recruits Bodie to kill Wallace (1.12). He never explicitly orders the hit, but simply asks him if he's built for the game and if he's "got heat." When Bodie affirms, Bell calls him a "good soldier." Likewise, in the same episode, Wallace explains to D'Angleo why he has returned to Baltimore after trying to leave the drug trade. His explanation serves as the epigraph for the episode: "This is me, yo, right here." For the students who "got it," the exercise enriched their writing and helped them think through how *The Wire*'s narrative structure makes a similar argument about social reproduction as Althusser's theoretical prose. There are some texts that could help, especially in providing models for students on applying a conceptual model to *The Wire*. Alisdair McMillan and Ryan Brooks have both employed Foucaultian readings of *The Wire* to understand how Simon's critique of institutions and their impact on individuals overlaps with Foucault's critique of the legitimacy of institutions. Paulo Friere's *Pedagogy of the Oppressed* provides a framework for understanding season four's critique of education in "Posing Problems and Picking Fights: Critical Pedagogy and the Corner Boys" by Ralph Beliveau and Laura Bolf-Beliveau.

Outside of the humanities, the touchstones for students can be less immediate, and the key texts are somewhat less accessible (although not as difficult as Althusser). I should point out—before getting into some useful texts—that the show has enabled upper-class students to productively apply learning from other courses. In particular, students from anthropology and ethnic studies are equipped to apply concepts from those fields to reading the show—a sophisticated writing move and one of the most difficult ones to convey and master from Harris's *Rewriting*. I have had students apply Clifford Geertz's method of "thick description" and James Scott's readings of "hidden transcripts" to analyze the show's project. The experience of cross-disciplinary fertilization is difficult to convey, and examples of it do not always drive home how productive such borrowings can be. A workshop-based writing course creates a space for students to make their own discoveries and, more important, witness and critically evaluate the same process in their peers.

As I have suggested above, *The Wire* excels at raising questions of metacognition and attention to form. When students compare the relative rhetorical effectiveness of *The Wire* to the academic literature that informs some of its themes, they develop a critical attention to the relative contributions of narrative realism vs. data-driven analysis. In the first iteration of my course we viewed seasons one and four, which address the lives of young teenagers who deal drugs in "The Pit" and four middle-school students and their different experiences of "The Game," respectively. I paired this with the work of Jonathan Kozol on education inequality and reform. In another iteration, we combined seasons one and two, the first investigation of the Barksdale organization and the docks investigation, with *When Work Disappears* by William Julius Wilson, Jr. As I expected, most students found the academic writing more inaccessible than the *The Wire* because of the style and sheer volume of data. This was especially true for Wilson's work compared to Kozol's, although I suspect Kozol's approachability stemmed from the shared experience of school rather than anything inherent to the text. Both works make interesting use of a synthesis of quantitative and qualitative data, and both attempt to document the effects of structural inequality—

in particular, the way that institutions of inequality can become self-perpetuating.

The possibilities for independent research do not end with the social sciences. *The Interrupters* (2011), the recent documentary about Chicago's anti-violence organization Cease Fire, raises issues of psychology and public health for students interested in health professions. The founder of Cease Fire, epidemiologist Dr. Gary Slutkin, models the organization on public health efforts by likening disruptions of violence to interventions preventing the spread of disease. In season four of *The Wire,* Dr. Parenti echoes Slutkin's ideas when he explains to retired major Howard "Bunny" Colvin that he hopes to research the possibility of "inoculating" inner-city youth against violence (4.3). Furthermore, the main narrative of *The Interrupters* resonates with the character of Dennis "Cutty" Wise, an incarcerated gang enforcer who struggles to adapt to life outside of prison until he starts a boxing gym for at-risk youth. The documentary spends a year with three "violence interrupters," former gang members who work in Chicago to prevent retaliatory violence by direct mediation. Like seasons one and four of *The Wire,* the documentary emphasizes the stressful conditions school-age children experience, arguing ultimately that violence is a learned behavior that stress, trauma, and other mitigating factors greatly exacerbate. The documentary complements *The Wire* both visually and thematically. Furthermore, students pursuing healthcare professions can then draw connections between the show and their disciplinary interests, in particular social psychology, epidemiology, addiction treatment, and public health. Peter Beilenson and Patrick McGuire's recent book *Tapping into the Wire* provides a helpful resource for students interested in these issues. The volume contains several explicit models of using *The Wire* to explore issues of public health and medicine, ranging from addiction treatment to nutrition to gun safety.

A former student, Justin Leder, published his work from our class in a student journal, and it provides an excellent model for the kind of interesting inter-disciplinary research that can emerge from student engagement with *The Wire*. As a high school student he read about the Stanford Prison Experiment, in which Dr. Philip Zimbardo transformed the basement of Stanford's Jordan Hall into an ersatz prison populated by volunteer students to test the psychological effects of incarceration on prisoners and guards. Leder wished to explore some of the implications of the experiment in his writing for the course. His finished product synthesized several sources from a variety of fields—he traveled from Zimbardo to Wilson and several other theorists—to argue that context ultimately explains violence better than any other factor.

He also drew on season four because, in his words, it showed how the inner-city violence serves as a "Jordan Hall of violence." In particular, I appreciate the way Leder establishes his argument by laying out the disciplinary approaches he will adopt and how they relate to Simon's approach:

> Building on Zimbardo's findings, this essay synthesizes the insights of contemporary sociology, psychology, and fiction to shed light on the causes of African American inner-city youth violence....[Simon] fills a void that science necessarily leaves behind in its understanding, exploring the underlying causes of the African American inner-city youth violence problem from a humanistic perspective, rather than a scientifically detached one. The season revolves around the stories of four eighth-graders: Namond Brice, Michael Lee, Randy Wagstaff, and Duquan Weems. Through their eyes, Simon shows the prevalence of youth violence in inner-city Baltimore.... The ultimate roots of the violence are grounded not in the dispositions of the individuals, but in the deep pathologies of the environment in which they live.

Leder goes on to argue that the narrative in *The Wire* explains some of the theories undergirding Zimbardo's (and others') social psychology by showing the phenomenon in a meaningful context. In other words, both the data and the narrative become essential for fully appreciating the impact of context on behavior.

The Wire *as Revision*

As discussed above, during the first half of the semester, I encouraged students to take into account the multiple texts that contributed to the show's plot, characterization, use of setting, and visual style. David Simon combined several sources—his own reporting, oral history, court records, fieldwork—in his non-fiction book *Homicide: A Year on the Killing Streets*. The best-selling book then became the basis for the serialized NBC drama *Homicide: Life on the Street*, which adapted many of the stories, but changed the characterization of the book's real-life protagonists (although many of the names stayed the same). David Simon and Ed Burns's *The Corner: A Year in the Life of an Inner-City Neighborhood*, which the authors termed a non-fiction novel, took a similar approach. When it was adapted into a miniseries, the director chose to film the book as a documentary, although a fictionalized one insofar as actors portray the subjects of the book. *The Wire*, then, can be seen as a synthesis of two revisions—a kind of multimodal project—that refines and transforms the arguments and effects from the earlier sources. It's of note that the real-life drug investigation that inspires season one's story was only alluded to in

Homicide: A Year on the Killing Streets. And the engagement with sources doesn't stop there, since the writers of the show also draw on academic research and other crime fiction, most notably by employing novelists like George Pelecanos, Dennis Lehane, and Richard Price.

Writing exercises and class discussion called attention to how *The Wire* transforms (for better or worse) these sources and considers the uses and limitations of a serialized drama for portraying the social life of an American city. Not only do these exercises pose complex and challenging questions about the relationship of form to meaning and argument, but in establishing source engagement and revision as ongoing and ambitious dimensions of the writing process that radically reshape argument and audience, the exercises enable students to break away from their accepted norms of revision as tweaking and polishing.

Of course, space on the syllabus is at a premium, and both the *The Corner* (535 pages) and *Homicide* (642 pages) are long. Not to mention that the TV version of *Homicide* yielded 122 episodes and a TV movie. So, unless the course is designed to focus on issues of adaptation, one must be selective about which materials to include. It is important to select portions that illustrate techniques available to prose that take different forms in a visual narrative. This can be useful at dispelling the idea—common among students—that a visual medium inherently connects with an audience and inspires empathy more than the written word.

Asking students to discuss and/or write about similar "scenes" in *The Wire* and *Homicide: A Year on the Killing Streets* empowers students to construct meaningful knowledge about different rhetorical effects of prose and televisual narrative. Some of these are direct quotes from *Homicide*. For example, some homoerotic banter between Jimmy McNulty and Bunk Moreland is quoted almost verbatim from a passage in *Homicide*. More interestingly, students can compare different handlings of similar themes. In one of the most famous scenes from season one, McNulty and Bunk investigate the murder scene from a case that has gone cold, but may relate to the special detail's pursuit of the Barksdale gang (1.4). As the detectives lay out photos of the victim, they look around the room for clues that might help reconstruct the murder of Deirdre Kresson, but the only words they can muster are variations of "fuck." The scene conveys both the difficult, even soul-numbing minutiae of police work as well as the dark humor needed to cope with its morbidity, a major theme in Simon's earlier work. Students will quickly point out the difficulty of the scene. The cumulative comic effect of dozens of curses uncomfortably juxtaposes with the horror of the crime scene. And they will rightly point to the fact that the scene could not translate into writing.

The opening to *Homicide* explores similar themes that likewise could not translate to the screen. In the opening of the book, two detectives investigate a homicide scene, and the senior officer jokes inappropriately that the body has a "slow leak" (1). In the text, Simon supposes what his partner is thinking throughout, which immediately illustrates one of the chief benefits of prose: the facility with which it conveys inner thoughts. Several pages later, Simon switches to second person and pointed details to convey the drudgery of the job:

> This is the job:
> You sit behind a government-issue metal desk on the sixth of ten floors in a gleaming steel-frame deathtrap with poor ventilation.... You answer the phone on the second or third bleat because Baltimore abandoned its AT&T equipment in a cost-saving measure and the new phone system doesn't ring so much as it emits metallic, sheeplike sounds. If a police dispatcher is on the other end of the call, you write down an address.... You look at that body as if it were some abstract work of art, stare at it from every conceivable point of view in search of deeper meanings and textures. Why, you ask yourself, is this body here? What did the artist leave out? What did he put in? What was the artist thinking of? What the hell is wrong with this picture? You look for reasons [14].

The second-person voice continues for several pages, speaking directly to the reader to convey the feeling for the job with a compelling immediacy—it places you in the detectives' shoes. And while a TV show might be able to convey all of the details in the scene, it would not convey the same depth of meaning without the context and metaphors that prose furnishes. This attention to uses and limitations of different modes of communicating turns into a more attentive consideration of students' own writing. Analyzing the power of the photos in the scene from *The Wire* prompts students to consider when they need to use visual evidence. Seeing the power of detail and metaphor also translates into stronger implementation of those techniques in their prose. More importantly, having students think about why Simon revises his ideas into different forms and media translates into thinking critically about their own writing. In this way, revision becomes a process that not only repairs texts, but transforms ideas.

The Wire *and Form*

While I have tried to break down some of the benefits of teaching *The Wire* in a writing course, there is of course a great deal of overlap between them. Interdisciplinary inquiry and a broad conception of revision both point to larger and more abstract attention to form.

Ted Nannicelli's essay "It's All Connected: Televisual Narrative Complexity" usefully explains the role of form to argument in television in a way that students can grasp. Nannicelli argues that *The Wire*'s real innovations can be understood as threefold, in the areas of "narrative complexity, character development, and social commentary" (191). Most interestingly, in Nannicelli's view, the social commentary is enabled by the formal elements that are inherent to long form television. For example, the ongoing narrative of the show enables frequent cutting from storylines taking place in all of the strata of the city (192). Television viewers become accustomed to cutting from, for example, a Narcotics Anonymous meeting to a political fundraiser to a scene of cops in a bar, allowing the show to juxtapose these different classes without seeming contrived or didactic. The form of the story telling, as much as its content, is crucial to its ability to critique class stratification.

In conclusion, I offer a comparison exercise that crystalizes for students how context, genre, and form impact one of the central problems of the course: the ways cycles of structural inequality and their attending violence impact social structures. Wilson explains the cycle using data, controlling for various factors, and ultimately coming to conclusions about causality:

> Consider, for example, the problems of drug trafficking and violent crime. As many studies have revealed, the decline in legitimate employment opportunities among inner-city residents has increased incentives to sell drugs. The distribution of crack in a neighborhood attracts individuals involved in violence and lawlessness. Between 1985 and 1992, there was a sharp increase in the murder rate among men under the age of 24; for men 18 years old and younger, murder rates doubled. Black males in particular have been involved in this upsurge...
>
> Violent persons in the crack-cocaine marketplace have a powerful impact on the social organization of a neighborhood....As a result, the behavior and norms of the drug market are more likely to influence the action of others in the neighborhood, even those who are not involved in drug activity. Drug dealers cause the use and spread of guns in the neighborhood to escalate, which in turn raises the likelihood that others, particularly the youngsters, will come to view the possession of weapons as necessary or desirable for self-protection, settling disputes, and gaining respect from peers and other individuals [21].

Wilson goes on to show that while rates of violence were indeed higher among African Americans, that increase disappeared when controlled for joblessness, concluding that joblessness, not culture or race, should be seen as the cause of increased rates of violence. It's a tour de force of analytical writing, strengthened by the careful presentation of data. However, many students find it dry and incapable of evoking pathos. (A vocal minority of students and I disagree.) Most agree that Wilson's analytical presentation of facts makes it apropos for policy decisions and legislation.

The following comes from David Simon and Edward Burns's *The Corner*, and it begins with an attack on those very policy discussions. The passage urgently explains the impacts of the drug market on an inner-city neighborhood. The authors strip away Wilson's analysis and data, replacing it with the moral force of experience, and, I argue, the power of the prose itself:

> We can't stop it.
> Not with all the lawyers, guns, and money in this world. Not with guilt or morality or righteous indignation.... No lasting victory in the war on drugs can be bought by doubling the number of beat cops or tripling the number of prison beds. No peace can come from kingpin statistics and civil forfeiture laws and warrantless searches and whatever the hell else is about to be tossed into next year's omnibus crime bill.
> In the neighborhoods where no other wealth exists, they have constructed an economic engine so powerful that they'll readily sacrifice everything to it. And make no mistake: that engine is humming. No slacking profit margins, no recessions, no bad quarterly reports, no layoffs, no naturalized unemployment rate. In the empty heart of our cities, the culture of drugs has created a wealth-generating structure so elemental and enduring that it can legitimately be called a social compact....
> Get it straight: they're not just out there to sling and shoot drugs.... The men and women who live the corner life are redefining themselves at incredible cost, cultivating meaning in a world that has declared them irrelevant.... Here, they almost matter [57–58].

If students can relate these passages to each other, and use them to understand the murder of Wallace—not just the harrowing scene itself, but how *The Wire* contextualizes the murder in a larger narrative—then they can begin to understand the power of form (1.12). When we discussed such juxtapositions in class, students quickly grasped the different rhetorical situations of the writings and the way they might appeal to different audiences in different contexts. However, while I encourage students to make their own evaluations of the texts, I also insist that we do not prioritize one form of writing over the others. Instead, I ask that they go beyond considering audience and purpose to thinking about how the different forms shape meaning. The narrative context of Wallace's murder realizes Wilson's and Simon and Burns's causal arguments, and does so in such a way that it creates a different kind of knowledge about structural inequality.

Ultimately, if students can model their writing on examples like these to reach specific audiences, they have gone a long way to becoming effective communicators. When they can use the best parts of these styles to cross fertilize their own pieces, then they've learned to write.

Works Cited

Beilenson, Peter L., and Patrick A. McGuire. *Tapping into* The Wire: *The Real Urban Crisis*. Baltimore: Johns Hopkins University Press, 2012. Print.

Beliveau, Ralph, and Laura Bolf-Beliveau. "Posing Problems and Picking Fights: Critical Pedagogy and the Corner Boys." *The Wire: Urban Decay and American Television*. Eds. Tiffany Potter and C.W. Marshall. New York: Continuum, 2009. 91–103. Print.

Brooks, Ryan. "The Narrative Production of 'Real Police.'" *The Wire: Urban Decay and American Television*. Eds. Tiffany Potter and C.W. Marshall. New York: Continuum, 2009. 64–77. Print.

Chaddha, Anmol, and William Julius Wilson. "'Way Down in the Hole': Systemic Urban Inequality and *The Wire*." *Crime and Justice as Seen Through* The Wire. Eds. Peter A. Collins and David C. Brody. Durham: Carolina Academic Press, 2013. 29–54. Print.

The Corner. Dir. Charles S. Dutton. HBO Studios, 2011. DVD.

Harris, Joseph D. *Rewriting: How to Do Things with Texts*. Logan: Utah State University Press, 2006. Print.

Homicide: Life on the Street (The Complete Series). A&E Home Video, 2009. DVD.

"The Interrupters." *Frontline*. Dir. Steve James. PBS. 14 Feb. 2012. *Netflix*. 28 Feb. 2014.

Kozol, Jonathan. *Shame of the Nation: The Restoration of Apartheid Schooling in America*. New York: Broadway Books, 2005. Print.

Leder, Justin. "A Contextual Theory of African American Inner-City Youth Violence." *Deliberations* (2011). Web. 15 August 2013. http://twp.duke.edu/cms/aMediaBackend/original?slug=delib2011leder&format=pdf.

McMillan, Alisdair. "Heroism, Institutions, and the Police Procedural." *The Wire: Urban Decay and American Television*. Eds. Tiffany Potter and C. W. Marshall. New York: Continuum, 2009. 50–63. Print.

Nannicelli, Ted. "It's All Connected: Televisual Narrative Complexity." *The Wire: Urban Decay and American Television*. Eds. Tiffany Potter and C. W. Marshall. New York: Continuum, 2009. 190–202. Print.

Potter, Tiffany, and C.W. Marshall. *The Wire: Urban Decay and American Television*. New York: Continuum, 2009. Print.

Simon, David. *Homicide: A Year on the Killing Streets*. New York: Holt Paperback Editions, 2006. Print.

Simon, David, and Edward Burns. *The Corner: A Year in the Life of an Inner-City Neighborhood*. New York: Broadway Books, 1997. Print.

Wilson, William Julius. *When Work Disappears: The World of the New Urban Poor*. New York: Vintage, 1996. Print.

The Wire: The Complete Series. Prod. David Simon and Edward Burns. HBO Studios, 2011. DVD.

Closure in the Classroom
"Final Grades"
C.W. Marshall and Tiffany Potter

Like most consumers of television, students often focus upon their desire for emotional closure as a significant aspect of their engagement with a narrative. This focus can lead to intense and interesting responses, but can be difficult to translate into a useful pedagogical situation and into effective scholarship that puts those personal responses to good use, allowing students to move beyond the emotional and to locate sites of legitimate scholarly analysis. We can help students make this essential critical shift by providing them with a conceptual vocabulary to describe their experience of television narrative in a scholarly context, ideally one that they can also apply to other forms of narrative media. Narrative closure theory is particularly effective in facilitating analytical considerations of the intersections among audience response, narrative frameworks, and the ideological and cultural work that television series enact. This essay will discuss the ways in which closure theory can be used to teach *The Wire* and to facilitate higher-level critical thinking in the classroom. We will use a framework derived from the scholarship of closure developed following Frank Kermode's early theorization of fiction in *The Sense of an Ending*.

Closure theory examines how a literary work concludes, and considers the audience's sense of that conclusion as satisfying when "the questions posed in the work are answered, tensions released, conflicts resolved," encompassing both formal and affective qualities as well as their intersections (Fowler 3). Gestures of closure may emerge from within a text or may be imposed externally: within television, a season's conclusion is imposed by network demand, but needs to be justified within a satisfying emotional structure that makes sense in terms of the larger narrative arc. The forms and contexts of gestures of closure allow significant insights into both a specific season or arc and the larger critical and cultural issues that a television show engages.

The Pedagogy of Closure

The broadest scholarly understanding of closure has provided a critical framework at least since Aristotle documented the tendency for ancient audiences to prefer just, causally-derived endings that convey a sense of poetic justice for the characters (*Poetics* 18, 1455b-56a). Modern theorizations of closure begin with Kermode's 1967 development of that Aristotelian observation, in which he argues for the significance of what he sees as a largely natural human preference for orderly events reflected in narratives structured with clearly-articulated beginnings, middles, and ends. David H. Richter's *Fable's End: Completeness and Closure in Rhetorical Fiction* (1974) adds nuance by arguing for the critical distinction between "completeness" (where all that needs to be included has been presented) and "closure" (where the sense of an ending is felt). Such foundational distinctions can provide students with a process framework for moving from a simple emotional response to critical engagement with the pathos of Season Four of *The Wire*, and in particular its final episode, "Final Grades." In a seminar context, these distinctions can be reinforced through small group discussion of specific scenes in a key episode. In a larger lecture-based course, completeness and closure can be presented as tools to be used in a short writing assignment in which students document the elements that establish the "completeness" of a particular narrative arc, and then argue for the way in which those elements do or do not contribute to the creation of emotional closure for the reader. In both cases, one of the learning outcomes will be the ability to articulate in critical terms the narrative strategies involved in creating a sense of completion, taking into account audience response and narrative frameworks. Reading and applying excerpts from Kermode and Richter can give students a vocabulary for recognizing the ideological work being performed in those upsetting stories of mistreated corner boys.

Subsequent closure theory recognizes the conventional assumption that the last scenes of a narrative are somehow authoritative or carry particular retrospective determinations of the importance of what has come before: what Peter Rabinowitz calls the "rule of conclusive endings" where there is a "widely applicable interpretive convention that permits us to read it in a special way, as a *conclusion*, as a summing up of the work's meaning" (160). The theory also recognizes that "such an assumption naturally produces the inevitable rupture of this rule ... a convention like this one inevitably ensures that many readers will misread endings that fail to conform to their ideological expectations" (Richardson 253). While "Final Grades" (and its montage in particular, as is discussed below) provides clear closural gestures and creates a sense of the conclusive ending, at the same time the episode leaves certain narrative elements unresolved, practically to allow loose threads to pull forward into Season Five, of course, but interpretable also as moments of contradiction where, as Russell Reising has argued of several American novels, narratives "collapse into anti-closure because of historically specific concerns and narrative agendas" that cannot be brought to (conventionally) successful conclusions: closure functions "as a liminal moment, a threshold subdiscourse which simultaneously provides closure to the poetic [or narrative] utterance and initiatory openness to the postpoetic [post-narrative] world" (10–11).

Ongoing television series, of course, typically perpetuate a paradoxical relationship with closure, as the season finale must normally leave open the path to the continuation of the narrative in the season that will follow: gestures of closure and continuation must coexist in a way that will both satisfy audiences and leave them wanting more. Pressing the practical consideration of television production toward a critical space, however, closure without completeness embodies in an even more nuanced way what Brian Richardson argues of narrative closure in fiction: "The formal imperative of concluding these works thus clashes with the impossibility of genuinely resolving the ideological tensions within them; these works can't close, precisely because they are so deeply embedded within the conflicted socio-historical worlds of their genesis" (253).[1]

Such recognition of the way that structural closure and affective closure intersect proves particularly useful in studying an episode like "Final Grades" (4.13).[2] "Final Grades" challenges viewers with several conclusions that appear to be designed to be unsatisfying, and in that unsatisfying quality they illuminate the larger threads of cultural criticism that underlie *The Wire*. Bubbles's suicide attempt, Bodie's death, Carcetti's intransigent rejection of state funds for schools, and the bleak futures anticipated for Randy, Michael, and Dukie all drive the viewer toward a sense of Baltimore or perhaps American urban infrastructure as a dishearteningly deterministic institutional force that is beyond the power of individual children to evade. Series creator David Simon may envision *The Wire* as a call to arms, but the closural gestures are more consistently significant as evidence of disempowerment than of capacity for change.

Against these gestures, the rescue of Namond and McNulty's reassignment to Major Crimes do not offer the emotional catharsis that Western narrative has often been thought to require (since Aristotle, *Poetics* 1449b).[3] As a season finale, "Final Grades" exerts multiple gestures of closure, concluding—with varying degrees of horror, sadness, frustration, and redemptive pleasure—the stories of the corner boys and of the individuals and social institutions that act upon them. Closure and containment, however, are not the same. The closural gestures of the Season Four finale also create series-wide connections and signal the complications of the notion of closure as contained completion.

The closural gestures of "Final Grades" can also serve as a fulcrum to enable classroom discussion of the series as a whole. When the episode introduces Vondas to Marlo, for example, students can recognize the full extent of the criminal underworld shaping life in the city. They will also perceive that it is the awareness of these criminal networks that will ultimately justify McNulty's fabrications in Season Five. In courses organized around the series as a whole, students might be asked to consider the significance of the show's argument on the competition and collusion among criminal organizations and their effect on people not directly involved in the drug trade (assignments might focus on the dock workers in Season Two, the corner boys in Season Four, the news reporters in Season Five, and the families of police officers and criminals throughout the series); or they might analyze the ways in which problematic or incomplete closure in a case or in a character's narrative invites dishonest follow-up (as is seen, for example, in Herc's crookedly successful policework, McNulty's red strings, falsified news articles, and snitch violence).

The use of closure theory is not limited to examinations of whole series, however, and it is that flexibility that makes closure a particularly useful pedagogical approach to introduce to students. Strategies of closure can equally be considered in terms of a single episode, a narrative or character arc, or a single season. This makes it useful both in courses that focus wholly on *The Wire* and in those using the series in dialogue with other narratives, urban studies, or cultural histories. Television is ideally situated to provide opportunities to consider "cultural poetics of segmentation, the 'units of thought'" of a narrative (Fowler 15). The accumulation of those units of closural signals is a process that encourages viewers to look back and to reevaluate the significance of earlier narrative elements and character interactions, enabling and embodying the scholarly critical practices that we seek to foster in our students.

Using critical strategies of closure theory in the classroom provides one path to help students turn their innate emotional responses (perceiving "happy endings" or "sad endings") toward a critical engagement that can facilitate good student scholarship. Students recognize the difference between formal markers of closure (such as episode and season endings, montages and retrospectives) and affective qualities of closure (such as use or rejection of ideas of poetic justice and emotional appeals) even as they realize that closure in televisual narrative almost always requires an invitation to keep watching. Small-group collaborative learning processes in the classroom generate transactional perspectives on learning and narrative, which are based on the belief that meaning is constructed in the transaction between an individual reader and the text s/he consumes.[4] In transactional models, personal response is highly valued, as students bring their pre-existing knowledge and individual experiences into dialogue with a text. Meaning becomes a product of the reader and text, and reading is understood not as the consumption of a narrative with a known meaning but as the construction of meaning in the mind of the individual reader.

In college classrooms, however, we typically seek to teach our students to work through their initial emotional and cognitive responses toward a more formally critical perspective, emphasizing the dialogic relationships among texts and their social, political, and historical contexts and on the implications of those relationships for textual interpretation. As Carole Edelsky has argued, "being critical means questioning against the frame of systems, seeing individuals as always within systems, as perpetuating or resisting systems" (28). Articulating that process to students through the teaching of closure strategies grants them insights into the larger social and individual implications of all classroom practice, but particularly the practices involved in studying *The Wire* and its explicit cultural criticism.

Given its density and nuance, *The Wire* is particularly amenable to critical articulations of the relationships among individuals, systems, and resistance. By focusing on season-ending episodes and asking about closure, students will have the ability to apply a heuristic tool to a single episode that is also pertinent to the season and the series. Such cross-applicability provides efficiency for the allocation of classroom time while still granting students a recognizable methodology that is easily transferred both to other television contexts and to other serial media. Using closure theory would typically require having students read two to three excerpts from the scholarship (or, in a pinch, the overview offered by

Richardson) beforehand, with some classroom time devoted to explication and analysis of the theory. Following that introduction, a class might spend a week on a single episode like "Final Grades" or a month on a season, or a semester on the series, as one of our own classes has done, with closure forming one element of a longer consideration. We suggest here several exercises and questions for consideration that might be used in any of these situations.

Narrative Closure

In this section, we analyze the structure of "Final Grades" in a way that models the critical requirement of breaking free from the sequential or chronological-response approach that initially seems natural to many students. The implications of the episode are best identified by recognizing that the episode's cultural criticism is conveyed through the structuring of its narratives and by the way in which the character pairings through which the corner boys' story is told break down walls that appear to separate cops from kids from criminals—divisions that have organized aspects of the season located outside of the political sphere. This shift of narrative organization itself works as a closural gesture, as we are forced to take the next step in the series' argument against the conventional television notions of good cops versus bad drug dealers that typically drive police procedural programs.

The strict content of the episode addresses Richter's sense of "completeness," but other gestures and structures of "Final Grades" constitute the sense of closure. "Final Grades" operates on both an ethical arc and a geographical one, and the two intersect perhaps most importantly as Carcetti's movement between Baltimore and the state capital in Annapolis establishes the relationships between the personal experiences of the students about whom we care so much and the institutional structures of state and municipal government that seem so distant. Having been reminded by his staff that "kids don't vote," Mayor Carcetti ends his season-long struggle with the political "system" by choosing to decline additional state money for students. Carcetti's evident self-loathing is echoed by both his wife and his staff,[5] but the series contradicts the moment of blame-as-closure: a simple location of one level of responsibility among many in the series. Instead the narrative asserts that it is not Carcetti himself to blame, but the systemic dysfunction of political institutions of city and state, and their fundamental paradoxes: Carcetti cannot help the children of his city both now and two years from now, he believes, as doing one makes the other impossible.

As Russell Reising has pointed out, some conclusions are inconclusive, and "these include conclusions that not only fail to 'conclude' the generative thematic and ideological issues of their works' primary original concerns but actually exacerbate those very issues" (21). The Carcetti plot operates at the highest societal level in the series, and its inconclusive conclusion in "Final Grades" demonstrates first that status is no protection from the paradoxes of American urban social order, and second that such important conflict must of necessity burst beyond the narrative confines of the television season. The Carcetti plot demonstrates the connectivity between a handful of short scenes in a single episode and the larger critical lines of a season or series, a relationship recognizable even if students have not seen all forty hours of the series leading up to this point.

A similar effect emerges in the first of Bunny Colvin's two plotlines in "Final Grades." Colvin has spent the season working with educational theorist David Parenti piloting a streamed classroom for disruptive students. While most of the students in the program appear to have gained little from it academically, the scenes of Namond and Zenobia working studiously on their standardized tests and of their irritated ignoring of Albert's acting out on their return to the "gen pop" of Roland "Prez" Pryzbylewski's classroom, suggesting a benefit for some. Colvin and Parenti seek to institutionalize their intellectual project, but are snubbed by Carcetti, who skips their meeting, and treated disrespectfully by staffers, who flip through the report for a matter of seconds, name it streaming, and reject it outright. The stakes are instantly removed from the season's major social project much as they were in Colvin's last social experiment, Hamsterdam. In recognizing the parallels among the markers of closure in the Carcetti and Colvin plots and that of the Hamsterdam narrative of Season Three, students can build arguments for the outraged individual as embodiment of broader systems of social order and resistance rather than considering them as good, bad, or frustrating outcomes.

The institutional failures of education that Colvin witnesses lead him to seek an individual response: in the second narrative of cultural geography in the episode, he works to adopt Namond, eventually removing one boy from the drug corners and moving him to a safer neighborhood. Colvin's neighborhood is like the one in which both he and Namond's father, Wee-Bey Brice, grew up: where criminality may exist, but it exists alongside families and other communities. The shots of Namond's participation in the Baltimore Urban Debate League (5.9) convey that he has begun attending a better school, still urban, but of the sort that habitually stands in for economic and intellectual potential in American television, with well-groomed articulate children in fit-ted uniforms. The prolonged final shot of the season four finale, from Colvin's front porch, rests on a quiet intersection a world away from the corner where Bodie has been murdered earlier in the episode.[6] The audience has already seen the imprisoned Wee-Bey agree to surrender custody of his son, not because he agrees that Colvin's version of urban life is intrinsically better than that of the corners, but because Colvin persuades him that life in the city is not the one they shared when they were younger. Wee-Bey's street "word"[7] can no longer protect Namond from the new and increasingly violent modes of control introduced by the amoral economies of Marlo's organization. When his wife De'Londa venerates the life of being a "soldier"—one that he once valued and for which he has surrendered his freedom—Wee-Bey sardonically asks, "Who the fuck would want to be that if they could be anything else?" Wee-Bey recognizes that the game has changed and is willing to surrender his legal paternity to give his son the father that he needs to make his way in the new world.

The eventual pairing of Namond with Colvin reflects a narrative strategy used in this episode to convey closure without completion in the lives of each of the corner boys: Namond is paired with Colvin; Dukie with Prez; Randy with Carver; Michael with Chris Partlow; and, for a corner boy aged beyond his years, Bodie with McNulty. As we will see, the closural gestures used in "Final Grades" mark each member of the pair as growing up or maturing in some significant way. Some of these associations have developed across the season, others in a few episodes, and some really only in this episode. We end the season witnessing a series of interactions that embody the permeability of culturally naturalized barriers of suburban and urban, cop and criminal, white and black, adult and youth. In teaching *The Wire*, discussion of this episode and all of Season Four can helpfully be framed around separate narrative threads involving each of five young men. In the remainder of this section, we trace some salient points that reveal narrative structure and elements of closure in order to provide some resources for prompting on-topic classroom discussion. In thinking about teaching *The Wire* through collaborative pedagogical practices, specific conclusions are less important than modeling responsible critical process.

Namond. The Namond/Colvin pairing provides the one narrative close that saves the season (and many viewers) from descending into complete despair, providing a direct contrast to the Randy/Carver plot in which Carver struggles valiantly but fruitlessly to find a way to make Children's Services care for Randy in any way that will save the boy from the horrors of the Dickensian group home in which he ends the episode. Carver even offers to foster Randy himself at one point, but is informed that such a process will take months, even if he is approved. Colvin, on the other hand, works outside of institutional systems of childcare, seeking to have Namond's parents surrender custody of their son. As Wee-Bey notes, "It's a lot to ask," but Colvin persists: "But I'm asking."

Dukie. The next pairing is much less successful, as Prez tries to mentor Dukie to help him to stay in school and avoid ending up addicted like everyone else in his family. When Dukie walks by the burnt-out row house Randy had been living in, it is clear that "all the kids at this point are homeless in one way or another," as Nina K. Noble observes in the DVD commentary. We have seen the failures of the school system throughout the season, and the No-Child-Left-Behind testing scenes in Prez's class make clear that the best-intentioned teacher cannot overcome years of educational and economic neglect. Like Colvin and Carver, Prez too tries to compensate for his institutional failures by trying to save one boy; like Carver, Prez fails. His failure is not for lack of trying, but because, the series suggests, Dukie's fall to drugs is inevitable. Dukie acknowledges Prez's effort with his heartbreaking Christmas gift of a fancy pen set for his desk, though it appears that he will never see his teacher's desk as he drops out of Edward Tilghman Middle and fails to attend the school to which he ostensibly transfers. The Dukie/Prez pairing ends with Prez reminding Dukie that he is always welcome to return to the class, but the failure of this sort of passive support is evident. The two share their last scene of the season standing outside of the school, and when Prez searches for Dukie later, he sees him back on the corner as Prez drives away from Kenard's offer of drugs.

Randy. Less reassuring still is the closure offered for Randy Wagstaff, whose well-being is being pursued by police sergeant Ellis Carver. Having been labeled a snitch on the street, Randy has endured beatings and a firebombing of his foster home, as a result of which he is being put back into the system. As is true of so many of the institutions in *The Wire*, the systemic flaws of child protection services are exposed. Having already moved through the foster home waitlists once, Randy is now due to be sent back to a group home to begin to wait again. Frustrated at his inability to help, Carver desperately seeks a solution, but there is no room for small acts of heroism in the institutions of Baltimore. In contrast to the near-miraculous rescue of Namond by Colvin, neither Carver nor Prez can solve institutional problems by taking in a single boy, even if the foster system would allow such a thing. Later in the episode, we see Carver taking Randy to the group home and we watch him rage at his own impotence in the face of institutional force.

Michael. Of the four young men tracked through Season Four, the greatest failure is that endured by Michael Lee, who slides into the criminal life. Distrustful of adults generally, Michael's strongest emotional connection is not with a parent or with one of the police officers, but with Chris Partlow, who is Marlo Stanfield's primary enforcer and second in command. The burden of looking after his younger brother Bug is a responsibility Michael has shouldered with careful attention throughout the season. At first, he warily refuses the gifts and money that Marlo distributes among the children in the first week of school. Michael is the most articulate of the corner boys, and the one who has displayed the greatest independence and self-reliance; he is not, however, able to deal himself with the release of Bug's father Devar from prison. It is implied that Devar has sexually assaulted Michael in the past, and with Devar's return to their home, Michael's options narrow: to protect Bug, he has little choice but to accept Marlo's offers of help, including an apartment where he, Bug, and Dukie can live safely. On Marlo's orders, Chris kills Devar, beating him to death in an uncharacteristically brutal murder (4.10), which, along with other hints, suggests that Chris may also have been a victim of sexual abuse. Not long afterward, Chris assumes the role of a mentor to Michael. "Final Grades" sees Michael being established with responsibility for his own corner (one inherited from the murdered Bodie) as well as making his first hit, though at Chris's urging it is not against Bodie as Marlo had initially suggested.

In addition to its clear contribution to the structural patterning of Season Four and "Final Grades," the specific example of Michael and Chris can serve to facilitate classroom discussion about the authority of DVD commentary and its relationship to critical questions of authorial intent in literary scholarship. Just as students must learn to interrogate the notion that authorial intent and textual implication must be the same, classroom work on the methodologies of television studies might include exercises on incorporating interpretations with differing levels of authority into a critical discussion. In the DVD commentary for this episode, David Simon makes explicit the source of the brutality of Chris Partlow's attack on Devar, asserting of an understated scene late in the episode: "this is really an acknowledgement, unstated, between the two that both of them were sexually abused." DVD commentaries, like officially-sanctioned real-time tweets, time-synched podcasts, and "two-screen experiences,"[8] exist outside of the dramatic world of the series in a space of authority, staking claim to an insider's understanding of the episode that is both authorized and informal. Directors' commentaries in particular are often cited as evidence of a correct or true interpretation of specific scenes.

The types of para-narratives that can supplement and shape interpretation of a television episode also go well beyond director commentaries: other modes include reviews, publicity images, blogs, fan fiction, interviews with actors and creators, and even academic scholarship. DVD commentaries, however, somehow feel more authoritative as part of the hard copy "official release" (in one recording format). In the case of the hints that Chris has also been abused, Simon's DVD commentary makes the implicit explicit, undermining ambiguity and providing a canonical response that exists within a non-canonical medium.[9] Students must be encouraged to resist such apparent authority. As with literary texts where students can read against the grain, recognizing the important insights in the way that an author has perhaps unwittingly conveyed values and ideology, students can be encouraged to interrogate the assumptions behind the vision of the auteur as a part of their own critical processes on narrative. Again, it is in the transaction between product and viewer where meaning resides.

Whether or not we read them exactly as Simon intends, these rites of passage mark Michael's transition to adulthood, the end of one period of his life. Michael's rapid advancement emerges in part because of a misinterpretation by Marlo. Throughout the season, there has been a subplot about a ring, first owned by Old Face Andre. It passes to Marlo, who is robbed by Omar, who has it taken by the corrupt Officer Walker, who in turn is robbed by Michael. When in "Final Grades" Marlo sees the ring around Michael's neck, he assumes that Michael has taken it from Omar directly, exaggerating the young man's criminal potential. This misperception anticipates Michael's eventual role as a new Omar, which he secures by the series' conclusion (5.10). Omar is regularly presented as a destabilizing element in the criminal world of the series, and even when he sells back the heroin that he stole from the Co-op headed by Prop Joe (taking a modest 20 percent of the street value for the return of the merchandise), the greed and audacity he exhibits prove contagious. Prop Joe tells the others that the cost was "thirty on the dollar," as he schemes to pocket the extra profit himself. This world Michael is entering has rules (it is paradigmatically and persistently called "the Game"), but transgressions are frequent and violations are severely punished.

Bodie. The fates of all four friends find a counterpoint in that of Bodie. Five or six years older than the others, Preston "Bodie" Broadus has been a constant presence on the corners since the series' first episode. The pacing of his character's arc has been slow. Impulsive and at times unlikeable, he appears monstrous by the end of Season One when he murders the innocent Wallace (1.12). Nevertheless, subsequent seasons allow him to demonstrate loyalty (to the faltering Barksdale criminal organization) and reveal an unexpected optimism within his character. Bodie sees no escape from the life he leads, but even as he develops a relationship with McNulty he sees himself as a survivor.

Like each of the character pairings except Michael's, Bodie and McNulty are by this point in the season concerned with redemption. In closural terms, redemption stories offer an immediate emotional reward for viewers, providing a transitional moment wherein a character is again put on the right track. Bodie's impulsive nature continues to assert itself and he is arrested when he kicks in a police-car window when he sees a friend's body removed from a vacant by police. McNulty urges the arresting officer to cut Bodie loose and takes him for a sandwich. The short scenes at this point are very economical, and a few words bear a considerable narrative burden. When viewed in light of Season One's chess scene with Bodie, Wallace and D'Angelo (1.03), these scenes offer tremendous closure and non-closure for the series as a whole.

"Still in the city?" Bodie asks McNulty in the Cylburn Arboretum, the distinctive statue of Lady Baltimore looking down on them.[10] Even as the camera angles emphasize the personified Baltimore looming above, the arboretum is a sanctuary where the two can speak as equals. Each feels free of the apparatus that constricts their usual lives. Bodie's monologue offers an extended self-examination, justifying himself and his choices in life. For some viewers, the mere existence of such an *apologia* is enough to signal the inevitability of his pending death: it is a paradigmatic closural gesture, allowing the character to speak his own eulogy.[11] The scene evokes at least two previous moments in the series. First, this is not the only meal that Bodie and McNulty have shared: they have previously met by chance in a diner (4.11), and the scenes confirm their developing relationship. Secondly, when Bodie speaks of his own personal growth, he echoes a very early programmatic scene for the series in which D'Angelo Barksdale explains the rules of chess to Bodie and Wallace (1.03: pawns are "like the soldiers," out of the game early, "unless they some smart ass pawns" as Bodie notes, at a time when he still believed career advancement selling drugs could be meaningful). Sitting with McNulty, Bodie sees the futility of his existence as a corner boy, the impossibility of emerging into something else: "we like them little bitches on the chess board," he suggests. McNulty, unaware of the earlier discussion, tries to reassure Bodie that the thoughts he is having are taking him in the right place, "You're a soldier, Bodie." He has no idea that this simply reinforces the inevitability of Bodie's foreshortened existence.[12] The momentary escape from urban life affords a corner boy a sense of transcendent awareness.

Bodie is seen by one of Marlo's prospects emerging from the police station and getting into McNulty's car. When told about this, Marlo's response is clear: Bodie is to be killed. The audience next sees him standing on his corner at night, wary of any threat and ready to shoot at supposed movement in the darkness. As Nina K. Noble, executive producer of Season Four, observes on the DVD commentary, "This is a guy who was not going to go quietly." Bodie sees shadows coming at him, but is in fact killed at close range, shot twice in the head, having been abandoned by his crew on his corner. The death of a corner boy is not newsworthy, and McNulty only learns that Bodie has been shot when he comes in to work the next day. McNulty's self-blame and frustration anticipate that of Carver when he has to leave Randy.

All five of the pairs integrate the lives of an older and a younger man. In each case the character growth for the youngster is obvious. A parallel process of development can be traced for each of the older members of the pairs as well: Colvin becomes a father; Prez becomes a teacher; Carver becomes a better police officer; McNulty expresses genuine concern for someone other than himself, perhaps for the first time. Chris, however, displays no development; his amoral adherence to the Stanfield drug organization establishes a contrast with the other examples. He and Marlo continue as they always have, gaining nothing but a soldier from their relationship with Michael, and eventually not even that. The rigid formal structure of these five juxtapositions creates connections that themselves constitute a closural gesture. By drawing together all of these narrative threads, the episode invites a final assessment of each individual trajectory. Reading Season Four and "Final Grades" through closure can encourage students to look beyond what seems obvious about *The Wire*, and in doing so provides a slightly startling contradiction to what students often see as the series' default premise. As a whole, *The Wire* proclaims that social and political institutions are the primary determinants of individual success or failure in urban Baltimore. Examining the five character pairings in "Final Grades" challenges this implicit claim and proposes an alternative whereby personal family connections—particularly how a young man identifies with a single father figure—outweigh larger social forces. Those who lack healthy paternal alliances are the ones who suffer most.

Amidst all of these individual stories, bodies continue to be discovered in the vacants. While each once had a name and an identity, this group of demographically similar young men[13] all had stories like those of the Season Four corner boys. In death they become anonymous corpses. So many bodies constitutes a "red-ball" (a high-profile case that will garner intense media scrutiny), and the police have started a pool betting on how many bodies there will be in total. With this section, "Final Grades" brings together threads that have appeared narratively disparate for much of the season: from Mayor Carcetti's perspective, the media attention is desirable, as the murders will remove the underfunding of schools from the headlines and can be safely attributed to the previous administration as Carcetti's staff rejects Colvin and Parenti's educational plan. And these plots point to the inadequacy of the school system that has been the subject of scrutiny throughout the season. Special programs are not funded because there is not money even for basic services, and the standardized tests are geared so that "proficient" is reading only two grades below expectation.[14] The irony of the police using the gymnasium of a closed elementary school to collect the bodies found in the vacants in a kind of postmortem triage is apparent to the majority of the viewership. Lest it be missed, however, Col. Daniels identifies it as the school he himself attended as a child: "Back in the day, got a decent education..."[15]

Structural Closure

In addition to focusing on narrative elements, structural elements that help students describe the process of closure can be signposted for them. The presence of bodies in the vacants has been presented as the major case around which the season has been organized. Each of the previous seasons has had a single major case (always requiring a wiretap). The seasoned viewer expects some sort of closure as a result: the formula of the police procedural[16] usually guarantees closure of this sort near the end of each episode, and in *The Wire* viewers expect it at least by the end of the season (as had happened in Seasons One, Two, and Three). Indeed, another measure of overall season pacing in *The Wire* is when someone at Major Crimes is found to have probable cause to authorize a wiretap. As the series proceeds, it comes later and later in each season (1.6, 2.8, 3.10, not at all in Season Four, and only again at 5.5). Despite all the gestures of closure evident in "Final Grades," the absence of a new wiretap on the Stanfield criminal organization significantly frustrates viewer expectation. In the DVD commentary, Simon indicates that despite only being renewed for a single season, he knew the Marlo storyline would require two seasons to tell; the absence of new wiretaps throughout Season Four is indicative of that narrative openness.

By the end of Season Four, *The Wire* had also developed its own closural gesture that audiences have come to expect: an extended montage with musical accompaniment provides not only a structural indication of the series' final moments that can be identified as such, it allows the episode to offer a final image for each of many narrative threads. Accompanied by Paul Weller's 1995 cover of Dr. John's 1968 "I Walk on Gilded Splinters,"[17] the fourteen vignettes presented all offer forms of closure for the wide range of characters that inhabit the dramatic world:

1. in jail, Wee-Bey with a hug frees Namond to go live with Colvin;
2. overcome with guilt at Bodie's death, McNulty returns to Major Crimes;
3. Herc is sentenced by a police tribunal, causing him to leave the police force[18];
4. Marlo watches Vondas meeting with Proposition Joe as his mind seeks further fields for his criminal organization to grow;
5. at an academic presentation on the results of the school's project, Colvin walks out in disgust;
6. Bunk continues to gather evidence of the bodies as a map shows the growing extent of the problem;
7. Landsman is weary as he looks at all the red on the board listing the murders yet to be solved; the list has been comically extended below the board's frame in order to accommodate all the bodies in the vacants;
8. Deputy Chief Prosecutor Rhonda Pearlman is seen sitting down with her partner (and head of CID) to meet Mayor Carcetti for lunch, with State Senator Clay Davis sitting in the next booth[19];
9. Prez watches Dukie dealing drugs on Michael's new corner, and Kenard spits on his car;
10. in the group home, Randy's bunk has been graffitied ("snitch bitch") and his money taken, and he is unable to escape the rumors on the street;
11. Cutty is out of the hospital and sits in his gym with his former nurse at his side;
12. Carcetti is in a meeting, seemingly uninterested in the tables and graphs being displayed behind him;
13. a new generation of kids messing around outside are driven off by Carver;
14. Chris drops into a drain the gun used in Michael's initial hit.

The narrative function of each of these very short scenes could be usefully examined in a short active classroom exercise. Individuals can be asked to describe each moment of the montage, and then to explain its narrative function and its connection with the larger narrative (or could be done collaboratively in small groups). Students could be asked to develop a sense of how their scene relates to the season's end: does it add new information, reinforce what we have already seen, problematize what we thought we already knew, or anticipate something yet to come? And what is significant about the specific visual strategies used to achieve that effect in these scenes? For example, the children driven off by Carver (montage scene 13) constitute the next generation of children destined to be caught up in the drug world, doomed to be failed by the school system. The cyclical nature transitioning around the years of middle school is signalled by the graffiti on the back wall where the kids are playing, with tags celebrating the "Fayette Mafia Crew 4 evah" and signed by Michael, Namond, Randy, Dukie and (anticipating his importance in Season Five) Kenard.

As students may note, only two of the vignettes (1 and 11) point unambiguously to a positive development for the characters involved, both focused upon characters who are leaving the corner culture behind. Such tender moments are rare, and the viewer may remember Omar's humane farewell to Butchie earlier in the episode, as (it seems) he is finally escaping the Game. It is also clear that some of these vignettes are taking place in the months that follow the main narration of the episode, extending the time covered so that the final shot of Namond eating breakfast appears to be in the late spring, months after the pre–Christmas setting of what has preceded.

Even the opening credits can provide an indication of closure. The opening credit sequence of *The Wire* changes each season, as different musicians present a version of Tom Waits's 1987 song "Way Down in the Hole," which plays to a season-specific collection of images. Most of the images come from specific episodes that season (though some recur from previous seasons), and for the attentive viewer, provide a sense of foreshadowing, whereby individual moments are recognized from the credit sequence when they recur within the narrative. In Season Four, the montage of clips includes a sequence of five scenes of wheels spinning: a rotating protective barrier in a convenience store, a chrome wheel in a rim shop, a playground roundabout, a child rolling an old tire, and bags of heroin being planted in a spare tire. The recurring revolving images may suggest the cyclical nature of delinquency and criminality just described, but the wheel images also establish a set of expectations. Once a spectator is aware that the scenes in the opening credits will appear at some point, there is a sense of resolution when the last wheel image is revealed in "Final Grades." Since its presence in the narrative has been anticipated, its integration into the main narrative also constitutes a gesture of closure. When seen in context, it becomes a symbol of victory, as Kimmie prepares to leave Baltimore after having helped Omar successfully rob the Co-op. The drugs in the wheel are her reward, and the semiotic value of the drugs is different from what the viewer has expected.[20]

Offering students the tools to think about closure cuts to the heart of television narrative, which is governed formally by layers of closure at the level of episode, season, and series (as well as at other points, including the momentary raising of tension before a commercial break).[21] As a closing example, we consider the beginning of the end, the sequence immediately surrounding the title sequence of "Final Grades." The opening twelve minutes constitute a self-contained unit that represents the episode's themes in miniature. Bubbles is in police custody, having confessed to the murder of his friend, which he didn't commit. It's a tiny self-contained drama, where Bubbles vomits on police Sergeant Jay Landsman's shirt-and-tie as he is overcome by the combination of stress, grief, remorse, and withdrawal. As the police contemplate manufacturing a murder (exploring a motif that will become the dominant theme of Season Five), a number of visual elements provide anchors to other moments in the series. Landsman's tie and humming of Christmas carols roots the episode firmly in December, at the end of the second quarter of the Baltimore school system's academic year. It is also close to the broadcast date of the episode (10 December 2006), which reinforces for the first viewers the sense of immediacy, as if events in the fictional world corresponded closely to those in the real world. Landsman's tie is ruined, as he walks by a board decorated with ties cut from the necks of officers caught sleeping on the job. As he returns to the interview room, Bubbles, who has been left alone only for minutes, is found hanging (his belt serving as another kind of necktie).

This suicide attempt ties to larger stories of redemption and recovery, which are pursued after the title sequence. Bubbles begs, "Just lock me up, man"; his grief overwhelms him, as the series' moral center struggles like no other character with the implications of his inadvertent action. Landsman recognizes this and urges the arresting office to cut him loose. The morality of the moment is contagious. More than any other character, Landsman has driven officers to maintain their individual clearance rates (rates that are on constant display on a public white board, with unsolved cases written in red). Here, in a moment of Christmas generosity, he will forego the closure so necessary to police statisticians. "Fuck the clearance," he says, apparently surprised at the words coming from his own mouth. As Simon observes in the DVD commentary, "It's the triumph of humanity over the brutality of statistics."

When teaching *The Wire*, it is easy to be overwhelmed. There is so much occurring in any given episode, and so many episodes from which one may choose. Considering closure will resonate deepest when the series is considered in a literary context, but it is also an essential part of the television experience, and it can prove useful in other disciplinary contexts as well. "Final Grades" marks an important moment of closure for the series, while at the same time pointing forward to its own lack of completeness. *The Wire* inexorably recognizes that every formal and affective gesture of narrative closure concurrently embodies the recognition that imposes closure on unresolvable issues.

Notes

1. The section on endings and beginnings in Richardson's reference collection *Narrative Dynamics: Essays on Time, Plot, Closure and Frames* (249–328) prefaces his foundational articles on closure with an overview essay that would provide a concise summary for classroom use.

2. "Final Grades" is also the series' fiftieth episode, which further introduces a self-awareness that marks it both as a moment of significant transition (a landmark) and as an accomplishment (a milestone). Within the parameters of HBO television production, where the fixed lengths of network television need not be strictly enforced (Marshall and Potter, "Thinking Inside the Box" 196), the significance of the episode is demonstrated in part by its being the second longest episode in the entire series (78 minutes), a length exceeded only by the series' final episode "—30—" (5.10). "Final Grades" was written by series creator David Simon, who for Seasons Four and Five only wrote the opening and closing season episodes.

3. McNulty's conversation with Daniels about returning as a detective is not without its rewards for the dedicated viewer of *The Wire*. The scene repeats verbatim lines that the two had spoken in the series pilot (1.01, promising quick busts that are "fast and clean and simple"), but they do so with a knowing evocation of the closeness and trust that has developed in the intervening fifty episodes. By taking each other's lines from the previous conversation, the audience is treated to a charming intimacy that has developed between the two men.

4. On transactional perspectives in literacy and pedagogy, see Rosenblatt, for example; for a concise consideration of critical perspectives, see McKormick.

5. Carcetti's advisors end the episode drinking into the night (as classic a closural gesture in television as is the drifting sleep of children's fiction), debating which future candidate in which future contest will be least likely to turn into the same sort of disappointment as Carcetti.

6. Rabinowitz stresses the importance of a final moment such as this in fiction: "last sentences ... cannot serve to focus a reading experience (at least not an initial reading experience). But they do often serve to scaffold our retrospective interpretation of the book" (62).

7. In a subsequent conversation between Wee-Bey and Namond's mother De'Londa, Wee-Bey makes clear his expectation that his "word" can control her and those to whom she might complain about his decision.

8. As most prominently used on AMC's *The Walking Dead*, the first broadcast aired in synch with parallel content on the AMC website to augment the episode with additional shots and information.

9. As discussed in note 16, however, commentaries can also provide misleading or erroneous information, rendering more complex still their status as assertions of authoritative intent.

10. Four statues of Lady Baltimore (1880, sculpted by Herman D. A. Henning), a personification of the city itself, originally stood on the St. Paul Street Bridge, but were moved to various locations in the 1970s. Two stand in the formal gardens of the arboretum (see Kelly, 188 and 310). For viewers familiar with Baltimore, the symbolism of the statues points to the shared experience of the city.

11. As David Simon notes in the DVD commentary, "If you didn't know Bodie was doomed at that moment, you haven't been watching *The Wire*."

12. The momentary tranquility and promise of escape from urban life provides further echoes for fans of Simon's earlier series, *Homicide: Life on the Street*, when Det. Frank Pembleton takes another young man, Rock Rock, on an unexpected trip to Chesapeake Bay (*Homicide* 6.13, "Something Sacred, Part 2"). This is the first time Rock Rock had seen the water. In the DVD commentary, Simon observes, "I used this in an episode of *Homicide* years ago," and notes that it draws on his own personal experience of young men in Baltimore.

13. "Black males 15–25?" asks McNulty. "Some older," answers Freamon.

14. The outrage expressed by Simon in the DVD commentary on this point goes far beyond any journalistic neutrality: "*there* is the bane of modern education—standardized testing"; "the process has genuinely corrupted the whole notion of education"; "in Baltimore they redefined failure as success."

15. The DVD commentary during the scenes in the gym discusses Tilghman Middle School (which has been a focus of the season), in a case of apparent confusion by Simon and Noble. The closed school (Lemille) where the bodies are being collected must be distinct from Tilghman, even if the same actual school was used during filming.

16. On *The Wire* and police narrative, see McMillan.

17. The DVD commentary indicates that this is the first time in the series the song had been selected before filming, with the result that the pacing of scenes could be much more tightly regulated through editing.

18. Elsewhere, we have argued that the comic presentation of Herc in fact presents him providing crucial evidence in every season of *The Wire*. See Marshall and Potter, "Fuzzy Dunlop."

19. Since Daniels succeeded Colvin as commander of the Western District, the juxtaposition of his easy access to the mayor in contrast to Colvin's awkward and embarrassed inability to have contact is also pointed.

20. In another structural inversion this resonates with the scene where Herc, operating on false information, pulls over a minister's car looking for drugs in the trunk (4.10).

21. Marshall and Potter, "Thinking Inside the Box" 191–93.

Works Cited

Edelsky, Carole. "On Critical Whole Language Practice: Why, What and a Bit of How." *Making Justice Our Project: Teachers Working Toward Critical Whole Language Practice.* Ed. Carole Edelsky. Urbana, IL: National Council of Teachers of English, 1999.

Kelly, Cindy. *Outdoor Sculpture in Baltimore: A Historical Guide to Public Art in the Monumental City.* Baltimore: Johns Hopkins University Press. 2011.

Lewis, Cynthia. "Limits of Identification: The Personal, Pleasurable, and Critical in Reader Response." *Journal of Literacy Research* 32 (2000): 253–266.

Marshall, C.W., and Tiffany Potter. "The Life and Times of Fuzzy Dunlop: Herc Hauk and the Modern Urban Crime Environment." *Darkmatter* 4 (2009). darkmatter101.org.

_____, and _____. "Thinking Inside the Box: A Short View of the Immorality and Profaneness of Television Studies." *From Text to Txting: New Media in the Classroom.* Ed. Paul Budra and Clint Burnham. Bloomington: Indiana University Press, 2012. 182–213.

McKormick, Kathleen. *The Culture of Reading and the Teaching of English.* Manchester: Manchester University Press, 1994.

McMillan, Alasdair. "Heroism, Institutions, and the Police Procedural." *The Wire: Urban Decay and American Television.* Ed. Tiffany Potter and C.W. Marshall. New York: Bloomsbury [Continuum], 2009: 50–63

Rabinowitz, Peter J. *Before Reading: Narrative Conventions and the Politics of Interpretation.* Columbus: Ohio State University Press, 1999.

Reising, Russell. *Loose Ends: Closure and Crisis in American Social Text.* Durham: Duke University Press, 1996.

Richardson, Brian. *Narrative Dynamics: Essays on Time, Plot, Closure and Frames.* Ed. Brian Richardson. Columbus: Ohio State University Press, 2002.

Richter, David. *Fable's End: Completeness and Closure in Rhetorical Fiction.* Chicago: University of Chicago Press, 1974.

Rosenblatt, Louise. "The Transactional Theory of the Literary Work: Implications for Research." *Researching Response to Literature and the Teaching of Literature.* Ed. Charles Cooper. Norwood, NJ: Ablex, 1985.

Part III

Ethics and Rhetoric

"The gods will not save you"
Teaching Ethics with The Wire

James W. McCarty III

> "It's Baltimore, gentleman. The gods will not save you."
> —Baltimore Police Commissioner Ervin Burrell (3.3)

Between Omar's "code" and Marlo's lack of one exists a world of characters who are neither purely saints nor sinners, neither heroes nor villains, in their own minds or in the minds of viewers. Rather than meeting heroes and villains, we meet a cast of characters living morally ambiguous lives that challenge our notions of righteousness, criminality, and virtue. Wallace and D'Angelo and Bubbles and Frank Sabotka find themselves swallowed up by "the game" despite sincere efforts to escape it or rise above it. Similarly, McNulty and Kima and "Bunny" Colvin want to be good cops but are consistently unable to live up to their own virtues and/or the imposed virtues of the Baltimore Police Department. And the corner boys' tragic though predictable socialization into various roles in the game is especially difficult because we admire Michael's devotion to his younger brother, Randy's honesty, and Dukie's intellectual curiosity. Indeed, in trying to do what they believe is right these characters often perpetuate that which even they believe is wrong. In providing for his brother Michael hurts others; in telling the truth Randy is accused of snitching and indirectly hurts the people closest to him; in his dogged pursuit of his own vision of justice McNulty becomes a liar and puts innocent lives at risk. Whether on the corner or manning the wire, in the classroom or on the docks, almost every character in *The Wire* embodies the ambiguous shape of the moral life as it is lived in the midst of late-modern sociopolitical institutions in the United States. There are no heroes or divine interventions in the Baltimore we find in *The Wire;* neither are there any in the economic, political, and other institutions in which most twenty-first century humans live. Rather, we are products of our world even as we make it. At least, this is what I have proposed to my students in an introductory course in philosophical ethics.

The course was one of two required academic courses in a year-long academic program I directed at Oxford College of Emory University, titled the Ethics and Servant Leadership Program, which also included service-learning and community-based research components. During the first semester students took an introductory ethics course and in the second semester students took a social ethics course focused on the development and possibilities for a global civil society. In addition to their in-class work, students volunteered at one of three civil society organizations in the local community for the academic year. They also conducted a community-based research project relevant to the work of the organization at which they were serving that was presented to community and university leaders at the end of the academic year.

Because of the extended time students spent outside the classroom in service activities and conducting community research, we spent only one hour in a traditional classroom every week. Students enrolled in the program were freshmen and sophomores who applied and were selected to be a part of the fifteen student program. I taught the course two times, but only incorporated *The Wire* the second time I taught the course. I brought multiple video clips focusing on the development of specific characters from the series into the classroom as case studies for the key ideas, especially around moral formation and ambiguity, explored in the course. Due to the nature of the program, I assigned short, standard introductory textbooks in ethics as the primary course texts. These texts, Rachels and Rachels' widely used *The Elements of Moral Philosophy* and Pojman and Fieser's *Ethics: Discovering Right and Wrong,* introduce the field of ethics through short chapters, usually between ten and twelve pages, summarizing major approaches and questions in ethics. For instance, each textbook I used included chapters on the questions of universal morality and cultural relativism and the role of religion in ethics. They also included chapters introducing deontological, utilitarian, virtue, feminist, and other major approaches to ethics. In these ways, the books provide brief overviews of dominant theories, approaches, and methodologies in the discipline. Through the first half of the course we spent each week focused on one major approach to ethical reasoning.

Of course, these standard textbooks are limited in their use. They tend to make an ethical tradition, like utilitarianism, seem homogenous when there are a variety of utilitarian approaches to ethics. In addition, there tends to be a lack of primary sources in such texts. So, students read *about* key figures and approaches, like Plato or Thomas Hobbes or virtue ethics, rather than reading the writings and arguments of key figures and thinkers themselves. In the first iteration of the course I attempted to overcome these shortcomings with supplemental primary readings, but the short time in class meant that students focused on the textbook readings and skimmed the supplemental readings. It was not practicable, then, to complicate students' ethical reasoning by assigning lengthy primary readings from Aristotle or John Rawls, for example. Therefore, I sought to complicate the rather simple overview of the discipline of ethics and its primary approaches as presented in these texts by bringing other forms of scholarship and media into the course.

Toward an "Anthropological" Approach to Ethics

Ethics, whether philosophical or theological, covers the broad scope of human experience and attempts to answer what it means to live a good life or to build a good society. Its central questions are: "What is right and what is wrong?" "What is a good life made of?" and "What does a good society look like?" These are some of the most important questions one can ask, and are foundational questions in any liberal arts education. In seeking to answer such questions, however, the discipline of ethics risks being so abstract and theoretical that people dismiss it as a game of definitions or as irrelevant to the material lives that humans actually live. In its historic elevation of the Platonic Forms, the Christian heaven, Kant's categorical imperative, or other universalistic explanations about the right and the good, ethics can seem to be nice words spoken by boring people unable to understand what it means to have to steal a loaf of bread to feed one's family or to face a true moral dilemma. Ethics professors are, in many ways, those whom people have in mind when they describe professors as white men with beards who wear tweed jackets with elbow patches, smoke pipes, and pontificate from an ivory tower.

Ethics does not have to be taught this way, however. Rather than being composed primarily of abstract reflection, it can be a discipline that pays careful attention to forms of moral reasoning employed in various contexts and the ways that people live in the world and make moral sense of their lives. At its best ethics does not merely prescribe universal definitions of right and wrong; ethics at its best includes the principled study of what it means to be a human being living with other human beings (and with other animals in an ever-expanding universe) in light of how we actually live with others and how that living shapes who we are and might become. The discipline of ethics can prepare students to do the difficult work of understanding how others reason morally about their lives in the world.

In my attempt to teach ethics in this way I have found the work of medical anthropologist Arthur Kleinman especially helpful. In his text *What Really Matters: Living a Moral Life Amidst Uncertainty and Danger*, Kleinman argues that "what is moral needs to be understood as what is local" and that ethics are "values that transcend the local and that can guide us in living a life" (2–3). In other words, morality is cultural and contextual and is radically concrete (as in cultural *mores*). Korean children know that it is wrong to wear their shoes in another's house, for example. It is an act of disrespect to enter another's home while wearing one's shoes. This practice is understood and goes unquestioned. It is, indeed, a moral question for Korean households. Most North American children, however, know that wearing shoes in the house is a matter of preference at most, and to get it wrong is to be an occasion for laughter rather than shame. A new context removes the moral element of the practice of wearing shoes in the house.

Ethics, on the other hand, are universal norms that all people should abide by or strive for. In the late-modern world, we generally recognize respect for universal human rights as that which is truly ethical. (Even the strongest moral relativists I have had in my courses express a belief in at least *some* universal human rights!) For example, murder is always wrong; whether taking another person's life constitutes murder, self-defense, or a justified act of war, on the other hand, is contextual. Regarding the example of wearing shoes in the house, perhaps the ethical norm at play is respect or hospitality. Concrete practices of respect and/or hospitality differ in various cultural contexts, however. The distinctions between morality and ethics in this framework can be blurry, but most people live as if they know what these distinctions are.

The characters we meet in *The Wire* demonstrate that there are times and contexts, however, when morality and ethics conflict with one another. And in such times doing the "ethical" thing can make one "immoral" in one's own eyes or in the eyes of others in their local moral community. The moral code of "no snitching," for instance, can conflict with ethical norms against lying. It can also conflict with other moral codes that prescribe deference to governmental authorities like the police. How people negotiate between multiple moralities, or between one morality and their perception of the ethical, are particular sites when one's moral formation is simultaneously exposed and in process. It is in such conflicts that the ambiguity of lived ethics in the late-modern world is clearest.

Human life consists of the constant negotiation between the moral and the ethical. Most humans believe in some form of universal norms while recognizing that their implementation is varied and contextual. And we must negotiate their proper implementation while in the context of social, political, and economic institutions that shape our ability to perceive and respond to both the moral (local) and the ethical (universal). In addition, the experience of living, Kleinman reminds us, is "dangerous"—*The Wire's* Baltimore is clearly dangerous. There are countless experiences, many of which we have no control over, that can crash into our lives and reshape us or transform us into new people—sickness, falling in love, experiences of violence, new experiences of wealth or poverty, professional formation, religious conversion, etc. Human lives are fluid and constantly in flux. However, we pursue stability and an unchanging sense of self. In our mundane, everyday lives a stable sense of self is possible. However, almost every person experiences times when life goes from being mundane to being dangerous.

"Danger arises," Kleinman says, "when our most deeply held values and emotions are threatened or lost. And people themselves become even more dangerous when they feel that these things are at serious risk" (18–19). When our morality or our ethics are pushed to their limits, such as when we learn that our dearly beloved cultural practices perpetuate injustice or we feel it is necessary to use any means necessary to save a loved one, we become dangerous persons "prepared to do anything and everything to protect and defend what really matters" (19). Sometimes "what really matters" is that deeply held cultural practice or ethical commitment. At other times it is a loved one or even personal survival. In moments such as these, where morals and ethics are challenged by dangerous experiences, "the self can be reshaped" (19). And, it must be said, our sense of ourselves often undergoes multiple reshapings over the course of a lifetime. This reshaping of the self is evident in the lives of several characters in *The Wire*. D'Angelo, Stringer, Kima, Dukie, Bubbles, McNulty, Namond, Carcetti, and many others evolve into new selves who negotiate the moral and the ethical in a variety of ways that are both the result and cause of that reshaping.

This reshaping does not occur only because of individual circumstances or tragedies. Rather, often what is most "dangerous" for people desiring a stable sense of self are social and political institutions and/or evolutions. Any ability to understand the constant reshaping of persons in light of their lived experience must be "concerned with how the large scale disorganized and disorganizing historical forces of politics and political economy transform our moral life. That transformation results from the interaction between three very different kinds of things: cultural meanings, social experience, and subjectivity (inner emotions and sense of self)" (Kleinman 227). In other words, our moral lives are impacted by our cultural context, our experience within social and political institutions, our own subjective responses to these contextual experiences, and our sense of the "ethical." When these various "world shapers" do not align our world becomes dangerous and our selves are (potentially) reshaped. Making sense of the reshaping (or lack thereof), I teach my students, is the task of moral philosophy/ethics.

When I teach ethics courses I want my students to be able to understand the reshaping of the self in response to lived experience as a moral act. While I also want them to understand the difference between Aristotle's virtuous actor and Kant's rational actor, I do not want such questions to be the sum of their education in ethics. I also want them to be able to discern the various ways that humans make sense of their own lives in light of their individual experiences and their interactions with social, political, and economic institutions. I want them to understand how people are shaped morally by their material lives in the world.[1]

Teaching Ethics with The Wire

To flesh out his claims about morality and ethics Kleinman tells multiple "moral biographies" to demonstrate the ways that lives are reshaped and people make sense of that moral experience. In this spirit, I incorporated extended clips from *The Wire* featuring key characters as types of "moral biographies" that would help my students understand the shaping of the self through the negotiation between the moral and the ethical in the midst of dangerous institutions. Specifically, we explore moral formation in post-industrial American urban neighborhoods defined by racialized poverty, violence, and segregation.[2]

The decision to incorporate television into my course is not uncontroversial in the field of ethics. While it is increasingly common for such media to be incorporated in courses across a variety of disciplines, this practice is still relatively uncommon in the ethics classroom. The reasons for the dearth of film/television in ethics courses are multiple and varied, but perhaps the most salient is a disciplinary bias against emotion. Ethicists are generally skeptical of the possibility of good moral deliberation when agents are overly influenced by their emotions or too invested in a character or narrative to reason disinterestedly. They are especially skeptical because directors intentionally use cinematography, music, and the skills of actors and screenwriters to manipulate audiences to elicit particular emotions and reactions. How can one reach a disinterested, universal ethical prescription when caught up in intense feelings of love, fear, anger, or compassion? One cannot, many feel, and anything that would stir such emotions is therefore often left out of the classroom.[3]

Of course, *The Wire* is not a typical television show and the "happy ending" conventions of mainstream television do not apply to its story. Still, its use in an ethics class is far from the norm. Its rejection of the conventions of popular television, however, is what makes it so useful in a classroom. Its moral ambiguity, unresolved tensions, and long story arc in which moral "growth" is not the norm allows for students to enter a narrative more like the lived realities of people who are sometimes virtuous and sometimes not as they negotiate a dangerous world. In addition, it forces the audience to empathize with characters such as Omar—who do no evoke simplistic emotional or ethical responses—that they simultaneously judge as immoral in some way.

Thus, I use *The Wire* to teach ethics in a way that emphasizes moral formation over a lifetime. Students cannot judge a character's virtue based upon one action. Rather, they learn to take social, political, and economic institutions into consideration when analyzing moral reflection by learning how these institutions constrain the moral choices the characters believe they are able to make. They learn that humans are moral beings who continually negotiate between local norms and universal values that are not always applicable in particular institutions. Rather, we learn how to live within certain institutions and when those institutions change or are challenged, or we find ourselves in new institutions, our world becomes dangerous and we either learn to live in new ways (and reshape our sense of self) or live in such a way as to be viewed as immoral.

In using *The Wire* to teach ethics in this way I begin by explaining the five-season format of the show. Each season of *The Wire* emphasizes a different social or political institution and its role and connection with other institutions in the city. Season one focuses on the Baltimore Police Department and the Barksdale crime organization; season two on the stevedores and labor unions in the post-industrial United States; season three on Baltimore's political institutions; season four on public schools; and season five on the media, especially the Baltimore newspaper. This format is helpful because it allows students to focus on the particular moral logics that rule in each institution. Furthermore, it allows for students to compare the institutional logics explored and identify similarities and differences between them. Seeing characters negotiate the contradictions between these logics enables students to recognize their own moral-institutional flexibility and recognize it as constitutive of their own moral formation.

In highlighting the way the series is structured to emphasize various social and political institutions at different times, while also recognizing that these institutions are interconnected and are all present in nearly every season, I am able to demonstrate to my students that we are shaped as moral agents through our experiences in these institutions. Oftentimes, ethicists work from the Kantian assumption that ethics is primarily about individual reflection on universal truths that are understood and practiced through the exercise of reason. This is not the case, however. At least, it is not the whole story. Rather, morality is something that is learned through institutional participation.

Every social, political, and economic institution has its own moral logic. Sometimes those logics are transferrable across institutions; sometimes they are not. When they are not, and a moral agent uses the wrong logic within an institution, that actor is reprimanded in some way. This reprimand can be either formal or informal and can come in the form of shame, punishment, or exclusion. An agent's response to these reprimands is their moral response to a new and "dangerous" world. The goal of incorporating these various media is to help students be able to identify these responses as moral acts and the reshaping of the self as an ongoing process of moral formation.

Morality, or local institutional norms, is not the only determining factor in moral action. Ethics, or universal values or principles, also have an impact. When ethics challenge the moral, or vice versa, life becomes "dangerous" and individuals reshape their moral self in the midst of this interaction. How people negotiate this interaction, I teach my students, is the most interesting data in ethics because it demonstrates the various ways that people reason about morality. To make this point I highlight the experiences of several characters across the first three seasons of the show. In this essay I will focus on two: D'Angelo Barksdale and "Stringer" Bell.

I begin by having students study the life of D'Angelo. We watched several clips, in between which I explain the narrative arc of the story that the students miss and details that are especially relevant to these characters' development, and then organized into small discussion groups. In these small groups I had students discuss two questions: (1) Why do you think D'Angelo made the decision(s) he did in these scenes? (2) Would you have made the same decisions? Why or why not? Interloping between groups as they talked, I would gently suggest that students focus not so much on D'Angelo as an individual, as compelling a character as he is, but on the ways that his individuality is constrained by the institutions he lives within, and these institutions' corresponding moralities in light of their understanding of various ethical theories we had learned in class. In other words, they were asked to identify both how D'Angelo negotiates contradictory institutional moral logics (for instance, the institutions of the game, the criminal justice system, and his family) and whether his actions conform to specific ethical theories. I then asked the class as a whole to judge whether D'Angelo was an ethical or unethical person. The vast majority of students felt unable to pass such a judgment; they were able, however, to state that he was someone who was "moral" in the sense that Kleinman uses the term.

In preparation for the small-group and class discussions I had students pay special attention to the scene in which D'Angelo teaches two younger boys, key characters Wallace and Bodie, that "the [drug] game" is like the game of chess (1.3). Specifically, D'Angelo teaches them that the best that pawns can hope for is to stay alive until their king wins the game. Most pawns, however, will die in service of the king—and there is no moving up in rank from a pawn to a king. A pawn in the game, then, is taught that their duty is to serve the bidding of the king. Pawn morality is to abide by a hierarchical code in which they do what they are told by their superiors.

This lesson is later played out when Bodie and Poot kill their good friend Wallace after being told to do so (1.12). Their morality is pawn morality, and a pawn does what a king commands even if it results in the death of another pawn (with whom they are friends). They both struggle with the act of killing Wallace, Poot more than Bodie, but both participate in his murder in order to prove they belong in the game. While they may have had ethical reservations about killing a friend, they decided to ignore those reservations and embrace the morality of the game. Their decision to do so, and the act of murdering Wallace itself, contributed to the type of moral agents they became. In that "dangerous" moment they became a certain kind of moral actor. Being a member of a particular social institution, in this case a drug gang, contributed to their formation as moral agents willing to see killing a friend as a justifiable action.

Importantly, in another scene the students watched, D'Angelo confronts other members of Avon's crew about what happened to Wallace (1.12). In prison for another crime, D'Angelo repeatedly asks the crew's lawyer and Stringer Bell, the second-in-command, "Where is Wallace? Where the fuck is Wallace?!" They refuse to answer his question and tell him to "shut his mouth." D'Angelo refuses to do so. It is this moment, and another moment in which

D'Angelo tells his mother that he no longer wants the protection of Avon's crew, that we see D'Angelo make the decision to officially abandon the morality of the drug game for a vision of the ethical that values persons over power and profits.

In giving his chess lesson D'Angelo endorsed the rules of the game even as he recognized its restrictions on people like himself. It is not clear in the scene, but it appears that early on D'Angelo considered himself something more than a pawn—at least in the chess scene he views those under his supervision as more "pawn-y" than he is. Because he is related to Avon Barksdale, the "king," D'Angelo feels that he is something like a rook or bishop. He finds himself in a position in which the rules of the game are more complicated. In some ways, rooks and bishops also often end up off the board. They, too, die in service of the king. However, they can move a little more freely than pawns can. D'Angelo, too, believes he can move more freely than a pawn. Because he sees himself as being able to benefit in a certain way from playing the game, he embraces and perpetuates its moral code. However, we eventually learn that he is nothing more than a pawn. He winds up being murdered at the command of Stringer Bell (2.6).

A second scene from D'Angelo's life that is especially helpful is one in which he dines at an upscale restaurant with his girlfriend Donette (1.5). He has been earning a relatively large amount of money selling drugs for Avon and wants to treat his girlfriend to a night out on the town. In addition, he is beginning to seek to move beyond the game into a life removed from the violence of Baltimore's corners. He does not want to be a pawn. However, the entire experience at the restaurant is one in which it becomes clear to D'Angelo, and to his girlfriend, that he has not been formed in the norms and rules of the game being played at the restaurant that night. There are local moralities everywhere and they do not necessarily translate across contexts. D'Angelo, formed in the morality of the drug game, does not have a reference for functioning according to the rules of another game in another context. While he desires to achieve a new social status that he thinks is tied to a world where the more brutal aspects of the game he knows do not apply, he is unable to do so because he has been so formed in the norms of Baltimore's drug corners. From birth he has been shaped by social institutions to play only one game.

Over the course of the meal D'Angelo voices his discomfort in the upscale setting and displays his relative ignorance with the rules that apply in that setting. He is skeptical of the host who asks to take his coat. He is jumpy when the waiter reaches across the table to remove crumbs after they finish the main course. Between the entrée and dessert, while feeling especially out of place,

D'Angelo asks Donette if she thinks the other diners know that they do not belong. Donettee, misunderstanding D'Angelo's concern as one primarily about race, mentions that they are not the only black people in the restaurant. D'Angelo responds that it is "not about that" but about where they are from. Donette responds to D'Angelo saying, "[If] you got money, you get to be whoever you say you are." At this point the waiter arrives at their table with a dessert cart. D'Angelo reaches out and grabs the sample of the chocolate cake that Donette wants. The waiter then retrieves it and informs him that it is only a sample, and then pulls Donette's piece of cake from another shelf on the cart. D'Angelo sits back in his chair in frustration and resignation. He is unable to transfer the morality of the game, in this case physical assertiveness, into practices that are appropriate in a different context.

A third scene from D'Angelo's life I had students watch is a scene from his time in prison, where D'Angelo becomes a member of a book club that discusses *The Great Gatsby* (2.6). In one book club meeting D'Angelo tells his peers and the volunteer leading the discussion that he thinks the message of the story is that one cannot escape their history—that "the past is always with us. Where we come from, what we go through, how we go through it—all that shit matters." Where one comes from, and the moral code of that place, will always have a profound influence on who one is and can be. In D'Angelo's words,

> It's like you can change up, right. You can say you somebody new, you can give yourself a whole new story. But what came first is who you really are. And what happened before is what really happened. And it don't matter that some fool say he different, 'cause the only thing that makes you different is what you really do, what you really go through.

This is the case even for people like Gatsby—and D'Angelo—no matter how hard one tries to escape this formation.

Over the course of his brief time in the show, roughly one and one-half seasons, we learn that D'Angelo has ethical reservations about the brutality of the game and wants to remove himself from it. He is haunted by the death of an innocent man whose only crime was testifying against him, by the brutal torture and murder of the boyfriend of one of his crew's biggest enemies, and by the death of a woman who overdosed on drugs at a Barksdale party and was put in a dumpster rather than taken to a hospital. And he is furious that Stringer Bell ordered the murder of Wallace. He believes in an ethical code that transcends the morality of the game, but negotiating how to live by those ethics while still in the game proves impossible. For a time, he chooses to play the game and serves a lengthy prison sentence on behalf of the crew. However, as time passes and he witnesses more of Avon and Stringer's brutality he announces that he wants nothing else to do with his family and the organization. Sadly, the brutality D'Angelo abhors eventually reaches him when his murder is arranged by Stringer Bell because he recognizes that D'Angelo's ethical commitments threatened the survival of the rest of Barksdale's crew. His attempts to transcend the game proved futile, and despite his highest aspirations D'Angelo becomes another statistic of the war on drugs. D'Angelo's story helps students understand the powerful influences that institutions have on who we are and who we can become.

Stringer Bell, the second-in-command in the Barksdale drug organization, has D'Angelo killed while he is living with Donette in a romantic relationship. Stringer is who Donette wanted D'Angelo to be. He is a childhood friend of Avon Barksdale and takes over the daily operations of the organization while Avon is in prison. Over the course of the first three seasons we learn that Stringer sees himself as a businessman more than a gangster. He takes business courses at the local community college, has a copy of Adam Smith's *The Wealth of Nations* on his bookshelf, and uses the money he makes selling drugs to secure real estate deals. He believes that if he has enough money he can be whoever he wants to be. Specifically, that he can be a businessman and does not have to be a gangster.

During his time running the Barksdale organization he institutes reforms in its practices by incorporating lessons he learns in his business classes. As a part of this reformation he significantly reduces the amount of violence street-level drug dealers employ. Eventually, Avon is released from prison and becomes increasingly dissatisfied with the way that Stringer has reorganized their practices. Specifically, he believes that Stringer has become too soft and seeks to reinstitute many of the violent tactics that Stringer phased out while Avon was in prison. This tension escalates quickly throughout season three because Marlo Stanfield, the leader of a new, rival crew of drug dealers, uses especially brutal methods to take corners away from more established drug dealers.

The tension between approaching the game as primarily a business endeavor (Stringer's approach) or as a gangster war (Avon's approach) is distinctly demonstrated in a scene in which Stringer and Avon get in a physical fight (3.8). Before Avon and Stringer tussle, however, they have an argument about tactics. Stringer does not like Avon's consistent use of the language of war to discuss their work; Avon accuses Stringer of wanting to be Donald Trump. In the course of the argument Avon says that the difference between him and Stringer is that he bleeds "red" while Stringer bleeds "green." He calls

Stringer "a man without a country" who cares more about getting rich than about loyalty to one's compatriots or earning the respect that comes with controlling the corners. In short, Avon accuses Stringer of not living up to the moral code of the game as he understands it. Rather, Stringer is living by another moral code that does not serve the needs of the war between Barksdale's crew and Marlo's crew. Stringer's morality is the morality of the market; Avon's is the morality of gangsters.

This conversation is reminiscent of an earlier conversation in which Stringer attempts to persuade Avon of the merits of joining together with the other drug dealers in Baltimore to buy in bulk from the same drug supplier, divvy up the corners, end the violence, and reinvest the money they earn from selling drugs in real estate and other legal business opportunities (3.6). Stringer gave this plea in response to Avon's assertion that one does not "buy" corners but "takes" them. In short, he espouses a different moral code than Stringer—a code in which force is more important than money. Avon's moral code is one in which the strongest, not the savviest, survive. After listening to Stringer's argument on behalf of abandoning that code and committing to a more "businesslike" approach, Avon says that he's not a "suit-wearing businessman" like Stringer. "I'm just a gangster, I suppose. And I want my corners," he says. This is a rift that is never bridged and they each arrange for the downfall of the other.

When Omar and Brother Mouzone have Stringer cornered before they kill him, Stringer offers them money in exchange for his life. Their response is that Stringer still does not understand—the game is not just about money. It is about respect, power, and playing by the rules. Over the course of three seasons we see that Stringer regularly breaks these rules: he arranged for the brutal torture and murder of Omar's boyfriend as a revenge tactic; he lied to Brother Mouzone and put him in a dangerous situation in which either he or Omar would be killed; and he broke the Sunday truce that all Baltimore drug dealers had followed for years in an attempt to get Omar killed. Stringer's free-market ethics were antithetical to the morality of the game. Stringer assumed that the morality of free-market economic exchange was a universal ethic that could be imposed in any context. Others who played the game, however, did not agree with his negotiation of the relation of his believed universal ethic to the local world they shared. He (and Donette) was wrong. Money does not mean you get to be whoever you want to be. Stringer, seconds before he died, tried to combine a universal free-market ethic with gangster morality. His attempt to combine this perceived universal within his local context was a stressful one that eventually proved to be too dangerous for others, especially Avon, to embrace.

In reflecting on Stringer's life I encouraged my students to recognize the ways that the moral logic of the market is increasingly the default logic of many social and political institutions. I asked them to identify the ways that Stringer imposed the morality of the market onto the game. I also asked them to identify the ways they see the logic of the market in their own lives outside of traditional market exchanges—one place I identify this tension for students is the ways that the moral logic of markets and universities are different and in some ways in competition. I concluded these conversations by asking students to identify the ways that it is appropriate for institutions to have their own moral logics and the difficulties of living in a world where we are formed in a variety of logics that can often contradict one another. In doing so they identified with Stringer's desire to impose one moral logic across institutions, but also realized the ways that desire made his life and the life of others more dangerous.

These characters are helpful, as are Randy, Omar, Kima, McNulty, Lt. Daniels, Bubbles, Michael, Namond, and many others, in demonstrating the ways that our moral agency is in part determined by our interaction with social, political, and economic institutions. None of them are villains or heroes. They are not saints nor are they purely sinners. Rather, they are morally ambivalent characters who display both moral courage and weakness at various points in their lives. The ways these characters negotiate between the moral and the ethical in the midst of some of late-modernity's most unique institutions, such as the ghetto neighborhood, the public school, and a modern police department, provide parables for students to understand the way that ethics is lived in the world they inhabit.

Conclusion

David Simon, the creator of *The Wire*, has said that he is "very cynical about institutions and their willingness to address themselves to reform." He is not cynical "when it comes to individuals," however. Specifically, he believes *The Wire* extols those individuals who are willing to stand up to institutions and fight for what they believe is right. What *The Wire* demonstrates is that no one—whether one is the rebel killer of drug dealers (Omar), the hater of brutality and inhumanity (D'Angelo), or the face of the "real police" who will not juke the stats (McNulty)—is free from such institutions. Rather, we are shaped as moral agents both by the institutions we live in and the ideals we hold dear. More often than not we are able to hold the two in a tolerable balance that enables us to live in a world that makes sense to our most deeply held beliefs. Most people on most days are able to be ethical actors in whatever moral world they happen to live in. There are times, however, when our ethics come into tension with our morality. In those moments, our morality, more often than not, rules. There are times, however, when our ethics reshape our morality and we enter a dangerous world that must be reshaped as we are being reshaped. There is no escaping this danger, and there is no immediate salvation from experiencing this reshaping, but we can endure this tension and remain ethical moral agents.

I teach my students that it is at moments such as these—when D'Angelo decides he wants nothing else to do with his drug dealing family or when Stringer realizes that his money will not buy off Omar and Brother Mouzone—that the discipline of ethics is its most relevant. For it is in such moments that our moral formation in social institutions such as families, schools, and neighborhoods challenges our universal principles and vice versa. It is in such moments that ethical commitments become practical or they are discarded. And it is in such moments that we become the moral agents we are always already becoming.

NOTES

1. On the ways humans are shaped morally by institutions see Roger Friedland and Robert R. Alford, "Bringing Society Back In: Symbols, Practices, and Institutional Contradictions," in *The New Institutionalism in Organizational Analysis,* eds. Walter W. Powell and Paul J. DiMaggio (Chicago: University of Chicago Press, 1991), 232–63. On the ways humans navigate these institutions using multiple moral logics see Steven M. Tipton, "Social Differentiation and Moral Pluralism," in *Meaning and Modernity: Religion, Polity, and Self,* eds. Richard Madsen, William M. Sullivan, Ann Swidler, and Steven M. Tipton (Berkeley: University of California Press, 2001), 15–40.

2. On the various social injustices highlighted by *The Wire* see Anmol Chaddha and William Julius Wilson, "'Way Down in the Hole,'" in *Corners in the City of God: Theology, Philosophy, and The Wire,* eds. Jonathan Tran and Myles Werntz (Eugene: Cascade Books, 2013), 31–56.

3. Not all ethicists feel this way, and scholars have begun reflecting on how to incorporate film into the ethics classroom in a responsible and pedagogically useful way. For example, see Ellen Ott Marshall, "Making the Most of a Good Story: Effective Use of Film as a Teaching Resource for Ethics," *Teaching Theology and Religion* 6.2 (2003): 93–98.

WORKS CITED

Chaddha, Anmol, and William Julius Wilson. "'Way Down in the Hole.'" *Corners in the City of God: Theology, Philosophy, and The Wire,* 31–56. Edited by Jonathan Tran and Myles Werntz. Eugene: Cascade Books, 2013.
Friedland, Roger, and Robert R. Alford. "Bringing Society Back In: Symbols, Practices, and

Institutional Contradictions." *The New Institutionalism in Organizational Analysis*, 232–63. Edited by Walter W. Powell and Paul J. DiMaggio. Chicago: University of Chicago Press, 1991.

Kleinman, Arthur. *What Really Matters: Living a Moral Life Amidst Uncertainty and Danger*. Oxford: Oxford University Press, 2006.

Marshall, Ellen Ott. "Making the Most of a Good Story: Effective Use of Film as a Teaching Resource for Ethics." *Teaching Theology and Religion* 6.2 (2003): 93–98.

Pojman, Louis P., and James Fieser, *Ethics: Discovering Right and Wrong*, 7th ed. Boston: Wadsworth, 2012.

Rachels, James and Stuart Rachels. *The Elements of Moral Philosophy*, 6th ed. New York: McGraw Hill, 2010.

Simon, David. "Interview with Bill Moyers." *Bill Moyers Journal*, April 17, 2009. http://www.pbs.org/moyers/journal/04172009/transcript1.html.

Tipton, Steven M. "Social Differentiation and Moral Pluralism." *Meaning and Modernity: Religion, Polity, and Self*, 15–40. Edited by Richard Madsen, William M. Sullivan, Ann Swidler, and Steven M. Tipton. Berkeley: University of California Press, 2001.

Good Lives in Tragic Worlds

Nathan P. Gilmour

Some of the most important lessons about education come from watching people learn. In season four of *The Wire,* Howard "Bunny" Colvin, a former police whose unorthodox approach to narcotics crimes ends his career on the force, takes a job with David Parenti, a University of Maryland sociology researcher who wants to develop programs to help at-risk urban students. After a few episodes spent deciding the context for the study (middle school) and observing some classrooms, Colvin begins to theorize about the ultimate aims of an intervention program. In the episode "Alliances" he suggests a program that leaves "stoop kids," those capable of staying in one place and engaging in disciplined, self-motivated learning, without constant adult supervision, in normal classrooms while taking "corner kids," the ones apparently incapable of such self-discipline, into some program that helps them learn to be stoop kids (4.5). Though they are not sure at the outset whether such transformations in broad populations are possible, the idea developed across the series is that academic success for such students is far less likely, even if remotely possible, without a corresponding change in larger patterns of life. After assuring Mrs. Sampson, an English teacher, that the program would not be in the business of "warehousing" the corner kids, the experiment moves forward without a clear end and means but with a demographic and a general sense of purpose in mind. Further on in the season, in the episode "Corner Boys," Colvin accompanies Parenti into a classroom in which Miss Duquette, a doctoral candidate, begins the work with ten select corner kids (4.8). As Miss Duquette tries to get the students (who refer to themselves as "corner boys" in the course of the scene) in the classroom to imagine their future, Colvin notices patterns in the classroom's relationships that those more closely and routinely involved cannot see. Watching Namond Brice, a vocal eighth-grader, deny that he possesses a magazine in plain view, first saying there's no magazine and then that he found it there when he sat down, Colvin plays off of Duquette's lesson, noting that, in spite of the failure of the school system to teach reading and math, the corner boys are learning to survive in their own world.

As far as the kids can tell, there's no real benefit to be had from learning history or algebra (though Randy, a character who does not participate in the Parenti study, does eventually learn that probability theory is handy in a game of dice), but Colvin sees that the classroom itself is an education in on-the-field combat psychology for the kids: the games that they play with their teachers, forcing them up against the limits of their formal authority and their patience, serve to hone their edges when they go out to the street corners, developing certain capacities for quick thinking that will serve them well as they elude police and rival gangs. Over the course of "Corner Boys" and subsequent episodes, parallel story-lines evolve as the Colvin-Parenti team in the special classroom and Roland Pryzbylewski, a former police officer who has become an eighth-grade math teacher (but also not part of the Parenti study), discover that in order to educate West Baltimore students, corner boys and otherwise, they must invite students formed by certain moral narratives—usually defined as much by neighborhood as by race or class—into new, broader views of their own worlds to realize that the corner and the prison system are not the only realities open to them, if they're both disciplined and lucky. But the things they know as corner boys and small-time con artists are not going to get them there; they must learn to conceive of the formal education which heretofore has seemed entirely useless not as a worthless holding pattern, or at most a trial-run for their street-careers, instead as a gateway into something beyond. As the season evolves, Colvin and Parenti in one storyline and Pryzbylewski in another engage in a complex process of inviting the students into a world that they did not imagine before.

A plurality of educations happens in all sorts of institutional contexts, of course. By no means are most college classrooms the sorts of environments where students are learning to gain the upper hand on law-enforcement officers—our colleges are hardly hospitable when such kids want to join us—but just as Colvin discerns in the Baltimore public school classroom, two kinds of education happen in American college classrooms. We who teach and love core-curriculum introductory courses often desire to shape our students into more critical and dedicated servants of communities beyond the self, be those communities national, municipal, or ecclesial. But what the students learn in those contexts, too often, is how to play the games that yield more individualistic rewards, the incentive structures of gaining the degree with as little fuss as possible. Whether the aim is to transform given value-structures or to discover a set of obligations and desires that better fit a citizen than an atomized individual, an introductory philosophical ethics class could do worse than to convince those students that they actually desire something other than a quick diploma, whether they knew it or not when they enrolled.

In a college that fields a philosophical ethics course for core-curriculum humanities credit, *The Wire*, specifically season four, stands to be a strong conversation partner with Friedrich Nietzsche's *Genealogy of Morals* and Alasdair MacIntyre's *After Virtue*. Working with these partners to open up questions of what counts as good, the course oscillates between the students on the screen and those enrolled in the college course as they learn that the practice of reasoned deliberation on the good life does its best work when imagination crosses the boundaries of fiction and life-outside-of-fiction.

Narrative and the Core-Curriculum Humanities Class

One year, at the small liberal arts college where I teach, walking down the hall during final exam week, I saw learning happen and understood the terms of the games being played. In a small college like mine, students take exams in economics, psychology, literary criticism, theology, and history all in the same hallway; so while I lacked working familiarity with much of the jargon students were trading, I recognized a good bit of it from my own general-education courses, at a couple decades' remove. Ostensibly, the students were preparing to demonstrate their entry-level familiarity with vocabularies from a broad spectrum of disciplines and disciplinary histories. But a common structure emerged in the last-minute exam prep itself: one student would recite a noun-phrase, one that sounded somewhat abstract, and the other would recite a brief definition. Students would repeat the same process at all parts of the hall, this cluster for American history, that for abnormal psychology, another still for management theory. I have not wandered the halls of the music building or the laboratory complex as often as I have my own building, but when I have, I've heard the same.

Such scenes, which I have witnessed semester after semester, reveal a certain notion of what counts as a final exam: students should exhibit specialized knowledge, which consists in knowing a strange set of vocabulary terms which, at least in terms of what counts as mastery, requires a grammar of performance for exhibiting competence that does not differ from discipline to discipline. Such is not to say that those who major in this or that field do not also have laboratory reports and recitals and portfolios to demonstrate mastery in more specialized manners, but too often the ways that we professors ask general-education students to demonstrate their initiation into disciplines relies on a specialized answer as a sign of accomplishment while assuming entirely too much about what counts as a legitimate question.

My good fortune as a teacher has been to work at a college that rewards, not punishes, attempts to imagine creatively the ends and the means of core curriculum. In recent years our core assessment goals have shifted away from course-specific measures of low-level vocabulary-mastery towards larger, liberal-arts goals so that students must demonstrate their education not by answering multiple-choice questions correctly but exhibiting, in writing, abilities to keep a particular audience in mind, address a plurality of competing theories in the course of an inquiry, and otherwise demonstrate fairly complex dispositions of thought. In such an environment, many faculty have shifted their modes of teaching more heavily towards case-studies, simulations, and other such narrative genres for the sake of letting students engage in complex thoughts. In my own courses, I have often allowed students to help me determine the forms of the final long-term research projects and exam, making early stages of those projects proposals and group dialogues in which as a group we establish formal requirements as well as what will count as competence, excellence, and failure. That process has let me know a fair bit about what students regard as real learning as well as what kinds of assessment really let me know that students have learned to see reality as practitioners of rhetorical theory or literary criticism or philosophical ethics, in other words to see whether students have reached the intellectual goals that I set for such classes. My own institution, in other words, would likely welcome the hypothetical class presented here as a thought-experiment, largely because it continues the institution's larger project of thinking hard about what sort of phenomenon learning might be and what sorts of educational practices might best encourage and eventually account truthfully for what sorts of learning have happened.

When a teacher tries to re-imagine what it means to learn philosophy and thus what it means to teach philosophy, two especially good friends among moral philosophers are an unlikely pair, Friedrich Nietzsche and Alasdair MacIntyre. *Genealogy of Morals* and *After Virtue* are two books best read in conversation, the first a criticism of the post–Christian liberalism of nineteenth-century Europe and the latter an extension of that critique, an insistence that Nietzsche's reaching into the resources of classical antiquity are not headed in the wrong direction but rather do not reach far enough to provide an alternative to liberalism. Both books share a common project, namely the narration of their philosophical opponents' mistakes not as faulty steps in a syllogistic system but ultimately as partial narratives, the sort of deception that might indeed get the facts right but nonetheless lie in terms of the larger picture into which those facts fit. In other words, the disputes that Nietzsche and MacIntyre find most interesting involve the reader not in questions of who answers the given questions right but rather in why someone decided that this question rather than that one should be the given question, not whether a given scholar is dedicated enough to the pursuit of truth but rather who set the terms for what counts as truth in the first place.

By Friedrich Nietzsche's account, the language of "good" and "evil" itself emerges from a history of deception, a story in which the games that we play lose sight of their own structures. The rise of what Nietzsche eventually calls ascetic values begins with a rebellion of the weak:

> The slave revolt in morality begins when *ressentiment* itself becomes creative and gives birth to values: the *ressentiment* of natures that are denied the true reaction, that of deeds, and compensate themselves with imaginary revenge. While every noble morality develops from a triumphant affirmation of itself, slave morality from the outset says No to what is "outside," what is "different," what is "not itself"; and *this* No is its creative deed [472–73].

What's most interesting for this inquiry is not the historical verifiability or even the rhetorical force of this narrative but the fact that the theory even takes place in the form of narrative. Corrupt ascetic ideals emerge historically, and the middle of history's story, our moment, takes its own particular character from the beginning of the story (for Nietzsche, the decline of the warrior ethos) and from the ending (for Nietzsche, an open future which has no intelligible aim and might well return to what was before). Thus whatever moral future lies beyond the ascetic hierarchy of goods will necessarily emerge through historical means, not a system that arises in a vacuum, as if Christianity never existed, but as a post–Christian reality.[1] Fans of *The Wire* will no doubt sense a certain resonance here with the show's disdain for too-easy answers to complex questions: those who attempt to forge lives without reference to the systems within which those lives happen, as Colvin does in season three when he discovers that Hamsterdam leaves junkies just as hopeless as before and as Carcetti does when he runs an early city council meeting as mayor (4.11), soon enough discover that whatever work of living in a human community, as mayor or otherwise, happens only after the particular kinds of breakfast that folks eat in a given human community.

The particular rhetorical power of *Genealogy of Morals* lies in its unflinching insistence that abstractions that philosophers try to posit "beyond" the story ultimately come to pass not in the abstract but as the maneuvering of real people with real agendas, and thus deserve historical and genealogical treatment as well as logical analysis. Morality, in other words, emerges as one faction's moment of intellectual dominance gives way to the next, and the philosopher who denies such emergence is always oversimplifying and in many cases outright lying. The new morality, as Nietzsche hints at it, cannot simply lay hands on long-lost forms; only a philosophy that overcomes liberal democratic, Christian sentiments, only an *Uber-mensch* morality, is even intelligible as a possibility. Thus Nietzsche is no simple relativist or nihilist but one who insists on the historical character of human existence and an opponent of Platonic and Christian modes of morality that would deny their own storied pasts. Whatever the good human life looks like in a post–Christian moment, the philosopher's tools for conceptualizing that life must be historical tools, not pretending that Christianity never happened but overcoming the powerful rhetoric of *ressentiment* and proposing a new city built among its ruins.

Alasdair MacIntyre likewise practices a hard-nosed, uncompromisingly historical-social moral philosophy, rooting notions of good life not in the individual's choice but in communal dialectics. MacIntyre, in *After Virtue,* also insists that visions of goodness must be historical visions, insisting that virtues manifest themselves not in discrete situations, where technical terminology rules and which minimize situations in longer stories, but in long, narrative spans:

> Someone who genuinely possesses a virtue can be expected to manifest it in very different types of situations, many of them situations where the practice of a virtue cannot be expected to be effective in the way that we expect a professional skill to be. [...] And the unity of a virtue in someone's life is intelligible only as a characteristic of a unitary life, a life that can be conceived and evaluated as a whole [205].

MacIntyre's own project is also inherently narrative in character. In his account, those philosophies that would ignore the teleological character of human life do not merely get things wrong; their errors are the results of particular historical movements in philosophy, starting with the Enlightenment's attempts to conceive of morality abstractly and universally without reference to particular human communities. By ignoring the sociological realities that surround questions of truth and lie, of good and bad, those moral philosophies will become unwitting ideological instruments of particular, technologically dominant factions rather than a tool of the thinker who would examine those same factions with an eye for making this human community, in this historical moment, in these terms of good and bad, somewhat more intelligible as good or bad. In other words, ethics for MacIntyre is always the disciplined reflection of particular people on particular communities, not the universal assertion of "principles" stripped of local human particularity. So like Nietzsche confronting Europe's Christian liberalism, and like Colvin discovering what school is really for in the life of a corner boy, MacIntyre insists upon telling a story of cover-ups and deceptions that themselves pose as self-evident truths, insisting that only truth-telling about the real history of institutional expectations can have any hope of leading to something better. For students learning to write and discuss ethical philosophy with Nietzsche and MacIntyre and Colvin, the enterprise always starts with careful attention to the particular, never grand dismissals of contingency. And one fine starting place for such examination is precisely the narratives that make sense of "core curriculum" in the twenty-first-century American college.

Towards that initial aim, Nietzsche's and MacIntyre's work, both treating narrative as integral to ethics rather than a site for "application" or some other secondary activity, stand to take the work of philosophical ethics out of the realm of vocabulary lists in favor of something more like close-reading, the sort of story-reading that makes the course less a matter of "quandary ethics"[2] and more the kind of investigation that lets literary narrative reflect life and thus teach students to study life as a text and ethics as a repertoire of poetic moves. Students who learn not only from the virtue-ethics storytellers but also from the complex story of David Simon's Baltimore learn to see that abstractions like "education" and "politics" make the most sense when one pays the best attention to particular details "on the ground." And because season four of *The Wire* is not a one-shot motion picture but a thirteen-hour exploration of characters, the character of the series and the character of the moral philosophers both, in their central structures, draw readers and viewers away from attempts to summarize and reduce too easily the jagged narrative edges, preferring instead modes of analysis that do the work of tracing an intelligible "big picture" flexible enough to accommodate irregular shapes as well as expected ones.

The Game Is Too Much with Us: The Tragic World of The Wire

In the particular story that *The Wire* tells, good ideas never survive the wrath of the gods. Parenti's and Colvin's and Duquette's program evolves over the course of several episodes, hitting on the idea eventually that the "corner kids" need to experience things that put them on the edge of their own world, looking into another. The three teachers get their students to work together building models without instructions, to venture forth into a restaurant that requires menus and coat checks, to role-play interactions in a variety of public scenarios. The students at the center of that storyline appear to be on the verge of a genuine, free choice of what sort of lives they want to pursue. Such a confrontation with possibility at first chases the students back into moral and narrative concepts that they find familiar, leading several of the students towards a crisis-moment in which new learning becomes necessary if their choices are to be genuine.

As Namond so quickly points out in the episode "Alliances," Parenti's program, on its face, resembles American prison life: the kids who go into "solitary" can look forward only to re-emerging into "gen-pop" where the rest of the students/inmates serve out their school days/sentence (4.5). Thus, as he imagines the program, the end is not ultimately transformation but mere repetition, since human beings in Namond's world never really change. Parenti and Colvin and Duquette rise to that ethical challenge, using their time and resources to ask the students, in a relatively short span of days, into a new way of imagining the world, inviting the students to transcend the corner-prison-solitary ecosystem. Although the education has to do with neighborhood-level social responsibility rather than geometry and astronomy, something happens in that process analogous to the movement that Plato names in *Republic*: from a narrow view, one that only regards the particular manifestations of larger patterns, Namond and his classmates begin to approach a broader view that does not nullify the world of particular instances but negates the primacy of the particular by situating particular instances in an intellectual framework newly intelligible because it stands in relationship to larger patterns, concepts and ideas (in *Republic,* the cave is still there when the prisoner goes beyond it to look at a broader and truer reality, and the sun-gazer's duty is to return and give the folks living in that cave the benefit of the broader vision).

But the powers that be, the gods of *The Wire*'s very Greek world, will not abide a classroom not sufficiently devoted to standardized test scores. When administrators in the school district discover that the special class is not devoting the requisite proportion of class time to standardized-test preparation, they discontinue the program, leaving Parenti with a new presentation for academic conferences but the kids without even that. In an impressive scene Colvin visits Namond's father, a drug-gang lieutenant who goes by Wee-Bey, to ask permission to bring Namond into his own home, to continue the work of the program in the life of one young man and to help him go places where neither Wee-Bey nor Colvin has been able to go, into another realm of higher education, social opportunity, and perhaps to the kinds of service unimaginable to the "corner kids" for whom the height of achievement is to become a dominant drug dealer (4.13).

Like Colvin's fated drug-legalization program, Hamsterdam in season three, and like the Major Crimes Unit throughout the series, Parenti's program stands as a sort of Pandora's Box in the world of *The Wire*. Those moments of possibility, of doing things differently, even for a moment, are a site of hope within the Baltimore of the series, not within the storyline's institutional contexts but beyond them, and within the space that such imagination opens, *The Wire*'s viewers might start to imagine that our own classrooms and workplaces and other human communities might do things differently. To put such a plot line at the center of a philosophical ethics class would have as its main goal to provide moments in which education itself and the ends at which education points become objects of philosophical interrogation. Following Parenti and Colvin and Namond Brice and other characters into the school system of *The Wire* might, among other things, provide occasion for analogical thinking, providing opportunities for students to ponder, in class conversations and written projects, how education as a practice fits into larger narratives of human goodness in their own communities and moments.

A Dialectical Pedagogy for Inventing (and/or Seeking) the Good

In the spirit of *The Wire* and of Plato's *Republic*, I ask readers to imagine with me a one-semester course that embodies the shape of education that might emerge if, like Duquette and Colvin and Parenti, one might imagine ordering a semester so that it points towards different ends. A text like *The Wire*, helping us both as curriculum and as imaginative exemplar, allows instructors to field a philosophy class dedicated to making friends with Nietzsche and MacIntyre, neither mainly for the sake of preparing the elect for graduate school nor for shuttling the rest through a fill-in-the-blank final exam but so that the course might call everyone into the room to a moment of judgment, when one must reject some philosophical content in favor of other philosophical content and take a stand on what sort of narrative best makes sense of education, work, and other human realities facing the students. The aim of such a course, finally, would be to examine moral stories well precisely because the examiners already exist within and will always inhabit complex networks of moral narratives.

To begin the thought-experiment, required course materials for this kind of teaching ought to be relatively inexpensive. Some version of *The Wire* season four would be a required text for the class (hard copy or digital streaming would be fine, just as long as each student had easy access at any given moment to every episode), and each student would also buy a copy of Walter Kaufmann's translation of *The Basic Writings of Nietzsche* and the most recent edition of *After Virtue* by Alasdair MacIntyre.[3]

Within this hypothetical fifteen-week semester, *The Wire*'s fourth season will play one role in homework and another in classroom exercises, and at all points it will be in conversation with *Genealogy of Morals* and *After Virtue*. In class, for the first ten of those fifteen weeks, a normal, slow-pace philosophy seminar will happen, with students reading small chunks of Nietzsche for five weeks, then MacIntyre for seven, and watching roughly two episodes of *The Wire* per week as they go. Class discussions will be as lecture-heavy or as Socratic as the instructor prefers, but the main aim for the first three-fifths of classroom discussion will be to let students pose as many questions as necessary so that they can work on their own projects as homework, starting to lay out the basic movements of their written philosophical dialogues and letting their literary characters ask questions that emerge as the writers continue in conversation with Nietzsche and MacIntyre and *The Wire*.

In the course of those twelve weeks, students will, to greater and lesser extents, avail themselves of the skills and interests of a more experienced reader, each instructor balancing seminar discussion, brief lectures, and small-group interactions so that students see the instructor, the more-experienced practitioner of philosophical discourse, engage with scenes from the show and passages from the books, and receive the benefits of that practitioner's coaching as they learn the same disciplined modes of inquiry. Although the television episodes will no doubt figure in for the sake of example and exposition, the main focus will remain the books. So in a given class period, students might ask with Nietzsche whether Marlo Stanfield's conversation about dying with the crown on (3.6) is genuinely a step beyond the ethics of *ressentiment* or ponder with MacIntyre whether Bunk's rescuing Omar (4.8/9) constitutes a failure of the virtue of loyalty to his fellow detectives or an exemplary moment of the virtue of courage (or, more likely, a tragic moment encompassing both). But to the extent that the classroom moment calls for it, all such conversations should remain focused on the disciplined moves learned from *Genealogy of Morals* and *After Virtue*, with which students might make sense of the characters' ways of life. Up until the last three weeks, *The Wire* serves largely as a narrative handle onto which students can grab for the sake of understanding narrative-dependent theories of moral intelligibility.

The final weeks of class will fall into the hands of small groups of students, who will use whatever classroom video technology stands available to lead classroom discussions on *The Wire*, each session focusing on one episode in the season and leading the class in conversations of the narratives that make sense of acts, the large moral deceptions that make sense of characters' difficulties, and otherwise using the tools of ethical philosophy to conduct conversations, with the class, on the events in the episode. Each group will receive credit not for the speeches they give but for the combinations of clips and strong philosophical questions posed to the class, and the final exam for the class will consist entirely of questions posed by those small groups, modified as needed by the instructor but culled largely from those questions that arise in the course of groups' presentations. Such a move not only lends students a sense that their own processes of inquiry are worth investigation, and count as knowledge in their own right, but do some work against the too-common tendency for students to regard peer-presentation days as "free days" to skip or, perhaps even worse, spend playing on their phones as their peers present the fruits of their hard work.

Using classroom time this way, guiding the students for the first stretch and letting them take the reins for the last, takes advantage both of more traditional modes of teaching philosophy, with an experienced practitioner acting as the guide, and the experiences of research and careful thinking that presenting one's learning involves. The instructor in those closing weeks has the freedom to act as critical challenger to students' presentations and responses or as encouraging coach to students whose personalities make them more reticent to contribute, based on what the situation requires, and the relatively minimal class-session planning needed means that instructors can spend most of their preparation time responding to a series of short, staged writing assignments that will constitute the course's main writing assignment.

To omit a long-form essay (usually imagined as a ten-page, thesis-centered term paper) from a philosophy class might at first seem negligent, but this course replaces the long essay with assignments animated not by a desire to prepare students to take further philosophy courses (though some might indeed do so) but to think hard about the art of conversation by constructing a literary conversation. Practices like connecting elements of thought to compose complex concepts, focusing a range of thoughts to a field of inquiry fitting to a word count, and other such moments in the essay-composition process develop the virtues of rhetoric well, and this essay will not attempt to abolish that genre. However, for a core class trying to get students to ask new questions and seek new ways to imagine a good life, the long-form essay runs the risk of becoming, for the students who are already suspicious of required non-major classes, yet another hurdle in the long race to bring home the diploma. A philosophical ethics course with *The Wire* as conversation partner, and with dialectic rather than grad-school preparation for its main goal, would leave the long-form writing for the students' major classes. Here, at the core-curriculum level, these students will write short responses and revisions that shuttle back and forth between instructor and student and between students, each constituting the content of the end-of-semester written project in the form of a philosophical dialogue. This dialogue's aim is not to advance one theory for the sake of educating one reader but the exploration of tensions between theories and the presentation of each in its own terms for the sake of leaving the class better able to appreciate the tension among the accounts.

Thus the instructor will assign and collect several short assignments, each constituting a "bounce" back and forth between students and instructor(s) as a practice in careful, deliberative ethical thinking and eventually extending the class's conversation beyond the bounds of the classroom session. Drafts of each segment will receive a brief instructor response, distributing the instructor's "grading" attention more evenly over the semester rather than concentrating it at the end after students have finished with the work. Even in a relatively large class, therefore, all students (not just the vocal ones) have opportunities to enjoy targeted responses to their thought processes.

The move from the term paper to shorter, more interactive writing assignments is not new by any means; John Bean's *Engaging Ideas* offers a range of shorter writing pieces that cast the instructor less as the judge who rules on final products and more as a coach who brings students along in the practice of complex thinking.[4] That approach, paired with seminar-style discussions of Nietzsche and MacIntyre, all brought to bear on any of the characters' narratives in *The Wire*, should provide a rich network of complex questions, storied answers, and student articulations of how those questions and answers work, the sort of environment that might have students doing ethical philosophy rather than merely reciting abstract definitions of guild-jargon.

Instead of composing a formal research essay, students will engage in a five-bounce sequence of writing assignments for the Internet, each manageable in as few as 250 and certainly not more than 500 words. Eventually each student will arrange the resulting sequence of "bounces" into a philosophical dialogue to be published on a simple website or social-network space of the student's choice and design. Such public-intellectual work will change the stakes of the "term paper" and render the instructor not as the end of the text's career but as one evaluating how the student brings philosophical dialectic to a reading public.

Over the course of the semester, each student will work through the following sequence of assignments, each consisting of 250–500 words for the student or 100–250 for the instructor and eventually adding up to a longer literary dialogue:

1. Each student, having viewed all thirteen episodes of *The Wire* season four and read *Genealogy of Morals* by week ten, will write a brief narrative treatment of one character in season four, telling the story in the character of Nietzsche or a twenty-first-century disciple of Nietzsche. The instructor will distribute a rubric that values the strategic deployment of Nietzsche's vocabulary and concepts without merely "name-dropping."
2. The instructor will make comments on the philosophical content of these reviews and return them to the students for revision. Comments should focus not mainly on professional correctness (grammar and usage and such) but on places where the student accurately and skillfully reflects the sort of philosophy that *Genealogy of Morals* is doing; and letting the student know where their "Nietzsche-characters" have stopped sounding Nietzschean. The commentary will eventually become part of the final project, so some thought will have to go into its composition.
3. Each student, having read *After Virtue* by week twelve of the course, will write a blog-style response to a randomly-chosen, revised Nietzschean review from a different student, this time from the perspective of Alasdair MacIntyre or one of his disciples. The instructor will again distribute a rubric that values both getting MacIntyre right and responding truthfully to the content of the Nietzschean pieces.
4. The instructor will provide comments on the responses, once again focusing on the places where each student brought MacIntyre to bear skillfully and suggesting places where the treatment could be more precise, more complex, and so on.
5. In the closing weeks of the semester, each student will combine all four of the previous texts (the narratives and the commentary provided by the instructor) into a philosophical dialogue, arranging the existing material into a more give-and-take sort of encounter. In the process, each writer will figure out how the dialogue's characters might cite both Nietzsche and MacIntyre and at least two other online treatments of *The Wire* season four or who talk without citations but whose dialogue gets footnoted by the editor. The dialogue's aims are to examine the competing notions of good in one of the major story arcs in the series and to give each character as strong an argument as possible for how to understand the character. Students will be free to provide "intermediate" lines in the dialogue to clarify concepts and to improve the narrative movement of the piece, but the core of the philosophical work is already done by the time the student gets to this step. The aim here is not simply to "choose sides" but to represent and to situate both books' central points relative to each other and either expand upon or counter them with

reasoned argument. This should be the longest assignment of the course, but since the instructor has seen the work leading up to it, evaluation can proceed on the basis of intellectual development as well as disciplinary standards of mastery.
6. The student uploads the finalized version of the dialogue to an online environment of the student's choice, allowing readers beyond the course to have a say on the project, leaving open possibilities for further interaction with a reading public. The grade on the final version is the last written-project grade for the semester.

The aim of this sequence of writing assignments is not merely to piece elements of Nietzsche and MacIntyre together in some sort of easy eclectic pastiche; instead, the aim is to set up a tense conflict of philosophies, one that will lead any given student into a moment of informed responsibility. Students might by this point "like" one version of moral inquiry better than the other, but the project of constructing a dialogue will reward those students who take both seriously.

A series as complex as *The Wire* offers students a wide range of intersecting narrative arcs from which to choose when they examine the long-running discovery or invention (depending on which philosopher one favors) of goodness. In the course of the semester's discussions, presentations, and written projects, the possibilities for ethical examination, along an extended storyline that allows for values to be invented and virtues to be manifest with constancy, include but do not stop with the following:

- Kima Greggs's ongoing search for what makes "good police," given the complex of games that make up Baltimore police work
- Tommy Carcetti's rise to the mayor's office and the competing goods of public duty, public image, and personal ambition
- Namond Brice's attempt to navigate a future amid the expectations of his mother, Colvin, and other characters in the season
- Roland Pryzbylewski's ongoing struggle to establish (or to discover) the persona that will let him serve the actual students in his classroom
- Marlo Stanfield's rise as the "young lion" of West Baltimore and the moves he makes to establish his prominence among gangsters, police, and other characters
- Jimmy McNulty's life as a "domesticated" romantic partner and the draw of his former/future existence as the self-destructive but exceptionally competent detective

As the students encounter all of these story-lines in common, genuine collaboration on classroom discussions and written projects become possible without all the students focusing their efforts on the same things. And because, like Nietzsche and MacIntyre, *The Wire* is interested in telling true stories about systemic deception and the ways in which human goodness arises in moments of *aletheia*, an un-ignoring of the complexity of reality, the entire course stands to be a single, intelligible dialogue, a story that instructors, students, and texts tell together about how the students' moment might (or might not) lead to something more truthful in days to come. With three good friends along for the journey, the instructor can and should turn attention to the course-design choices, not least of all what sort of verbal discussion and written thinking should happen, to enjoy more fully the possibilities.

The King Is Still the King: Socrates the Invisible Partner in Rhetorical/Dialectic Education

Although David Simon, Alasdair MacIntyre, and Friedrich Nietzsche have been the main conversation partners up to this point, the real model here is Socrates. David Simon has noted on a few occasions that the literary influences behind *The Wire* are Greek tragedies.[5] The course I conceptualize here attempts to take on the role of Socrates, taking an artistic, narrative force that's already political and theorizing about how it exerts its force on imagination and further how disciplined investigation might lead to reading stories more intelligently. Like Socrates in *The Republic*, one's initial temptation might be to say that life in the streets of David Simon's Baltimore, as compelling as they are on the small screen, are still too removed from our students' quotidian reality to be of much use for ethical discussion.[6] But after noting that objection, perhaps we instructors can play Aristotle and suggest that *The Wire* is just what a good introductory college class calls for, not a list of abstractions but an involved, interested investment in narratives, not taking them as identical with human lives but certainly as reflections whose *mimesis* stand to help us look at reality differently.[7] Thus in the process of beholding performances, tragic at their core, and performing the rhetorical task of advancing forensic (in the ancient sense) accounts of what happens in those narratives, then engaging in the dialectical process of negating the rhetorical assertions and suggesting counter-interpretations, the students in such a course might, like the characters in *The Wire*, discover that there are realities that transcend the school/prison axis (or, for our students, the school/job axis) that call us into a world capacious enough to encompass but not limit its denizens to what they've always known.

If this course works as I hope it might, students will experience two masters of moral theory as contenders for their philosophical souls as they pull with all of their might (helped by a teacher dedicated to facilitating the struggle) on the questions at hand, and students take some sort of stand on what possibilities are better and what worse in a field of competing accounts of moral goodness and badness. But one who teaches these courses, especially one who endeavors to teach them better, should remember that, if the tragic visions of life set forth by MacIntyre and by *The Wire* are true, every course of this sort is part of a struggle and a trial, a narrative still unfinished in which the ending is still up for grabs. Like the students in Parenti's study, students might well decline the opportunity to step out of the world of French fries into the world of French cuisine, but the offer is still there. A course like the one I'm imagining, in the face of such contingencies and possibilities, hopes to set before my fellow teachers something different, a measure of goodness different enough from the way that many of us practice that we should have at least the chance to think carefully about what counts as a good class. The best classes should present these sorts of challenges to students, should offer some exposed, unfolded truth about reality, for the sake of letting students invent or discover (depending on whether they ultimately find themselves more Nietzschean or MacIntyrean) notions of visions of goodness that were not available to them at the outset. For students to walk away from the final exam better equipped to converse intelligently about good and bad is the aim, and these texts and tasks should point towards that aim. The good course should confront students, make them acknowledge at the very least that their lives can be better and worse, and that, while their circumstances give shape to the array of possibilities for good and bad lives, that their own conceptions of what count as good are at least partly responsible for what emerges next.

Notes

1. The third essay of Friedrich Nietzsche's *Genealogy of Morals*, which would be part of this hypothetical course's required reading, begins to point towards just such a post–Christian philosophy while heaping no small scorn on the liberal atheists of Europe, who think it a virtue not to believe in God but still to order their lives according to Christian morality.

2. Paul Wadell's book *Friendship and the Moral Life* proposes a narrative-rich virtue ethics as a more adequate alternative to what he calls "quandary ethics" (18–23), the sort of ethical theory that does all of its work on the level of the problematic episode abstracted from the longer narrative.

3. Though they're not by any means the only editions available, the editions of *The Basic Writings of Nietzsche* and *After Virtue* listed in this essay's bibliography have served me well in teaching core-curriculum philosophy.

4. College-pedagogy scholarship has become far more readily available in the last couple of decades, and two books that have helped me (and the new faculty in the Writing Across the Curriculum workshops that I lead) are Ken Bain's *What the Best College Teachers Do* and John Bean's *Engaging Ideas*. Both books make strong cases for embedding the "content" of courses in complex, demanding intellectual environments, discarding old notions that "the facts" must precede reasoning and realizing that memory works best when learners have to deploy facts as they learn them, fixing them in meaningful structures rather than binging on context-less facts and forgetting them directly after the final exam.

5. In an interview with *Believer*, David Simon describes *The Wire* thus: "But instead of the old gods, *The Wire* is a Greek tragedy in which the postmodern institutions are the Olympian forces. It's the police department, or the drug economy, or the political structures, or the school administration, or the macroeconomic forces that are throwing the lightning bolts and hitting people in the ass for no decent reason. In much of television, and in a good deal of our stage drama, individuals are often portrayed as rising above institutions to achieve catharsis. In this drama, the institutions always prove larger, and those characters with hubris enough to challenge the postmodern construct of American empire are invariably mocked, marginalized, or crushed. Greek tragedy for the new millennium, so to speak." For a more lighthearted take on the Greeks and *The Wire*, the YouTube clip in the bibliography features David Simon and Dominic West riffing on several aspects of the series and landing, towards the end of the interview, on Greek tragedy as one stream of influence.

6. For anyone whose undergraduate education denied them a full read-through of Plato's *Republic*, I'm riffing here on the dialogue's exploration and critique of representational poetry. The critique happens during *Republic* 596a-608b. Remarkably, and ignored by many critiques of Plato, Socrates ends this section by implicitly inviting the reader to make a good philosophical defense of representational poetry, a task that I've often set before students as we" encountered this section.

7. My response to our latter-day imaginary Socrates, of course, borrows its main ideas from Aristotle's *Poetics*.

Works Cited

"Alliances." *The Wire Season Four*. Writ. David Simon, Ed Burns, Richard Price. Dir. David Platt. 2006. Amazon Streaming Video. Accessed 14 December 2013. Web.
Aristotle. *Poetics*. S.H. Butcher, trans. *Internet Classics Archive*. Accessed 11 March 2014. Web.
Bean, John C. *Engaging Ideas: The Professor's Guide to Integrating Writing, Critical Thinking, and Active Learning into the Classroom*. San Francisco: Jossey-Bass, 2011.
"Corner Boys." *The Wire Season Four*. Writ. David Simon, Ed Burns, Richard Price. Dir. David Platt. 2006. Amazon Streaming Video. Accessed 14 December 2013. Web.
Hornby, Nick. "DAVID SIMON, CREATOR-WRITER-PRODUCER OF HBO'S THE WIRE." *Believer* August 2007. Accessed 11 March 2014. Web.
MacIntyre, Alasdair. *After Virtue*. Notre Dame: University of Notre Dame Press, 2007.
Nietzsche, Friedrich. *Genealogy of Morals*. Walter Kaufmann, trans. In *Basic Writings of Nietzsche*. Walter Kaufmann and Peter Gay, eds. New York: Modern Library, 2009.
Plato. *Republic*. Robin Waterfield, trans. Oxford: Oxford World's Classics, 2008.
Wadell, Paul. *Friendship and the Moral Life*. Notre Dame: University of Notre Dame Press, 1990.
"The Wire—David Simon Interview." *YouTube*. 16 July 2009. Accessed 11 March 2014. Web.

Wallace's Choice

Tom Nurmi

Thin Lines

Of the many characters tangled in Avon Barksdale's web in Season One of *The Wire*, an empathic sixteen-year-old named Wallace demands viewers' attention in a singular way. Wallace, perhaps more than any other character in the first season, allows viewers to consider the implications of freedom, choice, and the limits of empathy amid the bleak urban landscape of West Baltimore. In fact, the relationship between Wallace, the Barksdale crew, and the Baltimore Police Department captures in one micro-narrative the ethic and tragedy of the entire series. Michael B. Jordan's delicate portrayal of Wallace exposes a central tension that motivates each of *The Wire*'s five seasons, albeit in different ways. Wallace's storyline stages for the viewer the paradoxical nature of choice in the invisible inner cities of twenty-first century America, offering an anatomy of the structural limitations of urban Baltimore life as well as the complex and unresolved ethical relation between Wallace and the viewers of *The Wire*.

This essay explores how an emphasis on *choice* provides a frame for reading *The Wire* in the undergraduate classroom, situating the series in two specific contexts: comparative law and literature studies and the dynamics of visual rhetoric. As the range of essays in this volume attests, *The Wire* can be productively approached from a variety of angles, but the relationship between the series' unflinching focus on urban crime and its visual narrative form (within a long tradition of crime fiction) invites a teaching framework that attends to both dimensions simultaneously. *The Wire* encourages viewers to see common patterns across criminal, legal and police forces: the same desires and fantasies, the same disillusionments and moments of helplessness. But

The Wire is unique among other urban crime fictions and police procedurals because its primary thematic and structural concerns are centered on the nature of watching and surveillance. *The Wire* is worthy of study in a college classroom not only because it sparks vital conversations about the many ways in which choice is limited in West Baltimore—for the Pit crew born into the drug trade and for the young children smuggled away in forgotten rooms of condemned housing projects—but also because its visual economy implicates the student viewer in the ethical dilemmas surrounding surveillance and in the consequences of *watching* at the heart of the series.

In *The Wire*, visual metaphor becomes the primary vehicle for the show's insights into the hypocrisies and ironies of West Baltimore communities. Although a number of specific scenes are examined in this essay, the opening sequence to the episode "The Wire" provides the paradigmatic example of *The Wire*'s visual politics (1.6). The opening shot finds the mutilated body of Omar's lover Brandon in full view of the low-rise housing projects. The shot continues uninterrupted to give viewers a literal window into the inner worlds of the low-rises. We watch young Wallace wake the abandoned children he cares for and hand them lunches before escorting them out the door on their way to school. The camera lingers on the boarded up door behind them, emblazoned with the Baltimore City Public Works stencil: "If animal trapped call 410-844-6286." The visual metaphor is stark; trapped possums and stray dogs deserve a hotline and a citizen's call, not the invisible children who live as animals, trapped in the houses by the same cycles of poverty and crime that hedge the choices of the older boys who feed them, Poot and Wallace.[1]

The Wire is crisscrossed with repeated visual metaphors and internal allusions that stitch the show together in strange and complex patterns. The final shot of "The Wire" lingers on Lieutenant Daniels bathed *film noir* in a swath of light before finally closing on a photo array of Brandon's dead body. This image deepens Police Commissioner Ervin Burrell's observation to Daniels in the next episode: "In this state, *there's a thin line between* campaign posters and *photo arrays*" (1.7). Burrell, of all people, links the parallel worlds of politician and criminal under the same visual economy used on screen in the previous episode, all the while echoing Bubbles's parting words to McNulty in episode four: "There's a thin line between heaven and here." This small example suggests how intricate *The Wire*'s writing and visuals really are: how the thin lines between character and viewer seem to dissolve under interrogation.

To scaffold my examination of choice and visual rhetoric in Season One of *The Wire*, I draw on my experience teaching a cross-listed English/Criminal Justice course at Elmira College during a condensed summer session. The interdisciplinary course, "Law and Literature," was designed to offer students in the social sciences and humanities an introduction to the thematic and formal relations between legal and literary texts, especially their shared foundation in language, rhetoric, narrative, and interpretation. Engaging a variety of texts, from novels to TV shows to judicial opinions, students considered law *as* literature, as well as law *in* literature, to explore how legal systems structure—and are structured by—our conceptions of crime, punishment, justice, and ethics. By reading and watching imaginative works that stage these issues in different ways, students began making fascinating comparisons between unlikely writings across genres and time periods. For example, *The Wire* appears worlds apart from Sophocles's play *Antigone* (442 BC) or Dostoyevsky's novel *Crime and Punishment* (1866). But by the end of the term students saw how certain texts "map" one another, as if in perpetual conversation and revision, and developed surprising and powerful insights between them. The aim of this essay is to help teachers across disciplines creatively incorporate *The Wire* into discussions of visual rhetoric, social theory, legal studies, and comparative literature by offering course planning, sample final exam questions, and pedagogical strategies that have worked well in the law and literature setting.

Law, Literature and The Wire

Before students even approach *The Wire* in a law and literature course, it is important that they recognize the narrative and rhetorical foundations of law and jurisprudence, including legal reasoning, argumentation, and analogy. This approach enables students to understand how language and poetics work to shape narratives across disciplines, from legal arguments to teleplays to their own essays. Although legal reasoning and philosophy of law only indirectly bear on the main plotlines of *The Wire*, the series is clearly invested in the deeper philosophical dilemmas that the Western legal tradition has grappled with for centuries: e.g., the nature of rights and the various logics of legal reasoning. Figure 1 shows the learning outcomes of the course across five related domains: (1) reading, (2) writing, (3) public speaking, (4) recalling content, and (5) researching. These goals are measured (and later assessed at the course level) by specific linked assignments: (1) random reading quizzes, (2) three essays with different sub-learning outcomes, including a research essay for outcome five, (3) a formal discussion leader requirement, and (4) a comprehensive final exam (see Figs. 3–5). The first unit of the course, "The Philosophy of

> **Figure 1.**
> **ENG-CRJ 1980: Law and Literature – Learning Outcomes**
>
> After successfully completing this course you will be able to:
>
> (1) **Demonstrate** careful and critical reading of literary works, visual texts, and legal documents, with attention to rhetorical strategies, narrative techniques, reasoning, and argumentation.
>
> (2) **Articulate** your perspective on a text or problem in law and literature with clear and effective writing in service of a reasoned, evidenced argument.
>
> (3) **Present** the historical, political, and philosophical issues raised by the relationship between law and literature.
>
> (4) **Identify** the major claims and problems within the field of law and literature, with reference to specific authors and works to support your positions.
>
> (5) **Produce** a research-based essay on issues related to criminality, law, and literature using primary and secondary sources (special emphasis on digital Humanities tools).

Law and Legal Reasoning," gives students a foundation in the basic philosophical trends in legal thought, from natural law, legal positivism, and legal realism to more nuanced philosophies that guide contemporary jurisprudence.[2]

Students take reading quizzes and we discuss the answers as a class as I integrate lecture material in response to questions about the quizzes. Each question is designed to direct discussion toward a specific aspect of the assigned reading, encouraging students to see the law as both a mode of social organization and an application of knowledge—*juris* (law) *prudence* (knowledge)—as well as a political system particular to a given set of social relations.[3] Shuttling between close readings of landmark decisions and contemporary examples, we track how the concept of natural law provides the touchstone for a variety of legal philosophies, particularly legal realism's investigations of the nature of reading, narrative, and reform (Culver 196). For example, in *Pavesich v. New England Life Insurance Co.* (1904), Justice Cobb famously ruled that "the right to privacy has its foundation in the instincts of nature."[4]

The right to privacy has a long and complex history, one that has specific relevance to the surveillance tactics in *The Wire*, but in the opening weeks of the course it is crucial for students to see that judges often use "value-judgments" in addition to formal argumentation strategies to decide cases (Golding 58). Legal reasoning can slip into "goal-oriented justification" (48) for a certain line of argumentation, as in *Joyner v. Joyner* (1862) where Chief Justice Pearson argued his decision on a specific conception of the family in which "the wife must be subject to the husband." For Pearson, the family is "a social institution in which the husband is the governing authority" (Golding 54). After studying Pearson's reasoning, students discern in the inner working of legal decision-making how social, cultural, and ethical values are coded and embedded in the language of the law. Martin Golding's book *Legal Reasoning* (1984) is invaluable here. Golding's case law approach pays special attention to the rhetorical, logical, and structural techniques that shape legal arguments, and we spend several classes working through the difference between formally valid and sound arguments, the role of precedent and decision theory on legal reasoning, and specific cases that help illustrate abstract principles.[5]

Figure 2. Assignments & Grading

Reading Quizzes (10)	20%
Essay 1	10%
Essay 2	10%
Essay 3	20%
Discussion Leader	10%
Final Exam	30%

The fact that "judges have to justify their decisions to an audience of rational persons is a highly significant feature of judicial argumentation" (Golding 9) because the law is now circumscribed in the world of rhetoric. If law, narrative, and rhetoric are bound together—lawyers argue cases, jurors interpret evidence, judges reason and decide—then legal arguments are a species of narrative, and can be understood in a literary way. Students begin to see that legal decision-making is not hermetically sealed from the messy world of perception, bias, and interpretation that characterizes the larger social dynamics of which the court is a part.[6] This insight allows legal theorists to consider how the court is "necessarily maintaining the law

> **Figure 3.**
> **Sample Final Exam Questions**
> **Matching, True/False & Fill-Ins: 20% (1 pt. each)**
>
> (1) T/F: An inductive argument can never be formally valid. [T]
> (2) T/F: The formal validity of an argument depends on the truth of the premises. [F]
> (3) T/F: For Judge Cobb in *Pavesich v. New England Life Co.* (1904), the right to privacy is an aspect of natural law. [T]
> (4) An argument with a suppressed premise is called an _____. [*enthymeme*]
> (5) The Latin phrase meaning "let the decision stand" is _____. [*stare decisis*]

and order implied in the particular system of class relations of which it is the expression" (Laski 161–2). If wealth and means of access become key elements to judicial practice, then "the bias of the law will be toward the interest of that few" (168), a trend that *The Wire* shrewdly investigates over five seasons.

This attention to bias directs our reading in Unit Two, "Dissent and Control," where we turn from the formal legal realm to the ways in which art, literature, and philosophy have critiqued legal concepts and their ethical contradictions. Students read selections from Aristotle's *Nicomachean Ethics*, Sophocles's *Antigone*, Kafka's "In The Penal Colony," Mill's *Utilitarianism*, Nietzsche's "Truth and Lie in an Extra-moral Sense," Goldman's "Anarchism: What It Really Stands For," Foucault's *Discipline and Punish*, Rawls's *A Theory of Justice*, and sections 213–216 of the 2001 *US Patriot Act*. These readings provide a rich set of problems that bring classic issues of justice, ethics, and legal order from Ancient Greece into the twenty-first century. We also watch a set of films to contextualize our readings, including the Wachowskis' *V For Vendetta* (2005) and Christopher Nolan's *The Dark Knight* (2008).

Students often struggle with these challenging texts, so we spend extra time diagramming on the white board—in different colors—how each reading builds on, relates to, or critiques the previous one. For example, our discussion of the *US Patriot Act* centers on Sections 213 (delaying notice of warrant), 214 (trap and traces on U.S. citizens) and 215 (access to records). These sections enable students to see how the very same goal-directed reasoning Justice Pearson used in *Joyner v. Joyner* is deployed under the rhetoric of "national security" concerns that can be linked to critiques by Foucault and other theorists. The linkages between, for example, Kafka's "Penal Colony" and the public display of Brandon's tortured body in Episode Six of *The Wire* are too complex to detail here. Other questions posed to the class include: Does Wallace act according to Aristotelian virtue? How does John Rawls's conception of justice as a "fair bargaining position" (246) relate to the representations of justice in *The Wire*? How does the Joker in Nolan's *The Dark Knight* articulate or distort anarchist views on freedom advocated by Emma Goldman?

> **Figure 4.**
> **Sample Final Exam Questions**
> **Short Answer: 40% (8 pts. each)**
>
> * Answer five (5) of the eight questions with 3-4 concise sentences for each question.
>
> (6) Identify and explain two forms of legal reasoning used by Chief Justice Pearson in *Joyner v. Joyner* (1862).
> (7) Define the following terms: natural law, legal positivism, and legal realism. Then explain how each term relates to the previous one.
> (8) Drawing on at least two other cases to support your answer, explain the legal significance of Judge Cardozo's decision in *MacPherson v. Buick Motor Co.* (1916).
> (9) David Simon's *The Wire* employs a number of visual metaphors. Define visual metaphor, then identify and explain the significance of one visual metaphor of your choosing from Season One.
> (10) Dostoyevsky's *Crime and Punishment* has often been read as a novel of competing social theories. Explain the differences between how Raskolnikov, Luzhin, and Lebezyatnikov think that society should operate.

When we come to the third unit of the course, students have a rudimentary background in the philosophy of law, legal reasoning, and the ethico-political critiques of legal practices. This allows them to see the creation of values in legal decisions and how the law is embedded in wider systems of knowledge. I approach *The Wire* by asking students how appeals to natural law—as in *Pavesich v. New England Life Insurance Co.*—can ground legal reasoning, particularly in cases dealing with right to privacy. This returns our discussion to the earlier sections of the course but also opens a conversation about the politics and ethics of surveillance, the nature of security, the erosion of the private sphere in twenty-first century America, and the technological innovations that support all three topics.

Season One of *The Wire* is only tangentially about law. It is deliberately in the background of the primary narratives, yet McNulty's choice to visit Judge Phelan in the very first episode motivates the action of the entire season, initiating the surveillance on Franklin Terrace and launching the Barksdale case. There are, of course, important moments set in courtrooms, like William Gant pointing out D'Angelo in Episode One (and later being murdered because of it). Avon Barksdale's shady lawyer Maurice Levy plays a pivotal role protecting his clients' rights throughout the series, to the scorn of McNulty and other detectives. Occasionally, however, *The Wire* does take on the systemic failures of the legal system directly. As Bodie says to Herc and Carver after escaping a juvenile facility, "The juvenile court system in this city? It's fucked up, yo" (1.7). We also see how Judge Phelan's circuit court has the power to extend the wiretap surveillance for Daniels's unit, yet even Phelan is entangled in the politics of reelection later in the season.[7] And finally, Season One concludes with Levy negotiating a structured plea deal for the entire Barksdale crew (1.13). Still, *The Wire* is often far subtler in its treatment of the legal issues surrounding the Barksdale case, usually in brief scenes where McNulty and

Freamon prove "exhaustion" to Phelan or when Freamon and Pryzbylewski argue over "pertinent" and "non-pertinent" conversations on the wire.

The tension between background legal procedures and the foregrounded action-driven narrative parallels the visual rhetoric of the entire season. Surveillance and watching provide the visual paradigm by which the viewer is interpellated into the series. When Kima Greggs begins rooftop surveillance in Episode Two, viewers intuitively (if unconsciously) recognize how the *theme* of watching is doubled by the *structural relation* of viewer to character and the many visual metaphors the show deploys. When we examine certain scenes from Season One in the classroom, students begin to see how *The Wire* is simultaneously about how the law can prevent a protagonist-detective from building a slam-dunk case against Barksdale and how the issue is more explicitly about the right to look, watch, and surveil. Given its specific attention to surveillance as theme and form, *The Wire* stages a meta-commentary on the television medium and the realm of hyper-visuality that so clearly delineates the twenty-first century from the twentieth. To help students recognize these complex issues, we read short selections from recent media criticism. Horace Newcomb and Paul M. Hirsch's essay "Television as a Cultural Forum" (1983), although somewhat dated, gives a clear outline of TV as visual medium in which dominant messages are disseminated through a symbolic-visual matrix wherein the field of public thought can be unified via communal rituals of watching (362).

In *The Wire*, the variegated complex of relationships related to surveillance and counter-surveillance operate within the show's thematic arc and between the show and its viewers. On the one hand, Sydnor's undercover reconnaissance of the low-rises in Episode Three is paralleled by Omar's patient counter-surveillance of the very same Baltimore PD efforts as he hunts the Barksdale crew's stash. And in Episode Five, Wee-Bey calls Avon "paranoid" for worrying about surveillance, but of course, as we know, Avon should be worried. So on the other hand, viewers' relation to the themes of *The Wire* puts them in an ambivalent position toward the knowledge they gain about the criminals and the police. At the heart of the show is a strange paradox for the liberal viewer who is granted access to the criminals' private lives and encouraged to empathize with them at crucial moments. For example, in Episode Eleven, we are shown Wee-Bey's dedication to his exotic fish collection in the immediate aftermath of Kima's shooting (by Wee-Bey and Little Man). But ultimately, *The Wire* aligns viewers with the police, particularly after Kima's shooting where the audience's emotional investment in Kima is amplified by McNulty's sudden vulnerability and visible pain. The visual sympathy engendered by the hospital scene—between Rawls and McNulty especially—is in stark juxtaposition to the intercut helicopter aerial night-vision surveillance tracking over the alleys where Kima is shot hours before.

Kima's shooting pivots viewers toward the police perspective, giving us pause to remember her words to stripper-turned-informant Shardene Innis in Episode Nine: "They use people, then throw them away."[8] The ethical complexity of *The Wire* demands that viewers return again and again to Kima's hard Aristotelian insight, in which she simply unveils the violence and murder that are status quo for the Barksdale Organization.[9] She shows us the cost, as Bunk puts it, of "all them bodies" (1.13). When students identify how *The Wire* places them in an ambivalent position, and then resolves the ambivalence, they are forced to develop their own perspective on the rhetorical power of the series and the issues of surveillance it installs within its narrative arc.

Unpacking this relationship between the problems of surveillance and the medium of television is central to the second learning outcome of the course: "Articulate your perspective on a text or problem in law and literature with clear and effective writing in service of a reasoned, evidenced argument." The reflexive nature of *The Wire* offers students the opportunity to tie visual and narrative rhetoric together to articulate their own relation to the material in Essay 3. When students can recognize that their own positions are mediated by the very institutions *The Wire* addresses in each season—the police station, the union, the courthouse, the school, and the newspaper—they begin to gain the critical awareness the show invests in its braided plotlines. A nuanced reading of *The Wire* hinges on the relation between viewer and narrative, and my course develops students' visual literacy and meta-visual analysis primarily by looking at the character of young Wallace and his choices, which sets up a tidy storyline to track in class discussion. I plan a note taking workshop before students watch *The Wire*, where we brainstorm strategies for outlining and jotting notes while viewing the show with three categories in mind: (A) What are the visual metaphors and patterns that recur? (B) How is surveillance both a thematic and structural element of the show? (C) What's happening with Wallace? The note taking is the basis for quiz questions, and since *The Wire* questions are open-note, students with better notes are more successful.

Wallace's Choice

Wallace's storyline really begins when he and Poot stare into Brandon's mutilated eyes, his body sprawled on the hood of an abandoned car. "Fucked up, yo," Wallace mumbles (1.6). In the previous episode, we first see Wallace playing with action figures in The Pit before he and Poot identify Brandon to Stringer and start the chain of events that leads to Brandon's death (1.5). The juxtaposition of Wallace's child-like tendencies with the brutal torture and murder he helped orchestrate in Episode Five anticipates Wallace's reply to D'Angelo in Episode Nine: "I just don't want to play no more."[10] In Episode Six, D'Angelo counsels him to forget Brandon: "All that shit is in the game ... sell that shit and move on." Wallace replies: "He sees everything." "Just let it go," urges D'Angelo. Brandon's face—and his ghostly vision—haunts Wallace for the rest of Season One. Wallace's empathy for Brandon and his guilt over his own role in the murder are his twin weaknesses in Franklin Terrace, resulting in his drug abuse and then his own murder. D'Angelo knows it—"You got a good heart" (1.9)—and Bodie admits to Stringer that Wallace's "heart pump[s] Kool-Aid" (1.12). Even the young kid Wallace helps with his math problem in Episode Eight better understands the law of the street: "Count be wrong, they fuck you up."

We understand the depths of Wallace's guilt more clearly because *The Wire* offers dark doubles of Wallace in Poot, Bodie, and Kevin Johnston, the fourteen year-old blinded by Pryzbylewski (1.2). D'Angelo and the corner boys see Wallace's decision to get out of the game as a free choice; "Ain't nobody holding a gun to his head or nothing" (1.8). But when the detectives hear about Wallace through Poot's conversation with his girlfriend on the wire, they see the opportunity to turn a kid "all tore up about the dead stickup boy" (1.10). Wallace chooses to confess to McNulty, even though McNulty has no charge or leverage over him. Shipped to his grandmother's house on the rural eastern shore of Maryland, Wallace misses the city and ultimately returns to the projects, where Stringer Bell is tying up loose ends as the unit closes in. "Country scenery just too slow for me," Wallace says striding through the low-rises. "This is home" (1.12). When Bodie, on Stringer's order, raises the gun to kill Wallace, he declares: "You brought this on yourself" (Ibid). In a brilliant concluding flourish to Wallace's story, the next day Poot has his girl call emergency services and report Wallace's death as a trapped animal inside the building, which returns the viewer to Episode Six and the visual metaphor we examined earlier: "If animal trapped call 410-844-6286."

Even after Wallace's death, he continues to play a role in the game. D'Angelo breaks with Stringer when he is picked up for possession in New York, and McNulty uses Wallace's murder to flip D'Angelo. In response, D'Angelo has one of the most memorable monologues of the season: "All my people, man, my father, my uncles.... It's just what we do. You just live with this shit, until you can't breathe no more. I swear to God, I was courtside for eight months, and I was freer in jail than I was at home" (1.13). In this moment, D'Angelo confronts the limits of freedom on the streets of West Baltimore, and, with Wallace's murder scene photos arrayed in front of him as he delivers his speech, the show links his words with Wallace's choice to return to the low-rise projects from his exile in rural Maryland. The fates of these two characters bring into sharp relief the limits of choice for inner city Baltimore youth, particularly because D'Angelo's mother eventually convinces him to stand with Avon at the trial later in the episode (and D'Angelo is murdered by Stringer in Season Two). The constant oscillation between freedom and determinism that characterizes *The Wire* is never fully resolved. Its characters remain guilty, indifferent, and full of an ironic sense of inevitability. But Wallace's choices—to call in Brandon, to confess to McNulty, to return to the low-rises—suggest that Season One of *The Wire* takes seriously the structural over-determination of the lives of young black men in urban American cities.

In fact, Slavoj Žižek claims, with his usual flair, that *The Wire* should be read as a classical Greek tragedy, or a "self-representation by the collective community" of the social paradoxes that define their experience (Žižek "*Wire*"). For Žižek, *The Wire* should be considered in the realist mode not because it depicts the "real" conditions of West Baltimore but because, like Greek tragedy, it stages itself.[11] But Žižek's most incisive critique centers on *The Wire*'s spatio-visual representation of class struggle. The police, criminals, and citizens of West Baltimore occupy the same geographic space, but there is little direct interaction between them: "You know they're there but you don't see them." There's a thin line, in other words, between the heaven of the upper classes and the "here" of the urban poor. *The Wire* simultaneously penetrates the "carefully screened universe" that designates the urban space from the rest of the city and, as noted earlier, largely aligns the viewer with the detective force, not the urban youth. *The Wire* "isn't about America, it's about America left behind... It's about a war on the underclass, not drugs" (Žižek "Wire").[12] The strength of *The Wire* lies in its ability to uncover the structural and institutional mechanisms that determine choice and often reduce the individual to, in Kafka's words, "nothing more than a piece of business" (*The Trial* 90). Yet this reduction is, ironically, precisely how the Barksdale crew treats its enemies and former employees alike.[13]

A number of scenes in Season One deal with the economic strictures on freedom in a post-industrial capitalist America. In Episode Two, as Wallace and D'Angelo are eating Chicken McNuggets, D'Angelo explains that the man who invented the McNugget is "just making money for the real players ... the nigger who made 'em nuggets still working in the basement." After D'Angelo makes $22,000 in a week working The Pit in Episode Three, Stringer quietly says: "This shit right here ... is forever." In this scene, Stinger is not only talking about the money in his hand, he is also commenting on the structural conditions of heroin addiction and the circulation of capital that supports the perpetual cycle of the drug trade.[14] This is why Stringer's paper-copy front business is such a perfect touch. His trade in paper supports the piles of bureaucratic files that litter the detectives' desks, and Avon continues to get rich (to the tune of a million dollars a month!). "The money is real and it's everywhere," Freamon reminds us in Episode Nine.

On the flip side, *The Wire* is also an anatomy of the political economy of the Baltimore Police Department, particularly in the later seasons. In some ways, *The Wire* is a straightforward procedural, a narrative organized around "the execution of a process, an orderly and to some extent standardized set of practices" (von Mueller 97). The police procedural is "most frequently about the trials, triumphs and occasional travesties of police work as *work* ... [It] is, moreover, an industrialized process: there is a complex division of labor ... and like many industrial laborers, police officers are often alienated, both from their constituency ... and their ostensible masters" (97). Both Daniels's and McNulty's storylines in Season One deal largely with bureaucracy and the nature of a police career: position, promotion, and rank. Major Rawls's singular vision on the department's murder clearance rate stymies McNulty, and Deputy Burrell's precarious position between the political elite and the day-to-day operations of the department causes him to shut down Daniels. Daniels understands this, finally, in Episode Eight:

> See, this is the thing everyone knows and no one says. You follow the drugs, you get a drug case. You start following the money, you don't know where you're going. That's why they don't want wiretaps or wired CIs or anything else they can't control. Because once that tape starts rolling, who the hell knows what's gonna be said.

The limits to choice we see in Wallace's storyline are refracted within the Baltimore Police Department, an institutional space where well-intentioned detectives are often thwarted by political and economic pressures from the top brass and (seemingly) blocked by the legal scaffolds protecting the criminals' rights. *The Wire* shows us that detective and criminal are locked in an endless dance, inviting parallels to military operations like counterinsurgency. Nicholas Mirzoeff contends that "the ultimate paradox of counterinsurgency is that the measure of its success is its permanent continuation" (302), a claim that seems to hold true at least in Season One of *The Wire*.

Crime, Genre and Social Realism

In addition to its other dimensions, *The Wire* is firmly part of a long tradition of crime fiction, a genre whose elements of escapism and fantasy have often masked the ideological dynamics that structure the experience of reading (and thinking) about crime. As Andrew Pepper suggests, recent crime fiction criticism has focused on "the ways in which ideology functions through and on the crime novel and determines or at least 'hails' both the subject in the fiction and the reader" (211). Following critics like Stephen Knight, Dennis Porter, and Ernest Mandel, Pepper considers the claim that crime fiction "is at best a conservative genre that reflects the needs and desires of its predominantly middle-class readership insofar as it ultimately depends upon a restoration of the status quo and a reaffirmation of the existing social order" (211). But Pepper finally concludes that the crime novel is in fact "an uneasy mixture of contradictory ideological inflections, or, rather, is coded to both resist and re-inscribe the dominant cultural discourses" (211).

Reading *The Wire* this way places it in a much broader context of social realism, particularly nineteenth-century American realism and naturalism, and resurrects old literary characters like Twain's Huck Finn, whose "moral growth" has been read as a con of the white liberal reader: a form of "bad faith" in which the reader's guilt is assuaged by projecting her own racial anxieties onto Huck, thereby alleviating moral responsibility once she closes the book.[15] Although *The Wire* may not fit neatly into this interpretation—the structural and logistical demands of the medium of television and variety of *The Wire*'s plots complicate a straightforward reading of the series' ideological functions—it is nevertheless fundamental to introduce undergraduate students to the literary history of social realism and crime fiction in order to position the series in an ongoing set of debates over the relation between reading (and viewing) communities and the material they consume.

To do this, I give students a short excerpt from Chapter 31 of *Huckleberry Finn* (1885)—where Huck decides he'll "go to hell" rather than turn Jim in—to spark discussion about the desire readers have to see characters make an ethical change. Then I use a discussion leader assignment (see Fig. 2) that asks students to choose one scene from *The Wire* episode assigned for that particular class and connect it to some other "digital object" from their own world of experience and explain the connection with a direct quote or shot. The students introduce a wildly different set of objects into the conversation that heighten students' awareness of their own expectations of the text and other students' different expectations. We see that social realist texts are largely about subverting expectations. Crime fictions like *The Wire* often "foreground social disintegration and undermine the tendency of narratives (and detectives) to achieve unproblematic control and closure" (Pepper 211) and simultaneously introduce utopian visions while undermining their practical application. Thus, *The Wire* becomes less about how the reader is implicated in the show's critique and more about the comparative ability of televised fiction to stage and deconstruct long-standing issues in Western culture.

Thinking about *The Wire* in a comparative approach this way invites contrast with the classic existential examination of crime, choice, and city life: Fyodor Dostoyevsky's *Crime and Punishment* (1866). Raskolnikov's meditations on criminality and guilt are framed by long conversations over competing social philosophies, most notably his talks with Luzhin, Razumikhin and Porfiry. The novel wrestles with socio-spatial determinism, the existential malaise of modern capitalist life, guilt, punishment, and, ultimately, the real possibility of choice. Read in the context of *The Wire*, Dostoyevsky's novel deepens the historical and philosophical roots of the apparently intractable problems facing West Baltimore and the show's viewers. To implement this pairing in the classroom, I spend at least one entire class closely reading David McDuff's excellent "Introduction" to the Penguin edition of the novel. We examine McDuff's claim that, in "Dostoyevsky's view, there is something profoundly wrong with a social order that needs to imprison, impoverish and torture the best people in it" (xvii), and then we compare Dostoyevsky's novel to the many plots of *The Wire*. When read together, these two texts—at first so different historically, culturally, and stylistically—inter-animate one another to produce remarkable insights.

For McDuff, "Dostoyevsky is the defender of freedom" (xxvii) even as he acknowledges the limits to choice in nineteenth-century St. Petersburg. "Raskolnikov feels little remorse for having killed the old woman," he writes, "but suffers under a crushing, life-destroying weight of misery at what he has 'done to himself,' to use Sonya's words" (xxviii). This nuanced understanding of freedom and existential guilt is often difficult for students to grasp, but with Wallace's story firmly in their minds, they begin to see Raskolnikov's condition as a different version of modern urban determinism. Tracking the complex unfolding of contingent events, characters, and plots is the reader's task in *Crime and Punishment* (how and why does Raskolnikov murder Alyona) just as it is in *The Wire* (how are these many characters related and why). This line of inquiry allows us to see how contingency is not only a central theme in both texts, but also a guiding formal principle that shapes the visual economy of *The Wire*. In both texts, readers don't know where they're going.

Giving students open-book group quizzes in which they choose one character from *The Wire* and explain how his or her role in the series gives insight into the intersection of law and social problems in West Baltimore fosters a class discussion that can easily pivot to a comparative analysis of characters from *Crime and Punishment*.[16] Second, both texts are largely concerned with how suffering and guilt compromise choice. For example, in Part VI, Chapter II of *Crime and Punishment*, Porfiry describes Mikolka's self-imposed "suffering" as a "Raskolnik" (or self-exiled wanderer) in ways that are echoed in a number of characters in *The Wire*, particularly Omar and Wallace. Finally, *Crime and Punishment* and *The Wire* are fascinating investigations of the role of art in illuminating social problems. Early in *Crime and Punishment*, Razumikhin gives a drunken speech about the value of "talking nonsense" to imagine alternatives to the over-determined social reality of everyday life. Both Dostoyevsky and Simon draw on fiction as a mode of collective meditation on serious problems, and both writers use the local dynamics of a specific urban space for social critique that emerges from the perspective of those usually unseen and from the voices of those usually unheard (like Wallace).

The comparative approach to *The Wire* and *Crime and Punishment* provides a platform for the Final Exam Essay Questions in which students are asked to marshal a host of material and advance a specific perspective that ties the course together. Figure 5 gives sample questions that require students to wrestle with the broad themes of the course while providing specific details to evidence their claims. Although the questions may seem daunting, students

---

Figure 5.
Sample Final Exam Questions
Essay: 40% (40 pts.)

* Answer one (1) of the two essay questions. "C" essays must have at least 4-5 paragraphs and basic essay structure (introduction with a working thesis, body paragraphs with development, and conclusion).

[1] A major theme in this course is the idea that choice may not always be totally free. Choose specific examples from three different texts we've studied this term – one of which must be *Crime and Punishment* – and explain how each text deals with the problem of choice and its implications for responsibility and justice in addressing social/criminal issues. Then make a case for the one text you feel offers a possible solution or productive way forward through this difficult problem.

[2] Another theme in the course is the emphasis on the law as a sociocultural construction. For example, in her book *Law & Literature: Journeys from Her to Eternity* (2007) Maria Aristodemou writes:

> Both law and literature are artificial constructs, concepts, or abstractions like time or identity, aiming to create, and, especially in law's case, to impose, order out of chaos: to write on the bodies and very souls of the subjects and fulfill as well as replace their unfillable desires. (1)

This insight makes us think about the role of art in understanding the law. Drawing on Aristodemou's quote and two other texts we've studied this term, explain how law and art "create… and impose order out of chaos" in different ways. How can "talking nonsense" (to borrow Razumikhin's phrase) lead us to truths about social problems?

have routinely submitted excellent responses, even under time constraints, and it seems that a written final exam demands a different form of understanding that they are able to retain even several semesters later.

Disobedient Reading

In Episode Five, D'Angelo and Stringer Bell discuss the choices available to the low-level Pit crew. Stringer's stinging response has tremendous resonance in the college classroom, where some students are confronted with an uncomfortable truth that their access to and presence in college is a privilege not afforded to everyone who might want it or who could succeed in the university setting. Of course, this line is ironic given Stringer's enrollment in a section of macroeconomics at the Baltimore City Community College (1.8), but the salient point is that the limits to Wallace's choices now appear, in ghostly outline, within our own classroom. Students often finish *Crime and Punishment* and *The Wire* with a sense of unease. They understand more clearly that social problems are densely layered and lack immediate or even individual sources of blame.

The two texts challenge not only their ability to take action in a meaningful way but also their own identity (sometimes hinging on guilt) as students on a college campus. These closing discussions are the most fruitful and substantive days of the course. But it is important to return to the texts themselves and the power that art has to disrupt and disturb, to challenge and spark debate. For example, what are Jimmy McNulty's choices in Season One? He made the choice to initiate and advance the case even at the expense of his own job, and after Kima is shot he admits that his reasons were (to some extent) egotistical. Did McNulty make a choice that mattered? Avon and most of his crew is behind bars. Open murders were solved. Yet, as the final montage attests, Stringer has only consolidated his power beyond the reach of the law. And to end the course, I ask: to what extent have things changed since Season One premiered in 2002? Is *The Wire* a historical relic, a reminder of the past, or must we still grapple with the issues of choice and freedom raised by the series more than a decade ago?

In "Civil Disobedience" (1849), Henry David Thoreau urges his readers, "Let your life be a counter friction to stop the machine" (234). McNulty was, certainly, counter friction to the machine, and within *The Wire*'s unyielding landscape of limited choice, there are moments of counter-friction and possibility. Despite its foreclosure on the viewer's hope for Wallace in Season One,

The Wire develops even more complexity in later seasons to maintain a hard kernel of possibility for change. Thinking about works like *The Wire* and *Crime and Punishment* against the usual disciplinary boundaries and expectations of liberal viewership requires a kind of disobedient reading that challenges the assumptions that structure our experience of these texts. Although I am not nearly so naïve to suggest that simply watching *The Wire* can engender substantive change, the students who take it seriously in the classroom realize the truth to Stringer's words and the profound effects of their own choices. They might be also haunted, as I am, by a few of Wallace's final words: "This is me, yo, right here" (1.12).

Notes

1. The phrase appears throughout the series, in Bunny Colvin's Hamsterdam in Season Three and Chris and Snoop's row-house tombs in Season Four, serving as the opening quote of the final episode of Season Four ("Final Grades"): "If animal trapped call 410–844–6286.—Baltimore, traditional." The visual metaphor is also a juxtaposition of an underground economy with a formal one: the bags of chips Wallace hands out to the children were bought with profits of the drug trade, while the building Wallace lives in is condemned by the formal economic and political structures of the city government. Another obvious visual metaphor in Season One is the desk wedged in the door of Lt. Daniels's unit in the opening scene of episode four, "Old Cases." The detectives do not clearly communicate which direction to push the desk, one side working against the other, countering brute force with brute force. The metaphor for police inefficiency is clear.

2. Keith Culver's *Readings in the Philosophy of Law* (2008) provides students with excellent overview essays, including introductions to "Natural Law Theory," "Legal Positivism," "Integrity," and "Legal Realism."

3. Both law and narrative, students realize, are attempts to give an "account of historical being": attempts that end up shaping the very world they describe ("Law and Narrative" 274). Or, to quote Henry David Thoreau in "Civil Disobedience," "The lawyer's truth is not Truth, but consistency, or a consistent expediency" (244).

4. In *Roberson v. Rochester Folding Box Co.* (1902), the issue before the court was "whether a certain claimed right (a person's right not to have his or her picture used for commercial purposes) should be recognized because it falls under a more general legal *right*" (Golding 65).

5. The three sections are usefully organized: Ch. I: "The Study of Legal Reasoning," Ch. II: "Types of Legal Argument," and Ch. III: "Precedent and Analogy." I spend extra time explaining how arguments by analogy are not formally valid (Golding 45) but are used often in the law: e.g., *Adams v. New Jersey Steamboat Co.* (1896).

6. Advocates of legal realism go so far as to claim that "the judge really decides by feeling and not by judgment ... an intuitive sense of right and wrong in a particular case" (Hutcheson, "The Judgment Intuitive," *Cornell Law Quarterly* 14, p. 274).

7. Omar's brilliant testimony against Bird in Season Two is, unfortunately, beyond the scope of this essay, and more work remains to be done thinking about the law across all five seasons of *The Wire*.

8. Rhonda Pearlman uses the very same phrasing to counter McNulty's rant about legal careerism and corruption in Episode Eleven: "You'll use anyone, won't you?"

9. Radical political readings of *The Wire* are possible (and perhaps seductive), given the

investment of the viewer in the lives of the police and the emphasis on the violence of the Barksdale crew. Beginning in Episode Five, we see that the Baltimore Police Department actually monitors every pay phone call in the West-side housing project, though Stringer later tells his crew to "tear them motherfuckers out" (1.7). For Italian philosopher Giorgio Agamben, video surveillance of the streets is troubling because it constitutes a "zone of indifference between the prison and the forum," a zone between the private and public spheres in which *The Wire* operates, *de facto*, as a television show. This indifference is linked to the historical development of the police force (and, concurrently, detective fiction) from the eighteenth-century onward. For Agamben, following von Justi, the police is "the relationship of a state with itself" 6. So when the Commissioner Frazier declares a victory against a "culture of death and drugs" at the press conference at the end of Episode Eleven, he publicly articulates the view of the police (and the state) toward the intractable social problems of West Baltimore couched in the rhetoric of culture wars. Whether the viewer's allegiances in *The Wire* are ultimately marshaled in support of police surveillance is another question, but an important one.

10. It also parallels Brandon's last moments playing pinball before his abduction, torture, and murder.

11. Certainly, the mostly black cast and numerous local Baltimore actors in the series support Žižek's reading, and the comedic and ironic moments in the series can be read, as Žižek does, as markers of a kind of realism (e.g., Bunk and McNulty's "fuck" scene).

12. This reading is supported by the dinner scene between D'Angelo and Donette in Episode Five that suggests that the structural obstacles the characters face are not racial but class-related. D'Angelo admits he feels like he's trying but "still ain't going no where." Donette responds: "You got money, you get to be whoever you say you are."

13. Žižek is influenced by his Marxist-Lacanian perspective, and the excerpts from Žižek's lecture we listen to in class provide students a launching pad to wrangle with this point of view. David Harvey writes that "Marx's essential ideological objective is to pinpoint the duplicity that lies at the heart of the bourgeois conception of freedom" (*Companion* 100). Marx wants us to confront our own "helplessness in the face of what [we] have made ... the alienated power wielded by humanly produced systems against the human beings who have produced them..." (Jameson 30).

14. In David Harvey's words, "The freedom of the market is not freedom at all. It is a fetishistic illusion" (42).

15. For more detail, see Forrest Robinson, *In Bad Faith: The Dynamics of Deception in Mark Twain's America* (Cambridge: Harvard University Press, 1986; 153).

16. Unfortunately, a fuller discussion of the comparative networks between *The Wire* and *Crime and Punishment* is beyond the scope of this essay. For more detail, see Malcolm V. Jones and Garth M. Terry, eds., *New Essays on Dostoyevsky* (Cambridge: Cambridge University Press, 2010).

Works Cited

Agamben, Giorgio. "From the State of Control to a Praxis of Destituent Power." Lecture in Athens. Nov. 16, 2013.
Aristodemou, Maria. *Law & Literature: Journeys from Her to Eternity*. Oxford: Oxford University Press, 2007.
Culver, Keith. *Readings in the Philosophy of Law*, 2d ed. Toronto: Broadview, 2007.
Dostoyevsky, Fyodor. *Crime and Punishment*. Trans. David McDuff. New York: Penguin, 2003.
Golding, Martin P. *Legal Reasoning*. Toronto: Broadview, 2001.
Harvey, David. *A Companion to Marx's Capital*. New York: Verso, 2010.

Jameson, Fredric. *Representing* Capital: *A Reading of Volume One*. New York: Verso, 2014.
Joyner v. Joyner. 59 N.C. 322. June 1862, Decided.
Kafka, Franz. *The Trial*. Trans. Mike Mitchell. Oxford: Oxford University Press, 2009.
"Law and Narrative." *The Routledge Encyclopedia of Narrative Theory*. London: Routledge, 2008.
Laski, Harold J. *The State in Theory and Practice*. New York: Penguin, 1935.
Mirzoeff, Nicholas. *The Right to Look: A Counterhistory of Visuality*. Durham: Duke University Press, 2011.
Newcomb, Horace, and Paul M. Hirsch. "Television as a Cultural Forum." *Quarterly Review of Film Studies* 8.3 (1983).
Pavesich v. New England Life Insurance Co. 122 Ga. 1905; LEXIS 156. March 3, 1905, Decided.
Pepper, Andrew. "Black Crime Fiction." *The Cambridge Companion to Crime Fiction*. Cambridge: Cambridge University Press, 2003.
Oxford English Dictionary. Online. Accessed April 2014.
Rawls, John. *A Theory of Justice*. Cambridge: Belknap, 2005.
Roberson v. Rochester Folding Box Co., 171 N.Y. 538, 64 N.E. 442. 1902, Decided.
Thoreau, Henry David. *Walden, Civil Disobedience, and Other Writings*. New York: Norton, 2008.
von Mueller, Eddy. "The Police Procedural in Literature and on Television." *The Cambridge Companion to American Crime Fiction*. Ed. Catherine Ross Nickerson. Cambridge: Cambridge University Press, 2010.
Wilson, Christopher P. *Cop Knowledge: Police Power and Cultural Narrative in Twentieth-Century America*. Chicago: University of Chicago Press, 2000.
Žižek, Slavoj. "*The Wire* or the Clash of Civilisations in One Country." Lecture. February 24, 2012. The Birkbeck Institute for the Humanities: Clore Management Centre, University of London.

PART IV

Education and Literacy

Reading the Scene
Discourse, Literacy and Pedagogy Through The Wire

Daniel Listoe

> All words, written or spoken, are a translation that only takes on meaning in the counter-translation, in the invention of the possible causes of the sound heard or of the written trace: the will to figure out that applies to all indices, in order to know what one reasonable animal has to say to what it considers the soul of another reasonable animal.
> —Jacques Rancière, *The Ignorant Schoolmaster*

> It is experience which shapes a language; and it is language which controls an experience.
> —James Baldwin, "Why I Stopped Hating Shakespeare"

> Now he frontin' with all them books but if we pull one down off the shelf ain't none of the pages ever been opened. He got all them books and he ain't read near one of them.
> —D'Angelo Barksdale, *The Wire*

One will be hard pressed to recall vivid and vital scenes of reading during the five complete seasons of *The Wire*. Even though one season features the life of public schools and the other that of a city newspaper, focused presentations of literate activity are rare. Those that appear essential to character and plot are themselves brief. In perhaps the most important of such scenes, D'Angelo Barksdale and his fellow prison inmates sit around a library table to discuss their reading of and responses to *The Great Gatsby* (2.6). There is the glimpse we have of Omar Little, after passing through the thick crowd of inmates threatening to kill him, alone in his jail cell, reading *Ghettoheat*, a self-published collection of poetry and prose by the Harlem-based artist Hickson (4.7). Then, adding to the aura of the armed enforcer, there is Brother Mouzone sitting on a bench outside one of the public housing towers at night, flipping through his political and cultural periodicals, insisting on the need to have *The New Republic*, *The Nation* and *Harper's* at hand (2.10). This allows him to reference—and from the exasperated looks of his assistants, not for the first time—an old adage that the most dangerous thing in America is a Black man with a library card, a line he punctuates with an all-too-knowing chuckle.

In contrast, when detective Kima Greggs recites a bedtime story to her ex-partner's son, Elijah, there is no book. She holds the boy on her lap as they sit at a window sill and the familiar cadence of Margaret Wise Brown's *Goodnight Moon* becomes a soothing lullaby to Baltimore: a soft wish for the po-pos, hustlers, hoppers, and scammers, the nobodies and everybody of the city, a "good night to one and all" (5.7). The students featured in season four have books, but even then the institutional dynamics of education revolve around homeroom and a math class. Outside of school, there are flashes of smaller kids encouraged to do their homework while the older ones tend to other routines. In the opening of that season our first look at Namond Brice does show him distractedly staring at the hip-hop magazine *Don Diva* while on the job. But much closer to the heart of that season is Sherrod, Bubbles's young, street-business protégé who Bubbles enrolls in school when he learns that he lacks basic math skills. At one point, Sherrod turns from Bubbles and takes from his backpack a tattered algebra book and a student's paperback dictionary, pretending that the two go together in a clumsy performance of diligent homework. Sherrod's choice of the dictionary is poignant, for it is a "complete" book, self-contained and perhaps the ultimate tool of what Jacques Rancière calls an "emancipated intellect," which is nothing more than, nor less than, a mind at work:

> One learns sentences and more sentences; one discovers facts, that is, relations between things, and still other relations that are all of the same nature; one learns to combine letters, words, sentences, ideas. It will not be said that one has acquired science, that one knows truth or has become a genius. But it will be known that, in the intellectual order, one can do what any man can do.... All knowledge of oneself as an intelligence is in the mastery of a book, a chapter, a sentence, a word [26].

In the scene, Sherrod turns the pages as if searching, as if preparing to read what he cannot yet read, as if ready to expand his vocabulary and comprehension. In the end, the dictionary, of course, isn't opened. In the hollow fakery of his gesture, we see clearly what emancipation means for a boy like Sherrod in such faint and fluctuating circumstance. Eventually his life, tracing that irresistible metaphor of the candle, proves easily extinguishable.

While the prison scenes of season two prominently feature the library where D'Angelo works, and wherein he engages Fitzgerald's novel, we see no one else cast as a would-be Malcolm X, making an education through an immersion in books; when a book is carried under the arm through the hallways, that book is likely ferrying drugs from one prisoner to another. Most of the written material consumed in the series is in the shape of police files old and new—the products of slow, distracted typing—that when re-read, bleed into the interpretation of crime scenes and vast arrays of stockpiled evidence. The icon of this is the ad hoc detail's expanding grid of information compiled through the use of a wire: image, drawn line or box, photo, pinned scrap of interest, and so on. Perhaps the most central act of interpretation or reading that takes place on the show is in fact numeric: the use of, and deciphering of, the paging code invented by Avon Barksdale for his workers.

Given the limited display of conventional book reading, using the show within a course focused on literacy studies and called "Strategies of Academic Writing"(generally populated by education majors) may seem like a stretch. After all, the show is deeply reliant on a rich verbal interplay for its relentless and rigorous explorations of political economy the way the show sounds generates much of the enticing pleasure in what painfully, even tragically, unfolds. There is the ever-evolving linguistic register (Agha 212) of the corners, what one of the show's writers, the novelist Richard Price, calls the apparent argot of the kids in the drug trade. There are also the aphoristic illuminations of Omar or the sobriety-sponsor Walon; the under-enunciated, rapid-fire ballistic references of Snoop; as well as the policy-girding rhetoric of politicians, police administrators, and educators. It might be tempting to think of the show's language as a surplus of signifying, somehow kindred to the chattering bareness of Samuel Beckett, or as with "the schizo-familiar" plays of Harold Pinter or Sam Shepard, presenting a manic effort to "rediscover a sense of unity amidst the ruins" (Kubiak 146).

The dissection of Baltimore's ruination within the era of late-capitalism—against which not one institution seems capable of offering a unifying authority—presents portraits of those caught up in what the anthropologist Elizabeth Povinelli calls "economies of abandonment." Within those conditions, the speech and dialogue of *The Wire* relentlessly denotes. It is a fundamental substance of the show; the rhythm and style of speech are the raw material for the Baltimore portrait. Each time a character speaks it seems as if they mark a place of origin, offer an act of interpretation, protect a position of power, or make some form of appeal. This is true even of the sly hissing disregard of Senator Clay Davis, the bullying roar of Deputy Commissioner Bill Rawls or the bar talk of Detective Bunk Moreland, which are never mere excess. For even as each of these characteristics suggest men who revel in the sound of their own voices, and what they can do with their words, they are still consistently signifying their roles within the world reflected by the show. One can draw on how these characters work verbally through conflict, contestation, and negotiation to find the show's realist heteroglossia: "the totality of the world of objects and ideas depicted and expressed in it, by means of the social diversity of speech types and by the differing individual voices that flourish under such conditions" (Bakhtin 263).

The version of "Strategies of Academic Writing" I am describing here relies on the now-well-established New Literacy Studies that—countering a cognitive and psychological approach to literacy that focuses on an individual's processing of signs on a page—is geared to understanding which voices flourish in which worldy conditions. It is, therefore, an intellectual and disciplinary vector "where sociolinguistic and anthropological theories of language and schooling meet ethnographic and discourse analytic methodologies" (Hull and Schultz, 584). In other words, New Literacy Studies guides a course that aims to help students become more aware of the "voice" they cultivate when they read and write within the particular context of the university. This is to help them sharpen their praxis, the self-conscious actions that give shape to that "voice" defined in part by given genres and conventions and in part through dialogue with others similarly engaged. Additionally, because the students are overwhelmingly education majors there is the chance to encourage their thinking about what it means to teach others and what happens when the "voice" of the teacher is in conflict with the "voice" of the student.

These students often bring to the classroom vague notions about literacy—a sense that it is about skills, abilities, and above all, the imperative that one not be illiterate. And these ideas go hand in hand with what they take will be their charge as teachers: to deliver those skills of literacy to the underprivileged who are seen as lacking the "proper" abilities. The course therefore attempts to de-naturalize these initial understandings. In the place of such divides as the written and oral, the literate and illiterate, the course attempts to deepen the students' sense of how literacy emerges through the intersections of language usage and context, directly or indirectly raising a series of questions related to both literacy and pedagogy: how does one account for and treat different voices? How does one work within uneven distributions of authority and control? How does one interrogate and understand otherwise unexplored assumptions about both what seems natural, right, and just plain common sense and, even more importantly perhaps, the well-intentioned but incomplete package of "best practices" and so-called cultural competencies they will carry into the classroom? And beyond the classroom, how will they position themselves in an environment where the tide of consensus continues to rise around the need for a particularly regressive kind of educational "reform"?

In light of the course goals, the language in *The Wire*, as it brings forth the social and political world we inhabit, allows for an approach to these questions precisely because it so starkly demonstrates the performance of interpretation, communication, and the collisions of various voices and social languages. The show becomes an important supplement to the large scale project of helping students see that expression and reception—including academic writing—are shaped by genre, expectation, social convention, and habit.

Before viewing and responding to a series of selected scenes from *The Wire*, students are assigned texts meant to lend appreciation of the socio-cultural context of literate practices. These include Plato's *Phaedrus*, Jack Goody and Ian Watt's canonical "The Consequences of Literacy," Walter Ong's "Hermeneutic Forever: Voice, Text, Digitization and the 'I,'" Ann Blair's "Reading Strategies for Coping With Information Overload ca.1550–1700," Hans Magnus Enzenzsberger's "In Praise of Illiteracy," Jan Assmann's "Remembering in Order to Belong: Writing, Memory, and Identity," Mary Louise Pratt's "Arts of the Contact Zone," Don Kulick and Christopher Stroud's "Christianity, Cargo and Ideas of Self: Patterns of Literacy in a Papua New Guinean Village," and John Szwed's "The Ethnography of Literacy." Finally, in conjunction with scenes from *The Wire*, selections from James Paul Gee's *Social Linguitsics and Literacies* and his article, "Reading as Situated Knowledge: A Sociocognitive Perspective."

Such readings, in the range and rigor of their analysis, might model the depth and pace and goals of academic prose, serving to both inform students about literacy and give them the chance to recognize the conventions of academic writing (at least as shaped at a particular intersection of the humanities and human sciences). However, as these readings define only to re-define ideas of literacy, they are likely to frustrate the students' desire to pin down the object of the course. Moreover, their authoritative language of analysis is foreign for the un-initiated undergraduate. Even if a class discussion begins with groups of three or four working through a small passage—preparing to present to the entire class a summary of its content, a key quotation and analysis of what the student deems the most vital terms, as well as questions the passage raises for them—the scope of a single observation is often extremely challenging.

For examples of the dynamics of competing concepts associated with literacy, as well as the language of analysis, we can look at selections from Goody and Watt and Jan Assmann. The course turns to Goody and Watt early since its claims for the consequences of literacy act as a prompt for much of what New Literacy Studies argues against. While Goody and Watt make the case for the expansive powers of literacy, they also suggest that a literate culture is burdened, among other things, by writing's expansive tendencies and the inevitable fragmentation of the social world with its cloistered cultural spheres. Compared to what they present as an enveloping oral culture, widespread literacy carries with it, they suggest, a collective inability to forget. Recalling Nietzsche's admonition that the weight of accumulated history left one unable to live and act in the present, they write, "Even if we dismiss Nietzsche's views as extreme, it is still evident that the literate individual has in practice so large a field of personal selection from the total cultural repertoire that the odds are strongly against his experiencing the cultural tradition as any sort of patterned whole" (335).

From this idea of an ever-expanding cultural repertoire, the course shifts to Assmann's refutation. In his view, we must recognize that despite writing's capacity for storage, writing and its record accelerate forgetting—the comparative mode that writing allows inspires innovation and change, the quest to write what has not been said before (83). This tendency toward expansion is in turn curtailed and constrained by the counter-forces of culture. For it is the gravitational pull of cultural values that shapes what will be read and how: what a culture deems as important ensures that only some, and not all, writing rises to the level of the communicable. The slowing down of change is established through what he calls a memory-based culture, or "the set of circumstances that ensures that writing retains its long-term readability and communication its elasticity" (87). He expands this to include the wonderful speculation, developed through an intersection of Freud and Deuteronomy, that some texts remain latent until the coming of their proper hour.

He, too, cites Nietzsche on memory. But working from Nietzsche's notion that the communal is built by binding each individual through a mnemonics of pain—the pain that instills the reflex of staying true to a promise and feeling responsible—Assmann turns to the ancient Egyptians and their concept of communal connectivity, or *maat, a concept that holds* out the ideal of a continued place in the community, even after death. Instead of the infliction of pain, there is a "gentle yoke" of cultural idea and practice that binds the individual to the community. A young initiate receives overt instruction and the tradition is reproduced through a myriad of signs and institutions, one of which was the monumental grave. The elaborate writing that marked the grave was an expression of *maat*, a scripted appeal for posterity. Assmann describes the inscriptions on the Egyptian grave as more than "effusive desire to talk," for like much of the talk in *The Wire*, it reflects "the pressure to provide an apologia, a response to a tribunal-like situation" (90). The "concept of writing" thus becomes "a convenient handle by which to sum up this world of signs, the different codes of cultural memory technique" (91).

This Egyptian example clearly shows how a hegemonic ideal might shape a cultural practice, but for the contemporary student, such a case from the ancient world may seem simply arcane. One can see here how *The Wire* might better illustrate a set of concepts having to do with how an individual must inscribe a public self into an existing ideological schema, allowing the students to witness and analyze the subtle distinctions that come into play when an individual navigates the social world.

Their evocative power notwithstanding, the way the students are asked to read and respond to the scenes are no different than any other text. In this course, they are attached to the readings from the linguist James Paul Gee (*Social Linguistics and Literacies* and "Reading as Situated Language: A Sociocognitive Perspective"). As for the practice of critical engagement, with Gee and *The Wire* the students apply the same method of exploration used to overcome, or make productive, the alienation that some may well feel from the highly academic assigned readings. This method stems from the Bakhtinian principle of dialogics, and in this case foregrounds the student's struggle to understand the formation of their voice through their engagement with words already spoken and established and ideological schema laid out before them. This is what Don Bialostosky called the need to "cultivate students' understanding of their ambivalent situations and to validate their struggles to remake themselves and the languages imposed on them" (17).

To keep the students mindful of the possibilities in their ambivalent situations, they are asked not merely to read and absorb content and concepts, not only to work through the content and concepts in dialogue with others, but to maintain a conversation with themselves about what they have read and how they have read it. Each student constructs a formal, critical notebook in which they create a catalog of short entries (a paragraph or two at the most) that translate the readings and focus their practice of reading. These notebooks are developed throughout the term, sometimes guided by a particular prompt or open question but most often guided by a set of broad instructions that ask the students to be alert to their own observations while reading. There is often time made in class to write, but they are eventually transcribed (and edited) and turned in as formal collections of multiple entries. There is no assumption that the student will be consistent since each entry is titled and dated, marking the limited nature of their insight as it relates to a particular idea, passage or links between readings.

The general prompts ask the students to provide abstract summaries in their own words; to identify a keyword or idea and explain how it helps them better understand the concept of literacy; to copy out a short passage with an attached explanation of its importance; to make connections and contrasts between texts. When they copy out a passage and then translate it into their own words they are asked to translate it again, this time self-consciously integrating some of the author's language in a weave with their own. In this way they practice developing their voice by drawing, in part, on the words and findings of others. Furthermore, because the notebook creates a kind of archive they can better track the evolution of their understanding of literacy, as well as its limitations, and utilize their developing insights and perspectives in the essays they're assigned to write. In this way they consistently return to their own voicings at a productively alienating distance or remove.

Before analyzing *The Wire*, the students have started to read the insistent and crucial voice of Gee. For him, understanding literacy means rejecting the primacy of the written. More so than any of the other course readings, he highlights the social function of language and the nuance of its performance more generally. He stresses a doing-with-words "to scaffold the performance of action in the world, including social activities and interactions." These announce and structure our "human affiliation in cultures and social groups and institutions." Thus we project ourselves outward and "entic[e] others to take certain perspectives on experience" ("Reading" 715). The key term in his framework for analyzing the array of human affiliations is Discourse. "A Discourse," Gee says, "integrates ways of talking, listening, writing, reading, acting, interacting, believing, valuing, and feeling (and using various objects, symbols, images, tools, and technologies) in the service of enacting meaningful socially situated identities and activities" ("Reading" 719). Such embodied communication, including within its sphere literate activity, requires that we perform these according to the expectations of a given audience in order to garner acceptance. To make a misstep in language, intonation, action or some fundamental variable betrays one as an outsider, someone who has not been properly or fully initiated into the contextually necessary Discourse.

Gee connects the shades of Discourse to familiar points of social transition: from the world of the child at home to school and beyond, introducing the distinction between primary and secondary Discourses. The former is more "naturalized," inherited through our earliest learning and experience within family and home life; one is effortlessly enculturated into them. The latter emerge in and around the many public, institutional spheres in which we might come to operate. As we mature we attempt to enter more and more Discourses, and are thereby able to perform more and more social roles, expanding our range of what Gee calls "identity kits." Such combinations of "Being-doing of a certain sort" are what mark the difference between the "physicist, gang member, feminist, first-grade child in Ms. Smith's room, special ed (SPED) student, regular at the local bar, or gifted upper-middle-class child engaged in emergent literacy are all Discourses" ("Reading" 718). Thus, through Gee and with help from *The Wire*, we see the folly of thinking of an independent skill with the written word imagined as "literacy." The concept, he writes, "has no effects—indeed, no meaning—apart from particular cultural contexts in which it is used, and it has different effects in different contexts" (*Social* 82). Literacy is only, says Gee, fluency in a particular Discourse, the ability to embody the right performance in the right context, an act which may or may not include reading and writing.

As undergraduates trying to find their way through the channels of the university—most at a school like mine having already adapted to the social sphere of their one and sometimes two workplaces while simultaneously poised at the cusp of being a professional teacher—the students should be able to see that the transitions and tensions Gee presents very much match their own (immediate) experiences. Many do. But this is not to say that they are immediately fluent in Gee's language, his academic Discourse on Discourse, or able to see their own naturalized Discourses as anything other than natural. The challenge is getting them to become confident enough to successfully translate—without falling back into notions of the authentic or core self—his notions of how we perform language and the social stakes of such performances.

The Wire helps them better see the living dynamics of his concepts. Presenting *The Wire* to students about to become teachers themselves might immediately suggest the need to focus on season four, in which the failed-detective-turned-educator Pryzbylewski learns the limits and possibilities of teaching in a public school system that is under extreme duress. For his students, the world outside the classroom is dangerous and delimiting. Inside the class, we witness uneasy performances on the part of both the kids and the teacher. Pryzbylewski eventually arcs from wide-eyed ineffectiveness to being, as best he can, the students' creative ally, but his early version of teaching math means parroting the language of standardized testing word problems. In the episode "Corner Boys" from season four, his students gently mock him for it and get him to lower the rhetorical register: don't use "distribute" if you mean "give out" (4.8). Just say so, they insist. Becoming more effective in communicating with the students means dropping the curriculum binder designed for the state test and the process of assessment. Needing to speak a language they understand, or lacking that, find a point of shared reference, he picks up a set of dice. He decides to use dice games—those of the neighborhood sidewalks and alleyways—to teach mathematics and probability. The kids know the rules, but he adds for them the principles as they pause in their play to reflect on what they are doing.

It can be no accident that the entire scope of *The Wire* begins with the shooting of a local known to get into a dice game only to grab the money, run, get chased down and usually beaten. This time he winds up dead. When one of the other usual players is asked why someone who almost always grabbed the cash would be allowed into the game, the response is simple: "This America, man" (1.1). And so again, four seasons later, the throw of the dice comes to stand both for a supposed radical equality of access to the contest and, at the same time, the loaded chances of a brutal end. What we will witness, the show's creators and writers tell us from the opening lines, is not a matter of tangled pathologies. Instead it is about lives and fates as casts and throws, the dire outlook of odds and probabilities.

Such extremes capture the echo of Foucault within Gee, an element that can be emphasized in the course to varying degrees. It is not necessary to include it explicitly in class discussions, for Gee's own angle on the dynamics of power will take shape—on their own and through *The Wire*—starkly enough. It is possible, however, to accent the core ideas of Gee's project by highlighting two observations by Foucault in his famous "The Discourse on Language." Foucault begins by pointing to those "great edifices that distribute speakers among the different types of discourse, and which appropriate those types of discourse to certain categories of subject." From this, he focuses on education as an exemplary site of a more general exclusionary economy, one in which only some speakers are allowed access to the dominant Discourse. In other words, as Pryzbylewski's kids would quickly realize, only a select few along the lines of distribution get the chance to use the word "distribute"; this despite the appearances of an open gateway. Foucault writes:

> Education may well be, as of right, the instrument where every individual, in a society like our own, can gain access to any kind of discourse. But we all know in its distribution, in what it permits and what it prevents, it follows the well-trodden battle lines of social conflict. Every educational system is a political means of maintaining or modifying the appropriation of discourse, with the knowledge and the powers it carries with it [227].

One of the risks in using *The Wire* in front of a predominantly white class, however, is that the differences in Discourses can be framed as a problem of African Americans alone, what Gee called the perspective that treats African Americans as "other," "deviant," and "non-standard" (*Social* 4).

Therefore, in order to extend the notion of Discourses beyond the specific example of the classroom—and the more obvious divide between teacher and student in the classroom—I choose to focus strictly on a constellation of carefully selected scenes featuring the drug lord's nephew, D'Angelo Barksdale. With D'Angelo, social exclusions are more subtle and nuanced and better gauged to what Gee demands we see. It is easier to discover through his figurative, and eventually literal, confinements the plights of a more general bind of entering adulthood, or trying to find one's way, of searching for the right words at the right time. For perhaps more than any character in the series, D'Angelo operates along the edges of multiple Discourses, as if his very character were an expression of the liminal lines between spheres of power—his life lived as part of a dominant family structure and yet in a kind of no man's land. From the shoddy couch on the dirty patch of his work days in the "pit" he can see well enough the disconnect between himself and the bourgeois world of peace and prosperity and that he is nonetheless not cut out for the life of his uncle. In other words, D'Angelo is perfectly positioned as a middle-manager of the low-rise courtyard. He supervises the teenage boys who distribute his uncle's drugs, but there are constant reminders that his position is a matter of birth more than a willful climbing of the company ladder (in fact, we meet him after he has "lost" control of the more lucrative towers). To the boys under his watch he demonstrates an ability to teach and cajole because without any overt sentimentality, he is sympathetic. But with his uncle, his mother, and with the police, he is vulnerable to the manipulative application of coercive appeals and outright pressure, as if all those power centers sense in his degree of empathy a vulnerability to exploit.

Focusing on selected scenes featuring D'Angelo has a strategic advantage to, say, watching the unfolding narrative of an entire season or the storylines that feature him as a protagonist. It concentrates the students' attention on very specific words and actions that are almost exiled from character and psychology. For the kind of analysis the students are asked to do regarding the illustration of Discourses in action and conflict, there is little back-story required. In fact, should the students be given too much background they might replace a focus on shifting Discourses to a response to D'Angelo, as if he were wholly individual and not serving as an illustration of competing voices. If the students watch the scenes with only the barest framing, the more they may hear just the competition to dictate and control essential meanings: of a game, social difference, a novel, and so on.

After rehearsing some of Gee's key ideas, I will first show a scene all the way through without comment. We then discuss what the students see and hear in the dialogue. The next time through, I will stop after important lines or gestures that mark a Discourse. We then watch each scene again so that the students can push their analysis forward with Gee in mind. Finally, I give them the chance to write out a critical notebook entry. In their writings on these scenes I often see the strongest traces of their initial applications of Gee's ideas.

The first scene I use comes from season one's episode "The Buys" (1.3). In it, D'Angelo finds two of his workers, Wallace and Bodie, biding time playing checkers with a chess set. They seem bored and distracted and not quite engaged with what they are doing. Chiding them, D'Angelo sits down and insists on telling them how to play chess properly. They don't know the rules of the game nor even how to identify the pieces and he has to explain to them how each moves according to its rank. Bodie is resistant at first to being interrupted and perhaps having to adapt to something new. But he begins to get interested when D'Angelo does not simply recite the rules in the language of chess. What gets and holds Bodie's attention is that D'Angelo is able to explain how the pieces move by analogizing each piece to a referent in a shared Discourse, that of their line of work: the King(pin), the fierce Queen (who gets things done), the muscle (that protects the drugs), the pawns (soldiers destined to be sacrificed). In the end, D'Angelo and Bodie are speaking the words of pawns and Kings and the objective of chess, and yet they are also talking about the realities of their profession and "the game." The two Discourses feed into each other within the dialogue, each sharpening the defining distinctions of the other.

What drives the dialogue forward is the shared Discourse of their mutual work. Without that communal language the references to the rules of chess would fail. This is not only reflective of the kind of translation work the students have been doing in their critical notebooks, but parallel to what Gee calls filtering: where crucial secondary Discourses have been integrated into the primary Discourse, therefore better preparing some students for the Discourse of school and its attendant performances (e.g., reading, writing, analyzing).

The second scene, from the episode "The Pager," shows D'Angelo with his girlfriend, Donette, after a meal in a moderately upscale restaurant in Baltimore's Inner Harbor district (1.5). It begins with D'Angelo, relaxed after the food, surprised by the waiter's gesture of crumbing the tablecloth. The waiter, seeing his reaction, explains the act. By explaining the gesture that is supposed to be discrete, or rather seen as discretely performed, the two are cast on opposing sides of a Discourse and D'Angelo is marked as the outsider. This commentary on a fairly reflexive action—describing for the outsider the gesture an insider would recognize—leads to D'Angelo looking around the room, sizing up the rhythms of the space and wondering aloud whether the people there "know what I'm about." It is a question about belonging: in the restaurant, at the Harbor, within, possibly, a banal world of pleasure and consumption. When D'Angelo measures the room he recognizes that the Discourse of the space and the one with which he entered are not aligned. In the words of Gee, "Discourses need not, and often don't, represent consistent and compatible values. There are conflicts among them, and each of us lives and breathes these conflicts as we act out our various Discourses" (4).

Sensing the misalignment, D'Angelo interrogates the relationship between his background and his context. First, there is the outsider status that is subtle, but real. What makes this scene effective is that the difference here is much less pronounced than when the police-lieutenant-turned-mentor, Bunny Colvin, attempts to take some of his students to a fancy restaurant in season four. In that case, the mismatch of Discourses is so extreme that from their very entrance into the place they are uneasy, nervous, overwhelmed, and wholly out of place in part because they have not (yet) been sufficiently mentored to engage that new realm (4.9). D'Angelo is none of those things. Fluent in multiple Discourses, he can generally navigate the differences he encounters. But in the second sense of his apprehension, he also knows, as he explains or tries to explain to Donette, that one cannot simply claim a status and *be* different. Otherwise, as he will say in a different context, it is a front, an unreal story.

Another quality that makes the scene effective in illustrating Gee's argument for the perpetual presence of Discourses and their subtle orienting necessity is Donette's resistance to D'Angelo's analysis of difference. For her, D'Angelo's concern over a sense of belonging is absurd. First and foremost, as she sees it, what matters most is that he has money. It is all a matter of one's money. If you have it, you get to be whatever you want to be. She tells him this as if looking right through him. She pointedly does not look at the room around them. She refuses to engage his speculation on the distinctions and gatekeeping functions of recognition. It is as if she is angry at him for raising the specter of them not belonging and indicating, by his very willingness to entertain the idea, the fundamental differences between their respective sensibilities and sensitivities.

When they are offered dessert, Donette shifts from her frustration with D'Angelo to the waiter and, sweetly and with a small hair flip (a move that announces that she has just changed Discourses), asks for chocolate cake. She then shifts back to an impatient tone to address D'Angelo. The quick pivots in and out of different tones that go with different social acts are just awkward enough to illustrate beautifully the constant tending that different Discourses require. D'Angelo, stymied in his ability to get recognition while trying to think through the difference of the Discourses at play, sinks into silence. When the waiter brings the dessert tray he grabs the chocolate one off the top and hands it impatiently to Donette. It is a wrong move that mistakes the sample for the real thing, leading the waiter to again explain to him the rules of where he is. The scene ends with the waiter asking D'Angelo if he would like anything. D'Angelo this time stays silent, merely raising his hand as if to say, at once, no and enough (trying to act the right way).

The final scene is from the episode "All Prologue" in season two (2.6). D'Angelo, now in prison, is part of a book group that has come together to discuss *The Great Gatsby*. The prisoners sit around several tables set next to one another. An instructor (played by the aforementioned Richard Price) is at the head of one side of the oval arrangement, D'Angelo at the opposite head. In this case, I do ask the students before showing the scene how many have read the novel. In turn I can pose a Gee-inflected question: how does one's situatedness impact how they might "read" such a novel?

In the scene, the first prisoner talks about Gatsby's victimization by Daisy, his tone suggesting his memory of some deeply felt sense of betrayal. The instructor, however, doesn't respond to the prisoner's clear claim of disappointment. He instead tries to carry on by saying something teacherly, offering them the Fitzgerald quote "There are no second acts in American lives." "Do you believe that?" he asks them. It is as if he does not know what to say in response to the prisoner's pain so he stays entrenched in the Discourse of a literature classroom. The obvious response to that question is a prisoner's joke that being locked up, they can only believe in second acts. There is some laughter and then, after a moment, marking patience to let the laughter play out as well as apprehension of saying what he is about to say, D'Angelo gathers himself and speaks, then pauses. He is ready to give the prisoners' point-of-view of what Gatsby might mean, but is clearly hesitant to take on the teacher's role. It may well be that he knows that he must translate their collective sense, for he is closer to the prisoners than the teacher, and closer to the teacher in his perceptions than the others.

When we re-watch the scene I have the students pay careful attention to a particular back and forth in which the teacher encourages D'Angelo to keep talking. The teacher is unable to pick up the pain of the first prisoner, but he hears enough in D'Angelo's initial commentary to know that he wants him to say more and that D'Angelo has more to say. Encouraging D'Angelo means surrendering his authority. Thus he lowers his register into a single contraction of "go head" (*g'ead*) with an added nod. In other words, unlike the rather stiff recitation of the Fitzgerald quote, here he shifts the language away from anything controlling—giving only a simple, signifying sound—and thereby opens a space for D'Angelo to enter. It is a small thing, but that register change and nod suggest to D'Angelo an intimacy, a connection, a degree of trust; a willingness to listen as if he is just another student and a message to D'Angelo that he can teach them all.

Exhaling and leaning forward in his own move toward that opened space, toward those with whom he wishes to communicate, D'Angelo in turn lays out his perception of Gatsby's refusals:

> Like at the end of the book, you know, boats and tides and all. It's like you can change up, right? You can say you're somebody new, you can give yourself a whole new story, but who came first is who you really are, and what happened before is what really happened. And it don't matter that some fool say he different because the only thing that make you different is what you really do or really go through. Now he frontin' with all them books but if we pull one down off the shelf ain't none of the pages ever been opened. He got all them books and he ain't read near one of them. Gatsby: he was who he was and he did what he did and because he wasn't ready to get real with the story that shit caught up to him.

This is all an expression of what, haunted with foreboding, he tells a refusing Donette in the restaurant—"the past is always with us," or put another way, no amount of money allows one the freedom to simply buy their way into a new Discourse and into a new way of being.

At that table, however, as the camera pans along the silent and still and listening faces, we see how his fellow prisoners are rapt, and so is the teacher, as if in awe of someone doing what he could not do, which was to translate Fitzgerald into the prisoners' situation. Where there was a divide between teacher, novel, and prisoners, the scene closes with the Discourse of a situated truth that they are sharing, even as that sharing is incredibly contingent. *If* we pull a book off the shelf, D'Angelo has said.

While only one of the scenes with D'Angelo features written material, and only two offer moments and methods of teaching, they help give resonance to Gee's insistence that literacy must be considered in the plural, as literacies. "Reading instruction," he says, "must be rooted in the connections of texts to engagement in and simulations of actions, activities, and interactions—to real and imagined material and social worlds" ("Reading" 716). Hopefully, the would-be teachers of my class come to see that even if their students eventually become enculturated by the language of the classroom, this does not mean that they won't struggle to reconcile their primary Discourse and what they experience in school, as well as feel the continual pressure of competing Discourses within an on-going education.

These three scenes with D'Angelo show, in very nuanced ways, the complicated human elements that go into any pedagogy and the necessity of becoming attuned to a multiplicity of merging, conflicting Discourses. They achieve this with much greater force than Gee's own examples because they demonstrate the flux of Discourses in dramatic time and pacing, making present his concepts of literacy as the lived and situated use of language and voice for particular ends. In what Rancière calls "universal teaching," there must be, before all else, an assumed emancipation of the intellect: "Speech and the conception of all works as discourse are, according to universal teaching logic, the prerequisite to any learning" (65). What follows from that prerequisite is the constant negotiation of real and imagined material and social worlds. The alert, alive, agonistic struggles of D'Angelo make human the "forum and the consciousness where [competing] languages meet and compete to be chosen" (Bialostosky 22). As Bialostosky insists, despite all well-intentioned hopes of any pedagogy, there is never a "blithe passage" from one Discourse to another and

> the participation in diverse knowledge communities opens a struggle among them that knowledge conventions and mannerly behavior cannot resolve. For Bakhtin, self-conscious participation in that struggle marks the free and education consciousness—the dialogic self. The writing course, like the novel and the public square, may be one of the forums in which that consciousness comes into being [22].

Integrating the show into a writing class demonstrates the unavoidable convergence of Discourses in the best teaching. For those would-be teachers and students of literacy, this is the unexpected lesson waiting along those liminal lines of *The Wire*.

Works Cited

Agha, Asif. "Register." *Key Terms in Language and Culture*. Ed. Allessandro Duranti. Malden, MA: Blackwell, 2001. 212–215.
Assmann, Jan. "Remembering in Order to Belong: Writing, Memory, and Identity." *Religion and Cultural Memory*. Stanford: Stanford University Press, 2006. 81–100.
Bakhtin, M. M. *The Dialogic Imagination*. Ed. Michael Holquist, trans. Caryl Emerson and Michael Holquist. Austin: University of Texas Press, 1981.
Baldwin, James. "Why I Stopped Hating Shakespeare." *The Cross of Redemption: Uncollected Writings*. Ed. Randall Keenan. New York: Vintage, 2011. 65–69.
Bialostosky, Don H. "Liberal Education, Writing, and the Dialogic Self." *Contending with Words*. Eds. Patricia Harkin and John Schilb. New York: Modern Language Association, 1991. 11–22.
Foucault, Michel. *The Archaeology of Knowledge and the Discourse on Language*. Trans. A.M. Sheridan Smith. New York: Pantheon, 1972.
Gee, James Paul. "Reading as Situated Language: A Sociocognitive Perspective." *Journal of Adolescent & Adult Literacy* 44.8 (2001): 714–725.
⸺. *Social Linguistics and Literacies*. New York: Routledge, 2008.
Goody, Jack, and Ian Watt. "The Consequences of Literacy." *Comparative Studies in Society and History* 5.3 (1963): 304–345.
Hull, Glynda, and Katherine Schultz. "Literacy and Learning Out of School: A Review of Theory and Research." *Review of Educational Research* 71 (2001): 575–611.
Kubiak, Anthony. *Stages of Terror: Terrorism, Ideology, and Coercion as Theatre History*. Bloomington: Indiana University Press, 1991.
Povinelli, Elizabeth A. *Economies of Abandonment: Belonging and Enduring in Late Liberalism*. Durham: Duke University Press, 2011.
Price, Richard. Interview with Terry Gross. *Fresh Air*. Natl. Public Radio. WHYY, Philadelphia. 17 July 2011.
Rancière, Jacques. *The Ignorant Schoolmaster: Five Lessons in Intellectual Emancipation*. Trans. Kristin Ross. Stanford: Stanford University Press, 1991.
The Wire: The Complete Series. Home Box Office, 2010. DVD.

The Wire at a Distance
The Socio-Cultural Determination of Meaning and the Challenges of Online Learning

MATT APPLEGATE

This essay investigates the pedagogical challenges of teaching David Simon's *The Wire*, and its associated critical material, in online learning environments. Further, I examine two obstacles inherent to the practice of online teaching—time and distance—and how these obstacles might be transformed as online teaching platforms change and contrast. My interests here emerge from a recently developed distance-learning course I prepared and taught entitled "Television Culture" in which *The Wire* served as the course's primary text. Seasons one and four of *The Wire* determined the shape and focus of the course content, although students were free to extend their analysis of the series beyond those seasons if they wished. The generational parallels between the two seasons, as well as each season's shared infrastructural challenges, served as the ground from which students drew connections between the formation of "television culture" in the United States and television's force as a socio-cultural site of production. However, in somewhat ironic, yet interesting ways, the institutional problems that come to the fore when seasons one and four are screened back to back manifested as challenges to the form and practice of online learning throughout the duration of the course (a 300-level course worth four credits taught in three weeks).

The parallels between the profuse institutional challenges depicted in *The Wire* and the material conditions of online learning are made manifest throughout this essay; however, my primary argument here is one of pedagogy and knowledge production in emerging educational spaces. Most specifically, I argue that online learning formats present a dual pedagogical challenge when they are mobilized to approximate "on-site" educational spaces. First, by outlining the complex theoretical traditions endemic to the study of television, I argue that online learning formats in their current state predominately encourage students to reduce multi-layered televisual environments and complex cultural interventions to a formulaic typology of character relations and plot. With reduced time and disincentive to complete each required assignment, students often interpreted *The Wire* specifically by comparison, i.e., McNulty and Bunk are likened to the detectives on *Law and Order* as they investigate drug crime and murders, evacuating the show of its specificity and dramatic nuance. Second, I argue that the conditions of online learning and their reductive effects parallel a common practice internal to *The Wire* as a series: juking the stats. Here, the show itself is mobilized as a metaphor that refracts back onto the conditions of online learning. Claims to "simplicity and flexibility," courses that require no technical knowledge, and courses that profess to "be all about you" mislead students, inspire mediocre work, and show little concern for student success. Indeed, at a structural level, many online learning formats present the pedagogical challenge of building basic literacy skills in new subjects and new media under institutional demands to do more with less. Further, many online courses present an unavoidable sacrifice in quality of student interaction and student-focused learning.

The focus of this essay is not limited to outlining the constraints or inadequacies of online learning in its current state. Much like its depiction in *The Wire*, institutional inefficiencies are not grounds for either the elimination of experimental pedagogical alternatives or the uncritical reformation of failing bureaucratic models. In season four specifically, both Roland Pryzbylewski and Howard Colvin implement experimental teaching practices in the spaces and times that bureaucratic educational imperatives consistently fail. Experiments like Pryzbylewski's dice game probability lesson and Colvin's classroom for troubled students are limited to neither standards of efficiency nor traditional models of educational exchange and relation. Rather, they are experimental landscapes from which new forms of knowledge and new modes of relation might arise. Similar struggles and tensions are currently at play in the development of online classroom spaces. The current contrast exhibited between MOOCs (Massive Open Online Courses) and DOCCs (Distributive Open Collaborative Courses) is a result of conflicting pedagogical desires: in the case of MOOCs, universities successfully extend their power to generate as much profit from a single faculty person's expertise as possible; in the case of DOCCs, the pedagogical imperative is to generate as much input and interest in a given topic from the expertise of all students and faculty involved.

In describing these effects and innovative qualities, then, this essay is divided into two primary parts. Part one details the ways in which I adapted *The Wire* to an online learning format, both methodologically and practically. Where I speak specifically about the kinds of assignments I required and the expectations I had for the course work, I also outline the course's theoretical framework and describe the experience of teaching *The Wire* online. Part two focuses on the impetus for and practical construction of experimental educational spaces. Where online learning is experimental by definition in its current state, I work to draw out and conceptualize the experimental traits of alternative pedagogies as they are depicted in *The Wire* to create a dialogue between both contexts. Given online courses' reduced time and what I term their inherent forms of distance, online learning is often a process of mimicking the onsite classroom writ large, rather than a process of rethinking and recreating it. This essay therefore culminates in an affirmative analysis of distributive open collaborative courses (DOCCS) and the innovative qualities they bring to online teaching and learning. In perhaps a more straightforward language, section two focuses on innovative pedagogical practices that make online learning functional, relational, and student-focused.

Methodology and Media

Despite its emerging popularity in Communication and Literature departments across the United States, the study of television and the cultures that it forms brings with it rigorous methodological breadth and a complex history of implementation. Where popular scholars like Fredric Jameson and Slavoj Žižek have specifically commented on *The Wire's* realism and critique of ideology for instance, scholars like John Fiske and Raymond Williams develop interpretive mechanisms with which to situate questions of realism and ideology through the study of television in a broader social context. I mention Fiske and Williams alongside Jameson and Žižek here because both thinkers place the study of television alongside the study of literature, philosophy, linguistics, and sociology, recognizing that the rise of emerging technologies and media alter the disciplinary scope of intellectual inquiry. As such, Fiske and Williams formed the methodological ground for my course in a more "meta" sense than the mere application of typologies and concepts to *The Wire*. In the effort to develop an interpretive toolbox where students could engage with the specificity of television's relation to cultural production in a broad disciplinary context, I assigned Fiske and Williams with the intention of performing two specific tasks.

First, when taken together, Fiske and Williams' methodological scope underscores the interdisciplinary character of television studies and places a demand on transferable interpretative skills. Inasmuch as the course was concerned with the study of television in particular, both Fiske and Williams are concerned with what might be broadly articulated as television's "socio-cultural determination of meaning." With this focus, the study of television acts as an access point to the study of, and critical reflection on, knowledge production across disciplinary divides. *The Wire* is an apt case study for this mode of inquiry. On a formal level, *The Wire* has been compared to both cinema and the novel, complicating its status and role in cultural production (Noah Berlansky's *Atlantic* interview with Sean Michael Robinson and Joy Delyria, "'The Wire' Was Really a Victorian Novel" characterizes this comparison well). On a thematic level, *The Wire* consistently provokes meditation on the production of social inequalities. Undeniably so, the show is driven by power differentials that stem from the unequal institutional valuation of race, class, and gender.

Second, and most importantly for this essay, Fiske and Williams' respective inquiries into television and culture provide a basis from which to theorize *The Wire's* reception and interpretation in the context of my online course. Fiske and Williams describe two phenomena—one general and one particular—that come to bear specifically on the pedagogical challenges I faced while teaching *The Wire* online. On the one hand, Fiske describes a complex methodological standpoint for interpreting television that dovetails with many of *The Wire's* socio-cultural interventions. On the other hand, Williams describes a process of interpretive generalization in his own classroom that parallels the generalization of *The Wire* in my course. On Williams' account, this interpretive generalization undermines the complexity that the study of television demands by relying on and producing cultural stereotypes that are simplistic and most often false.

Fiske opens *Television Culture* by examining the relation between realism and ideology, claiming, "The only way we can make sense of reality is by the codes of our culture" (4). This describes a constant tension for Fiske between the discourses that comprise our most intimate social relations and the power structures that order them. Following figures like Roland Barthes and Antonio Gramsci, Fiske frames this tension between realism and ideology as a tension between competing social powers and the discursive construction of those powers. In this way, Fiske writes that "realism is not a matter of any fidelity to an empirical reality, but of the discursive conventions by which and for which a sense of reality it constructed" (21). *The Wire* offers numerous examples of this complex discursive power. Donette's comment to D'Angelo in the episode "The Pager" from season one is perhaps one of the most recognizable: "Boy, don't nobody give a damn about you and your story. You got money, you get to be whatever you say you are. That's the way it is" (1.5).

Certainly, saying that one is rich does not produce wealth, and the conflict between the desire for wealth and the fact of poverty is a driving force in the series. What is important to note here are precisely the power relations that are constructed in and from a particular discourse. In Donette's case above, D'Angelo's wealth derived from the drug trade is precisely the social power that gives his words force. For Fiske, then,

> discourse, as we have seen, is not only a product of culture, it is also, in industrialized societies at least, a product of society, and the power of political relations within that society. A discourse will always stem from a socially (politically) identifiable point and will serve the interests of the groups around that point by making their sense of the real appear *common* sense: and common sense is, as Barthes (1973) says, "truth when it stops on the arbitrary order of him who speaks it" [150].

Take Clay Davis as another example from *The Wire*. In the episode "Took" from season five, Davis faces corruption charges that stem back to season one (throughout the series, Davis is shown accepting bribes from drug dealers and making backroom deals to his own financial benefit) (5.7). On the steps of the courthouse immediately prior to his testimony, Davis is shown carrying a copy of *Prometheus Bound*, likening himself to an inordinately punished Prometheus for "bringing light to the people." In the courtroom, Davis projects himself as a Robinhood like figure, taking money from the rich and distributing it to the poor, regardless of donor intent. In so many words, Davis is the personification of Fiske's writing on discourse in television culture; the inherent inequality and abuse of Davis's corruption is masked in the common sense of "helping" the poor, allowing him to be acquitted. With examples like these, it is easy to see how *The Wire* demonstrates the relation between what Fiske terms realism and ideology, drawing the series' social and political interventions into a broader context.

Whereas Fiske is ultimately more concerned with popular sitcoms in *Television Culture*, Williams comments on the crime drama genre directly. His concerns are also social and political, but also important for analyzing how *The Wire* was most commonly interpreted in my course. In an interview on

"Television and Teaching," Williams describes a course he taught entitled "Police Fiction" in which he moved through literary archetypes to describe and analyze the representation of police on television. What results is a struggle to articulate a broad social issue—what some have termed a crisis of modernity—concerning the collapse of conventional models in popular fiction. In describing his course, Williams states,

> What emerged was an evolution of the law-keeper from the highly respectable police figure, through the cultivated amateur who sold a certain social style along with detection, to this very interesting development in which the distinction between the law-keeper and the law-breaker is purely nominal in terms of manifest behaviour. You are told who is the criminal and who is the cop, but at most ethical and practical levels there is little to choose. In this work, the social analysis follows the formal fairly clearly because these are different *perceptions* of the nature of law and crime. It's also a social analysis of the production of stereotypes on which these perceptions operate [211].

In other words, the difference between "good" and "bad" as it is represented in two opposing popular figures, the policeman and the criminal, functions on both a social level and an archetypal one. On the one hand, the archetypes are pregiven. With any crime drama, the assumed difference between cops and criminals as one of inherently good and inherently bad personal characteristics is manifest. On the other hand, the social function of these figures is not as distinct or clear, largely because the discourse that produces these archetypes is culturally specific and under constant revision.

It is important to note here, though, that Williams's characterization of the police on television is identical to that of Frederic Jameson in his essay entitled "Realism and Utopia in *The Wire*." Williams's point here is that there is a discourse that orients the viewer in the genre and to the figures that comprise it. The cops are good, the criminals are bad, and the good guys are always already poised to win. However, this discourse breaks down at a fundamental level. Where Williams cites the failure of this discourse as a tension between stereotypes and the social relations that produce them, Jameson addresses this as an issue of epistemological crisis. Citing world-historical events like the Holocaust that blur the line between inherent good and inherent evil, and the event of Frederic Nietzsche's thought on the origins of "good" and "evil," Jameson writes that

> the melodramatic plot, the staple of mass culture (along with romance), becomes increasingly unsustainable. If there is no evil any longer, then villains become impossible too; and for money to be interesting, it has to happen on some immense scale of robber barons or oligarchs, for whom, to be sure, there are fewer and fewer dramatic possibilities today, and whose presence in any case

recasts traditional plots in political terms, where they are less suitable for a mass culture, that seeks to ignore politics [367].

I focus on Williams's and Jameson's arguments here for two reasons. First, from a methodological standpoint, these thinkers detect an inherent irony in *The Wire* and the crime drama genre. The very same stereotypes that viewers most often associate with the crime drama—indeed, the very stereotypes that the crime drama helps to construct—are inadequate for interpreting it. In other words, to rely on an overly simplistic "good vs. evil" model is to fail to understand the discursive power upon which the crime drama is constructed. It is also to uphold a dominant ideological standpoint that maintains social inequality. Second, in relation to my course, these thinkers outline the very nuances that were most difficult for me to teach in an online setting. These nuances were also the most difficult for students to detect. Here, then, the challenges and conflicts I encountered teaching *The Wire* online can be addressed in pedagogical terms.

The Wire *Online*

My course, "Television Culture," spanned a three-week period in the winter of 2013. I assigned traditional research paper assignments alongside blog assignments and discussion in digital lecture halls, as well as episode reviews. I intended each assignment to build on the course reading, allowing students to encounter the complexity of television studies while grappling with a set of concepts pertinent to the interpretation of *The Wire*. For instance, I provided prompts for each paper that explicitly asked students to connect Fiske's concept of ideology to the interpretation of a particular episode; I asked students to dialogue about the social and political dimensions of *The Wire* in relation to a quote from either Fiske or Williams; and I required each student to give episode summaries along thematic lines, allowing students to develop a body of writing that could be used in their research papers. Further, in addition to Fiske and Williams, I assigned several pieces of critical material that relate specifically to concepts and concerns I outlined above. For instance, I assigned several essays from Tiffany Potter and C.W. Marshall's *The Wire: Urban Decay and American Television* to give students broader cultural contexts and critical frameworks with which to interpret *The Wire*. The critical breadth of that text reinforced Fiske and Williams's theoretical approach to the study of television while it simultaneously focused students' attention on contemporary social issues. By way of example, Jason Read's "Stringer Bell's

Lament: Violence and Legitimacy in Contemporary Capitalism" accomplished this while also linking up with Jameson's concerns outlined above. C.W. Marshall and Tiffany Potter's "I am the American Dream: Modern Urban Tragedy and the Borders of Fiction" explains the cultural nuances of the series in a way that parallels Fiske's discussion of ideology and realism. My own lectures, however, focused on questions of plot and theme by applying Fiske's and Williams' work to an interpretation of the series.

On a practical level, these assignments were meant to address and teach several necessary skills: mastering college writing, learning digital composition, and critically engaging with a broad range of theoretical texts on television culture. As I have already indicated, however, time was a prohibiting factor for teaching television as a critical medium of expression; it was also an obstacle in terms of teaching *The Wire* as a unique expression of television's critical qualities. Yet, distance was perhaps more of an obstacle than time. While I made myself available for virtual office hours and responded to students' questions via email (often multiple times daily), several forms of distance, either produced or intensified by online teaching outlets, informed students' engagement with the course. I cannot address each form of distance equally here; rather, I will focus on the most pertinent. I should also note that my examples are anecdotal, and assume a direct relationship to the instructor as a figure of authority. While undesirable, I think this is a necessary assumption given the conditions under which the course was taught.

Cultural and linguistic divides are potentially present in every college classroom, but the cultural and linguistic distance that online teaching allows for (both literally and figuratively) proved to be an issue here for several reasons. Throughout the course, students had difficulty writing critically in online formats. They had either never used online learning technologies prior to the course or did not think it necessary to use correct grammar and spelling for online course assignments (this was partially due to the high number of ESL students in the course, but it also seemed to be a function of students' experience writing informally in digital contexts). This is to say, many students were not fully prepared to engage with the technologies that make online learning possible (i.e., Blackboard, blogs, etc.), and many students were not yet prepared to write under conditions where they received less personalized attention with regard to their writing. In fact, this online model, especially in a three-week winter term, is not designed for students to become better writers in English. It rather necessitates a proficient level of writing ability that if not already acquired will significantly reduce a student's ability to pass the course. Where this fact of online teaching is out of sync with the medium's supposed flexibility and student-focus, it identifies an inherent tension between what online teaching is supposed to allow and what pedagogical necessities prohibit a streamlined vision of technologized teaching from taking place.

My course did include opportunities for students to receive personal feedback on their writing, however. Under university guidelines, my course counted as a "composition" credit and general education requirement. Therefore, each student was required to revise each research paper. This allowed some students to focus on deficiencies in their writing and allowed me to offer guided feedback on their work. In many instances, though, students did not substantively revise their papers or implement my suggestions in their revisions. Rather, over and again, I was presented with long summaries of particular episodes or paraphrased versions of my online lectures.

The problem concerning composition certainly indicates a tension between differing pedagogical visions and the reality of student need; however, it is perhaps better situated as a thematic problem internal to the course that results from the tenuousness of current online pedagogical models. As I assumed that students enrolled in a 300-level course would be ready to read, discuss, and write about television in a complex manner, i.e., critically discussing the tension between realism and ideology in *The Wire*, the lack of proficiency in composition and writing in digital formats was only the first obstacle students had to overcome. In addition to teaching students an already complex set of methodological approaches, cultural analysis, especially among international students, proved to be more than a difficult task. *The Wire* is a complex American drama. Its cultural reference points and slang are specific to West Baltimore. International students voiced concerns throughout the course that they either could not understand what the characters were saying or could not adequately interpret the meaning of a particular word or phrase. The reduced time and distance inherent to the online model for my course severely limited my ability to explain fundamental reference points in the series as well as students' ability to discuss these issues with their peers. Even with assignments in which I compelled student interaction, I still found students simply summarizing particular episodes rather than addressing issues of comprehension and interpretation.

While the problem among international students might be identified as a form of cultural and linguistic distance, it also leads to a question of genre and tradition. To return to Jameson's argument above, *The Wire* is provocative precisely because it clues the viewer in to actually existing moral, political, and social crises. *The Wire* compels the viewer to question the supposed moral difference between the police and the drug gangs of West Baltimore and invokes a larger epistemological crisis when the differences among them are few. This is *The Wire's* socio-cultural intervention. However, where students had less time to engage with the material, they in fact relied on the supposed moral difference between cops and criminals, deploying it to the point that both the dramatic and cultural specificity of *The Wire* was lost in their analyses. Repeatedly, student discussion and research papers were filled with generalities and platitudes about how "the police always get their man," or, even more often, with unsupported comparisons to contemporary crime drama like *Law & Order* and *NCIS*. This is to say, when students were not summarizing a particular episode or paraphrasing my online lectures, they wrote about television shows or made comparisons to television shows that lacked the critical nuance and impact of *The Wire*, failing to understand the series' criticism of the good vs. evil, cop vs. criminal trope so common in crime drama. While my reasoning is speculative here, I assume this occurred precisely because comparison and generalization seem easier to students in a short time period, or perhaps more relatable in situations where they cannot decipher what they are viewing. It is my strong feeling, however, that the absence of critical engagement with and reflection on the course material is a result of the online model my course was made subject to. In so many words, time and distance proved to be obstacles too powerful for students to overcome in an online setting that approximated on-site teaching and learning. As a result, the work students produced mirrored what Williams identifies above as a mode of interpretive generalization, and therefore did not produce the critical discourse I desired, nor the critical discourse *The Wire* provokes.

Juking the Stats

While many decisions and situations could produce the inverse response to what the course reading and what the series itself provoke as a critical response to the representation of social and political inequality, the two common obstacles in the course, time and distance, played a larger role in its pedagogical makeup. I underscore these two constraints on the course because the challenges inherent to and produced by our most common online learning environments elicit an important pedagogical tension at the level of technology, i.e., how digital technologies best enhance pedagogical practice, but also intensify ideological differences at the level of class organization and content. At the institutional level, the material benefit of online teaching results in a discourse that supports what is, for the university, a series of identifiable goods:

faster time-to-degree rates, increased enrollment (many students enrolled in my course were actually enrolled full time at other universities without online learning programs), increased revenue, and the claim to innovation. At a pedagogical level, online teaching, in the format that I have described, presents a series of challenges: can one teach four months of material in three weeks? Indeed, this is a consistent refrain among those that taught online courses in this institutional setting (every course offered during the winter term at my graduate institution was limited to three weeks), but one that seems to necessitate alternative pedagogical approaches to online teaching. Further, how does one accurately assess students who struggle using the technologies that organize the course, or students who struggle with the course material because of linguistic and cultural divides?

At the institutional level, the online model my course was made subject to relies on an idea of education that belies in-depth analysis and critical thought. Online teaching in this format is not for the development of skills the humanities most often provide in this context; it is intended for the course content to be flexible and tailored to a student's time. This narrative and pedagogical imperative for online teaching not only fails to approximate the realities of the classroom, it simply attempts to command them from a distance. This was perhaps the most influential form of distance at work in my course: the institutional command of course time and course structure at an absolute remove from course content. The structure implemented by my university for online teaching did not allow for experimental pedagogies and teaching practices to shape the online model. Each class, regardless of discipline or course content, is taught in the same way and in the same amount of time. Given this, I was compelled to pack fourteen weeks of course material into three, write lectures as if I were teaching in front of students, and mobilize online discussions as a proxy for in-person discussion. What is lost under this schema is precisely the time and relational quality that an on-site classroom allows for critical thought and reflection.

The Wire provides a functional metaphor for this phenomenon: juking the stats. While the metaphor is developed and appears across the series in a variety of institutional contexts, its most pertinent appearance is showcased in season four. In the episode "Know Your Place," Roland Pryzbylewski, or "Prez" for short, shares a conversation with Grace Sampson, a fictional middle school teacher at Edward J. Tilghman Middle School (4.9). The conversation takes place in a faculty meeting where teachers at the school are told that school superintendents want to see a ten point increase from all city middle schools on a standardized test. As a result, all teachers, regardless of discipline, will have to teach "language arts sample questions," the area of the exam that Edward Tilghman students consistently score the lowest on. The strategy that administrators at Edward Tilghman impose consists of teaching the students sample test questions, compelling teachers to ask what is being taught: necessary skills or answers to standardized tests? In the midst of this conversation, Prez describes the process of juking the stats, or, methods he learned in the police department to downgrade felonies and other violent crimes to decrease violent crime statistics. At an institutional level, these practices manifest as a net-good: lower crime rates make the city appear safer and higher test scores on standardized tests make students seem like they are functioning at a high level.

The institutional vision for the use and function of online teaching that approximates the on-site classroom is akin to institutional frustrations depicted in this scene and described by juking the stats. Where pedagogy is made to address institutional demands on education before content, educational quality remains in question. The realities of the online classroom, therefore, seem to require an entirely different discourse and pedagogical practice: one that addresses the constraints imposed by the time and distance of online teaching and learning while also transforming them.

Experimental Pedagogies

Season four features two examples of pedagogical experimentation that can be taken as points of reflection and departure for online teaching and its potential for educational innovation: Prez's dice game assignment (4.7) and Howard Colvin's classroom for troubled students. I am not claiming that a one-to-one relationship exists here. Rather, I am interested in the representation of experimental pedagogies and what motivates these characters to think outside of the institutional demands they are confronted with.

In season four, Prez transitions out of law enforcement and into education, electing to teach eighth grade math at the fictional Edward J. Tilghman Middle School. Prez's immediate cache among faculty originates with his former career as a police officer; however, his efficacy as an educator is derived from outside of the institutional structures of police work and the middle school itself. In the moments where Prez is most effective, he is depicted teaching students to calculate probability by playing dice. In more minor moments, Prez discovers a computer and new text books in the school's basement, both of which offer students more up to date information and new learning platforms. However, Prez's experiment with teaching probability through dice games is important for at least two reasons. First, Prez's experiment taps into a common cultural experience for many of his students. If his students are not shown playing dice on the street directly, they are often shown hanging out in and among the places where dice is played on the street. Second, Prez's experiment disrupts the institutional norms for teaching eighth grade math while improving the students' ability to perform abstract thought. This is to say, Prez is willing to deviate from the institutional script in order to teach students a necessary skill in a format his students are more prepared to understand.

In another, more substantive, example, Howard "Bunny" Colvin, a former Major in the Baltimore Police Department, is conscripted into an experimental teaching program at Edward Tilghman that targets the most troubled and "at risk" students who are enrolled. It is important to note that Colvin is originally asked to participate in this program because of a prior event that spans much of season three: Colvin's attempt to create de facto legalized drug zones in West Baltimore, the most popular of which comes to be known as "Hamsterdam." It is precisely Colvin's willingness to work outside of institutional structures and norms that makes him desirable for the experimental program at Edward Tilghman.

Working with Dr. David Parenti, a fictional professor of sociology at the University of Maryland, Colvin creates a class space apart from the majority of Tilghman's student population. While this experiment might seem counterintuitive (one might imagine a situation in which troubled students would go through varying processes of socialization rather than isolation), it is meant to function as an alternative site of socialization. By separating troubled students from the larger student population, Colvin and Parenti attempt to teach students skills that they have either missed entirely or persistently fail to enact, such as speaking civilly and respectfully to each other and their elders, working in a team, managing their anger, and adopting unfamiliar decorum in uncomfortable situations.

The relational quality of these educational practices is their most striking quality. Both experiments prioritize communal learning and personal history, allowing students to learn with each other and from their own experiences. Indeed, these examples walk a fine line between institutional demand and what Paulo Freire calls "the practice of freedom": "Education either functions as an instrument which is used to facilitate integration of the younger generation into the logic of the present system and bring about conformity or it becomes the practice of freedom, the means by which men and women deal critically and creatively with reality and discover how to participate in the transformation of their world" (34). Colvin's "divide and conquer" strategy is an interesting pedagogical intervention when it is cast in this light. While it is clear that Colvin has a vested interest in funneling students through the education system, charting students on a path to college rather than to the drug trade, he does not fully condone the middle school's approach to teaching troubled students. His strategy is therefore not a question of enacting new ways to meet institutional demand in these instances, but a question of transformation within and against the practices Edward J. Tilghman has adopted to teach troubled students. The operative question here is precisely: how might one create a transformative space for education and critical reflection with and beyond the institutional constraints with which one is presented?

The very same concern has motivated experimental pedagogies in online learning environments. Rather than trying to make online learning environments approximate on-site teaching environments, some proponents of online teaching have created online structures that recreate educational space and practice. They have doubled down on online teaching's experimental qualities by practicing new ways of teaching and learning. One important example is Anne Balsamo's (dean of the School of Media Studies at the New School) concept for "distributed open collaborative courses," or DOCCs. Her concept went into effect at 17 schools in the fall of 2013. In describing the organization and function of a DOCC, Balsamo directly contrasts this educational space to a MOOC (massive open online course), which attempts to more closely approximate an on-site educational space. In a profile on her online model featured on Inside Higher Ed, "Feminist Anti-MOOC," Balsamo claims, "A DOCC is different from a MOOC in that it doesn't deliver a centralized singular syllabus to all the participants. Rather, it organizes around a central topic.... It recognizes that, based on deep feminist pedagogical commitments, expertise is distributed throughout all the participants in a learning activity."

With Balsamo's definition, DOCCs confront head on the problems of time and distance online teaching is so often made subject to. In reference to time, DOCCs utilize centralized topics as opposed to a universal syllabus. This allows students to focus deeply on a subset of course materials while also exposing them to a breadth of material as other students and faculty present it. In this case, one does not force students to learn fifteen weeks of course material in three, as was the case in my course, it allows students to develop competency in one area while still providing a broad picture of the object of study. In reference to distance, the DOCC model addresses two related problems. On the one hand, the DOCCs' decentralized syllabus gives students the opportunity to teach and learn from each other as they would from the course instructor. In terms of my own course, this mode of classroom organization would have compelled students to dialogue with each other on a deeper level, ideally inspiring more critical reflection on *The Wire* and the course reading. On the other hand, Balsamo's model reimagines the position of the instructor and frees him or her to give more attention to groups or individuals that need it. The DOCCs' decentralized model therefore enhances the possibility for a student-focused classroom as it allows the instructor to adapt and learn from student interaction. Indeed, this is one aspect of what Balsamo means when she refers to the DOCCs' relation to feminist pedagogy. To cite bell hooks, following Paulo Freire: "Engaged pedagogy does not seek simply to empower students. Any classroom that employs a holistic model of learning will also be a place where teachers grow, and are empowered by the process" (21). The relational qualities of Balsamo's DOCC is ideal, but at the very least these pedagogical experiments compel educators to create sites for teaching and learning that resist institutional command over course organization, and therefore the need to sacrifice critical inquiry to flexibility and economic pressure.

The realities of the online classroom and the ideological imperatives that attempt to direct it toward the expertise of the few over the many profit at the sacrifice of educational quality, and institutional good over student good are indeed opposed, but it is the experimental reinvention of these points of opposition that offer one final point of reflection on my course as a whole. Balsamo's DOCC aspires to establish an important precedent in online teaching and learning. Its relational qualities and structure are attuned to, and in fact driven by, a capacity for critical thought and action. In so many words, Balsamo's DOCC attempts to link the structure of online teaching to her intended result: a classroom space where students take command of their learning environment. One downside of the DOCC model is that it does not account for the variances in technological knowledge and competency that inform student success in an online setting. The DOCC model seems to assume that digital environments are spaces in which students feel at home, mobilizing new technologies as cultural reference points for better teaching and learning. Further, DOCCs are not a guarantee that a decentralized online classroom will compel students to a new experience of education; students might still emerge from the course without a firm grasp of the course material or course goals for a variety of personal and institutional reasons. However, Balsamo's model does create the conditions for, and indeed compels, students to take a more active role in their learning.

It was precisely this active component of student learning that became obscured and lost in the space and time of my own course. And yet active engagement was precisely what the course content necessitated. When studying television in any format, one cannot remain a spectator, but when studying television online, one must actively create the conditions for mutual interaction and understanding across numerable obstacles and divides. How this process might be assessed and measured in an online course that approximates on-site teaching is difficult to parse out, if it is even possible to enact. What the experience of teaching my course on *The Wire* provokes, however, is question for the future implementation of experimental pedagogies in online settings. In what ways can educators ensure that remedial technological skills are met and addressed while simultaneously creating an educational environment that challenges and stimulates the student? In reference to teaching *The Wire* in particular, this question might be reformulated: can educators teach competency in digital skills in tandem with the critical discourse the series provokes and demands?

Balsamo's DOCC is a provocative response to these questions because it is a working example of the experimental pedagogies depicted in *The Wire*. It is also a response to the ideological differences in play between institutions and educators who are concerned with the relation of course structure and course content in online formats. In the times and spaces where DOCCs remain unavailable, further pedagogical experimentation is demanded.

Works Cited

Berlatsky, Noah. "'The Wire' Was Really a Victorian Novel." *The Atlantic*. Atlantic Media Company, 10 Sept. 2012. Web. 3 July 2014.
Fiske, John. *Television Culture*. London: Routledge, 2011. Print.
Freire, Paulo. *Pedagogy of the Oppressed*. Trans. Myra Bergman Ramos. New York: Continuum, 2000. Print.
hooks, bell. *Teaching to Transgress: Education as the Practice of Freedom*. New York: Routledge, 1994. Print.
Jameson, Fredric. "Realism and Utopia in *The Wire*." *Criticism* 52.3–4 (2010): 359–72. Print.
Jaschik, Scott. "Feminist Anti-MOOC | Inside Higher Ed." *Feminist Professors Create an Alternative to MOOCs | Inside Higher Ed*. N.p., 19 Aug. 2013. Web. 2 Apr. 2014.
Williams, Raymond. "Impressions of U.S. Television." *Raymond Williams on Television: Selected Writings*. Ed. Alan O'Connor. New York: Routledge, 1989. 24–30. Print.
⸻. "Television and Teaching," *Raymond Williams on Television: Selected Writings*. Ed. Alan O'Connor. New York: Routledge, 1989. 203–215. Print.
Žižek, Slavoj. "Zizek on the Wire (2012)." *YouTube*. YouTube, 13 Aug. 2012. Web. 3 July 2014.

Using *The Wire* to Teach Cultural Competency in Higher Education

Tia Sherèe Gaynor

Culture, according to Cross, Bazron, Dennis & Isaacs, refers to integrated patterns of behavior including thoughts, communication, customs, actions, beliefs, and values of racial, ethnic or social groups. Therefore, cultural competency is "a set of congruent behaviors, attitudes, and policies that come together in a system, agency, or among professionals and enable that system, agency or those professionals to work effectively in cross-cultural situations" (Cross 13). In general, cultural competence refers to the ability to effectively interact with individuals from multi- and cross-cultural backgrounds. Individuals who are culturally competent not only understand their own culture and experiences, and the biases that come along with their culture and experiences, but also understand, are sensitive to, and respond thoughtfully to the varying cultures of others (Swan).

College is designed to expose students to the knowledge, skills, and perspectives that may shape their outlook and approach to life. Ideally, this knowledge, these skills, and perspectives are designed to put students in the best possible position to achieve their professional and personal goals. Developing the skill of cultural competence is vitally important for students so that they learn to consider differences in sexual and gender identity, race, religion, ethnicity, immigration status, ability, and socio-economic status, among other personal characteristics, are better able to understand experiences of those from differing backgrounds, and are able to navigate their professional and personal worlds while embracing difference. *The Wire* can be used in any higher education course as an innovative pedagogical strategy to help develop students' cultural competency skills.

The recommendations presented are grounded within my own empirical study that demonstrates how using the show in college and university classrooms can aid in developing culturally competent curricula and students. This study examined 20 syllabi from accredited public and private colleges/universities who offer courses that make primary use of *The Wire*. Primary findings reveal how the show is used to impart cultural competency skills. Although fictional, *The Wire* accurately portrays the complexities of urban life that "are very difficult to illustrate in academic works" (Wilson & Chaddha para 6). Therefore, use of *The Wire* in the college classroom serves as an innovative pedagogical tool that helps develop a culturally competent curriculum.

The Case for Cultural Competence

The changing demographics of the United States and the realization that communities and organizations are becoming increasingly more diverse has, arguably, ignited an influx of scholarship focused on the importance of diversity, equity, and cultural competency, particularly within education and curriculum development. The Census Bureau in 2012 predicted that by 2060 more than half of the American population will be of color. As those traditionally considered minorities become the majority in the United States, the Lesbian, Gay, Bisexual, Transgender, and Queer (LGBTQ) community becomes "out"wardly present, and American society as a whole evolves, it is increasingly more important to train students to be culturally competent. These shifts in American demography are changing the faces of those within society, providing evidence for the urgency to create and implement culturally competent curricula. Thus, the responsibility to ensure that students develop cultural competence, are exposed to varied perspectives within their discipline of study, and understand the cultural and social contexts for which disparity and discrimination occur falls to universities and colleges.

According to Rice and Mathews, the "higher education community is failing public sector and nonprofit organizations, because it does not impart the nuances of cultural competency to students in both teaching and training, leading to poorly working, failed, or inappropriate programs and the lack of organizational support systems to implement culturally appropriate and culturally responsive programs and services" (24). Historically, systems of higher education were predominately tailored to white, heterosexual males (Swan). Accordingly, pedagogical materials and strategies were designed to teach white, straight men. Traditional curricula significantly focused on white male theorists (White), largely ignoring the roles women and ethnic minorities played in the historical evolution of theory. Cross-cultural practices were not institutionalized in professional schools and did not adequately prepare students to service "minority clients" (Cross 7). Students were primarily taught "the thoughts of white, European males, while the thoughts of the diverse student body are not reflected in the curricula" (White 112). Classrooms experienced a "whitewashing of differences" with little to no exposure to alternative perspectives, experiences, and considerations (Ibid.). To combat the "whitewashing" implicit in higher education, institutions of higher learning must ensure that when students graduate, they are "culturally proficient" (Rice and Mathews 21). It thus becomes incumbent upon colleges and universities to ensure that students are well prepared, as professionals, with both scholarly and cultural knowledge.

The importance of culturally competent curricula is also evidenced by the increased attention of cultural intelligence by accrediting bodies. For instance, NASPAA (the accrediting body of graduate public administration and policy programs) requires programs to incorporate curriculum content that enables students "to communicate and interact productively with a diverse and changing workforce and citizenry" (NASPAA Standard 5.1). This standard directs curricula away from the traditional white, male, hetero-normative focused model and toward curricula that embodies diverse perspectives from varying theorists enabling students to better understand points of view other than those deemed dominant. To incorporate cultural competency over the long term, undergraduate and graduate programs must consider what changes they will implement into their programs in order to prepare students for careers that will inevitably require them to work within a culturally diverse workforce and ultimately build culturally competent agencies (Bailey).

A Framework for Cultural Competency Education

Principles of cultural competent curricula are evident in Rapp's framework for culturally competent medical curriculum. This framework is easily adaptable for any discipline and can be used as a guide to give faculty "a base through which to connect the goals for the learning outcomes to specific course practices across the curriculum" (Norman-Major 313). Rapp's framework is explored through a discussion of five curricula components: (1) knowledge-based; (2) community-based; (3) skills-based; (4) attitude-based; and (5) assessing student knowledge (Table 1). Through the incorporation of these

Components of Culturally Competency Curricula	Subject Matter (not exhaustive)	Skills Developed
1. Knowledge-based	Definitions/terms Data analysis	Culture Basics/Themes
	Demographics Communication Sexuality Roles (Gender/family) Spirituality/Religion	
2. Community-based	Service-learning Internship/Shadowing Community based projects	Establishing rapport Understanding socio-economic barriers Active, hands-on learning
3. Skills-based	Communication (language barriers) Planning Management Leadership Economics/Budgeting	Understanding socio-economic barriers Understanding cultural themes/practices
4. Attitude-based		Self-reflection Awareness of cultural/personal Biases
5. Student Assessment		

Table 1. Framework for Cultural Compentency Education.

conceptual approaches, undergraduate and graduate programs can impart upon students the skills needed to face new opportunities and challenges that often coincide with changing demographics (Carrizales).

The first aspect of an effective culturally competent curriculum is one that establishes a knowledge base through "the creation of early classroom experiences that teach students the basic principles germane to culture and cultural diversity" (Rapp 706). Through formalized instruction, students develop "culture basics" and learn foundational definitions and concepts that provide a basis for understanding cultural competency (706). Historically, pedagogical strategies sought to assimilate "the professional into the dominant society's value system, separating them from the very resources that are the greatest assets of their community" (Cross 7). Knowledge-based curricula combat this tradition and bridge student learning with a fundamental understanding of cultures and cultural practices. Through knowledge-based curricula, students are better able to determine the importance of cultural competency when working with a diverse constituency as they understand its varying definitions, the multiple levels of diversity, and its connections to social equity. Moreover, when curricula presents a base of culturally competent knowledge and is approached with the broadest brush stroke, students are reminded that diversity expands beyond race and gender and includes differences in religion, sexuality, age, class, education, ability, and so forth.

Curricula must embody complex "cultural themes" that expand students' understanding of varying perspectives and ways of life (Rapp 706). In this regard, incorporating aspects of a community-based curriculum promotes identifying and understanding the perspectives and experiences of clients, citizens, community leaders, and customers. Community-based curricula incorporate a practical component to the theoretical concepts developed through knowledge-based curricula, allowing for active learning and hands-on experiences. Through community-based activities, students can develop a fundamental understanding of the important role the community plays in one's professional life. As Carrizales posits, "Working with communities has critical benefits that should first be explored in academia" to effectively present students with a "critical introduction to diverse populations" (602).

The next component for a culturally competent curriculum is skills-based, one that explores discipline related skills through a culturally competent lens. A skills-based curriculum is designed to provide students with practical knowledge to identify socio-economic differences that may serve as barriers, assess clients'/stakeholders' understanding of services needed/provided, or identify relevant religious and cultural beliefs that may be pertinent to a specific situation/interaction (Rapp). Although cultural competency is not "imparted in the way that particular skills may be transmitted in training courses for technical competencies" (Rivera 277), Carrizales explains that the inclusion of cultural competency is not an independently taught skill in and of itself. Rather, it is incorporated within the teachings of existing skills related to each discipline. A skills-based curriculum builds upon foundational skills and "incorporates both the knowledge- and attitude-based curriculum to translate into cultural competent skills" (Carrizales 601).

In this respect, the instruction of skills such as communication, planning, evaluation, leadership, or management is done in such a manner that fosters cultural knowledge and awareness. For instance, when exploring communication skills, classroom instruction may recognize the diversity of languages spoken in the United States and cultural practices that extend beyond verbal communication. When learning Geographic Information Systems (GIS), planning students should understand community and cultural dynamics while developing plans for neighborhood development. A curriculum that embodies skill development aids students in becoming proficient in cross-cultural communication, developing an ability to identify solutions that address and manage cultural conflict, and learning how to assess cultural competency within an organization and specific programs.

Attitude-based curricula foster students' ability to make sound judgments and decisions by developing an awareness of their own culture, biases, and assumptions and how these biases and assumptions form their thoughts and ultimately influence their decisions. In this sense, developing an attitude-based curriculum encourages self-reflection and an understanding of societal biases. The awareness of one's own biases prepares students to work against their preconceived views and beliefs (Carrizales). Curricula using this framework foster an understanding of oneself and the society in which they find themselves which ultimately, develops cultural competency at the individual and organizational levels (Norman-Major).

Finally, appropriately assessing the achievement of learning objectives serves as the last component of a culturally competent curriculum. Faculty can employ objective assessment tools to effectively measure curriculum components to "demonstrate achievement of learning objectives" (Rapp 708). Assessment, Rapp argues, should first occur to "ensure that a basic fund of knowledge is present" (709). Once it has been established that students have foundational knowledge, applied projects can be used to assess skills in cultural competency. Tools that assess both students' knowledge and skill proficiency help to prepare students to thrive within culturally diverse environments.

The incorporation of culturally competent curricula is vital for continued training and learning which, according to Rapp, increases students' preparedness for addressing cross-cultural issues in any educational and/or professional setting.

Finding Cultural Competency in The Wire

Since the show's airing, social scientists have noticed *The Wire*'s critique of urban America through its portrayal of life in Baltimore. *The Wire* "has done more to enhance both the popular and the scholarly understanding of the challenges of urban life and the problems of urban inequality than any other program in the media or academic publication we can think of" (Chaddha 83). As a fictional piece of serial television, *The Wire* exposes "the side of the city that is scarred by vacant houses, hampered by a poor performing public school system, and plagued by a concentration of poverty that leads to high levels of illegal drug abuse and violent crime" (Schmoke para 2). Ultimately, the show, in its ethnographic presentation, challenges stereotypes: "While scholars of inequality often take these ideas as basic assumptions, Americans remain strongly disposed of the idea that individuals are largely responsible for their own economic situations...*The Wire* effectively undermines such views by showing how the decisions people make are profoundly influenced by their environment or social circumstances" (Chaddha and Wilson 165).

I examined college course syllabi that use the HBO television series to determine how the show can teach cultural competency. An assessment of 20 undergraduate and graduate level courses in U.S. based accredited public and private institutions (ranging between the Fall 2008 to Spring 2013 semesters) were used to determine aspects of Rapp's culturally competent curricula, particularly within course objectives, course descriptions, and graded assignments. Syllabi were identified by researcher's knowledge of existing courses using *The Wire*, Internet searches, and instructors volunteering their course for inclusion in the study. The disciplines represented are: religious studies, American studies, freshman seminar, criminal justice, sociology, TV/film/media/pop culture, law, public administration/management, public affairs, urban studies, and social work. Each course reviewed incorporated at least one full season of *The Wire*, although many of them covered multiple seasons.

Course Objectives

Fifteen of the 20 courses incorporated at least one of the four themes of a culturally competent curriculum within their course embedded objectives and outcomes. Knowledge-based content was most prevalently represented in the syllabi course objectives and outcomes (see Appendix A). An instructor (Rel–1) indicated that students will "leave the course with a functioning conceptual vocabulary that enables you to assess a given situation and formulate the appropriate questions to determine to what extent it is a product of structural injustice." The instructor of this course not only expects students to learn terms and definitions related to structural injustice, but also has set the expectation that when the course concludes students will be able to apply the concepts in real-life situations to ascertain the existence and extent of social disparities. An American Studies instructor (AS-4) defined one learning objective as the ability "to demonstrate mastery over the major issues, theories, and concepts within the field of American Studies, including urbanization, deindustrialization, failure of traditional urban institutions, the betrayal and pyrrhic nature of the American Dream and the frontier between urban and ex-urban." This course is designed to provide students with a normative understanding of the issues, theories, and concepts related to cultural competency and the need to develop competency skills. This learning outcome also incorporates aspects of social equity, inequality, and disparity: concepts all related to the knowledge-based theme. A First Year Seminar (FYS-3) course objective is "to examine the structural racism that corrupts American institutions." An examination of racism directly correlates with an imbalance of power between two groups; in other words, social disparities and inequality. These concepts are directly indicative of content associated with the knowledge-based component of culturally competent curricula.

Course objectives and outcomes included 13 references to attitude-based themes. Many of these statements related to evaluating roles, understanding the behavior of the show's characters, and understanding one's own thoughts. A course in criminal justice stated that students would be able to "explain obstacles prisoners face when reentering society" (CJ-5). By providing students with the ability to explain the experiences of those considered to be within a vulnerable population, particularly the obstacles returning citizens face upon re-entry, they become familiar with the physical and emotional aspects associated with facing those challenges, and may be better apt to make culturally competent decisions. A social work course sets out for students to "reflect on their own sources of privilege and personal assumptions regarding disadvantaged populations" (SW-14). By engaging in self-reflection, students are making themselves aware of the biases associated with one's own culture, privilege, and experiences. Cultural competency encompasses the ability to work with and provide services for varying demographic groups and one's awareness of the biases they have internalized allows them to make decisions in spite of personal biases (Swan). Finally, attitude-based content was presented in the outcomes of a political science course, which stated "students will develop their critical thinking skills and apply them to their political and social lives, allowing them to grow as persons and reflective citizens" (PS-19). Again, this course challenges students to apply skills taught in class in ways that allows them to engage in self-reflection. Through reflection, students may "acknowledge that cultural differences are critical in public service delivery" (Carrizales 597).

The final two components of culturally competent curricula were less prevalent in the course objectives and outcomes than the first two. Skills-based themes were evident within three course syllabi. One course asked students "to analyze *The Wire*...to develop effective arguments about the state of American city, and to present those arguments orally and visually to peers and to the general public" (AS-4). In this course, the instructor sought to develop the communication skills of enrolled students. This preparation builds upon the concepts and definitions learned, allowing students to formulate arguments and effectively communicate with cultural competence. A criminal justice class expects students to be able to "analyze the code of the street and urban culture" (CJ-5). The analysis of urban vernacular and culture increases familiarity with varying cultural traditions and helps to lessen the gap between the "suite" and the "street."

Only one course evaluated integrated community-based content. The one religion course included within this study encompassed external learning opportunities where students were told "there will be an active service learning component in the justice system" (Rel–1). This community-based learning experience brings students face-to-face with the challenges, obstacles, and issues that are presented to them in course material. This instructor chose to enhance foundational knowledge by incorporating connections to the community, which according to Carrizales is community-based content.

Course Descriptions

Overall, course descriptions included a substantially smaller number of competent references than course outcomes and objectives. A sociology course informed students, "we will use the television series *The Wire*, as a thread to integrate topics that form the basis of a thorough understanding of urban inequality" (Soc–7). The use of *The Wire* was explicitly linked to knowledge-based content in this course. This course, through the show, explores issues of social equity and disparity to increase student understanding. An urban studies syllabus indicated that "the course will examine the urban crisis through the lens of *The Wire*, exploring such issues as urban poverty, drugs, and the decline of the inner city neighborhoods, shrinking economic opportunity, the follies of political leaders, and the failures of urban institutions such as schools, police and the media" (US-17). The professor in this statement has chosen to highlight how *The Wire* will demonstrate the contextual issues that shape social disparities in communities and use the show to aid in her/his demonstration of these issues. Knowledge-based content is evident in this course's focus on providing students with information that aids their normative understanding of cultural competency and its importance. A public administration course includes knowledge-based content and demonstrates that "through the use of alternative perspectives and diverse methodologies, students will learn to think analytically about public issues and apply the skills of policy analysis to articulate realistic solutions that will be relevant for a vast array of stakeholders" (PA-19). The notion of using alternative perspectives in and of itself is using cultural competency; however, teaching students how to engage in policy analysis in such a way that the result is relevant for various stakeholders is keenly representative of knowledge-based course content.

Attitude-based content was only evident in the course description of one syllabus. This first year seminar indicated "our analyses of the show will challenge you to face prejudices, and we will push you to examine your assumptions and privileges" (FYS-3). Engaging in self-reflection may assist students in understanding how their assumptions and privileges are piece to decisions made as administrators. There was no content related to skills- and community-based components in the course descriptions.

Graded Assignments

The assignments section of course syllabi is the final section that was examined for culturally competent content. Unlike the previous two syllabi sections, the assignments sections did not include many examples of culturally competent content. This may be due to the fact that many instructors do not provide detailed assignment instructions in the syllabi themselves. Oftentimes, instructors provided a general explanation of the assignment and indicated that details would be provided at another time or indicated that a detailed description of the assignment was available via other outlets such as online course management systems.

The assignment content linked to culturally competent curricula represents two courses (religion and law). Three statements were linked to knowledge-based, one linked to attitude-based, and one linked to community-based content. There were no statements associated with skills-based curriculum content. A pre and post assignment associated with the religion course asks students to write a paper beginning "with raw statements of their understanding of social justice, and the take home final will be a reevaluation of those original statements in light of what they learned in the course. This may entail a "case analysis" where the students are asked to evaluate it in terms of the concepts they have learned" (Rel–1). Students in this assignment will indicate in their final exam how their initial statements have changed when taking into consideration the concepts of social justice that they have learned throughout the course. This assignment is associated with both knowledge- and attitude-based content. In the reevaluation of their initial statements, students are engaging in self-reflection that occurs with the application of learned concepts and theories. Also included within this course is a journaling assignment coupled with a service-learning component. Through service learning, students will work "with the judicial system where the characters from *The Wire* often end up" (Rel–1).

Interpreting Competence in College Courses

These data indicate that *The Wire* can be used to help create culturally competent curricula. Courses included within this study have used the show to help illustrate the concepts being taught, understand the value of interacting with residents, and expose students to the realities of life, particularly in urban communities. Overall, the majority of syllabi (15 out of 20) included within this study were linked to at least one component of a culturally competent curriculum. Knowledge-based content was found to be the most prevalent of the four themes.

Course	Knowledge Based	Attitude Based	Skills Based	Community Based
Religious Studies-1 (Rel-1)	7	4	0	2
First Year Seminar-2 (FYS-2)	0	1	0	0
First Year Seminar-3 (FYS-3)	3	3	0	0
American Studies-4 (AS-4)	4	0	2	0
Criminal Justice-5 (CJ-5)	4	3	2	0
Criminal Justice-6 (CJ-6)	0	1	0	0
Sociology-7 (Soc-7)	2	0	0	0
Sociology-8 (Soc-8)	1	0	0	0
Mass Media-9 (Med-9)	0	0	0	0
Mass Media-10 (Med-10)	0	0	0	0
Mass Media-11 (Med-11)	0	0	0	0
Mass Media-12 (Med-12)	1	0	0	0
Law and Social Policy-13 (Law-13)	2	1	0	0
Social Work-14 (SW-14)	3	1	1	0
Urban Studies-15 (US-15)	1	0	0	0
Public Management-16 (PA-16)	0	0	0	0
Public Administration-17 (PA-17)	1	0	0	0
Pubic Administration-18 (PA-18)	1	0	0	0
Political Science-19 (PS-19)	1	1	0	0
Political Science-20 (PS-20)	2	0	0	0
Total	33	15	5	2

Table 2. Cultural Competence in Course Syllabi (Totals).

As noted in Table 2, there were 33 examples of knowledge-based content within the syllabi, whereas there were only 15 examples of attitude-based content. Skills- and community-based content were far less prevalent with five and two examples, respectively. The prevalence of culturally competent content was not evident in any one discipline but rather was shared throughout. Where one public administration course included culturally competent material in four separate statements, a second course in this field included none. Similarly, a criminal justice course incorporated five statements of culturally competent content where the other course did not have any.

A key concept highlighted in several syllabi was the encouragement of self-reflection. In this regard, students learn how their own privileges and/or experiences shape the way in which they view scenarios and influence decision-making in the workforce. The depictions of a failed public school system, a police department employing hardworking officers and those who engage in illegal activity, a struggling union, and the questionable decisions of government officials present a reality that may be at the fringe of students' experiences, and help students understand experiences that may be different than their own. These images and the narratives embedded within these images present students with an increased awareness and responsiveness to "the nuances of cultural competency" while opening the door to foster new perspectives (Rice and Mathews 24). The show's content can be supplemented with readings from diverse theorists (all related to the specific discipline of study) building upon those traditionally taught. Presenting students with a diverse, well-rounded knowledge base invigorates topical discussions and embraces alternative perspectives. This ultimately builds comfort with the notion of difference rather than a fear of the "other."

The Wire challenges students' understanding of good versus evil and reveals the gray areas that exist in American society. Furthermore, the show expands student perceptions of urban poor and, for some, introduces them to the contextual conditions that often predate urban challenges. The exposure associated with the show develops an understanding of an individual's own culture, experiences, and prejudices and enables that person to better understand and address cultural differences. *The Wire*, therefore, serves as a unique (and for some entertaining) pedagogical tool to create a culturally competent curriculum. Its ability to demonstrate knowledge-, skill-, and community-based content within a course demonstrates its usefulness in college level curricula. Undergraduate and graduate programs should continue the trend of incorporating popular culture, particularly *The Wire*, as a means to develop the cultural competency of course material and the student body.

The Wire in higher education curricula aids in the reinvention of traditional educational practices that Norman-Major and Gooden argue are vital toward the development of a workforce that is qualified to develop initiatives for and work with diverse constituents. It is not enough, however, to include topics and material reflective of cultural competence. Programs and instructors must also engage in self-reflection and honest discussions to determine whether they teach, irrespective of course topic, cultural competence. *The Wire*'s content challenges instructors to acknowledge their personal experiences and prejudices and how they have shaped the ways in which they teach students. It cannot be assumed that instructors are culturally competent and do not bring their prejudgments into the classroom. Therefore, *The Wire* may prove to be beneficial in helping to craft curricula that communicates cultural competence. More needs to be done to ensure that culturally competent curricula are the norm rather than exception. *The Wire* can play a role in helping to facilitate this.

Using The Wire

To illustrate the role *The Wire* can play in fostering students' cultural competence, the following list provides examples of how the show can be incorporated into course material. The illustrations are not meant to be specific lessons, assignments, or class exercises but are meant to provide a general demonstration on how *The Wire* fits into varying higher education courses.

General Education Courses

Season one of *The Wire* introduces students to the main characters of the show and the conditions in which they find themselves. The opening scene of the show depicts Detective McNulty discussing the details of a murder with an eyewitness. The victim was known to routinely engage in a game of craps with the same individuals, grab the money that is being bet on the game, and run away. McNulty asks the witness why they continue to let him play in the game if they knew he would try to rob them and run away. The eyewitness responds, "Got to. This America, man" (1.1). Instructors can use this scene to evaluate the exchange and lead a discussion that centers on this statement. Questions the instructor may ask include: what does the eyewitness mean?; what does this statement foreshadow about the show?; how can this statement be applied in a larger context?; how does this statement relate to American society or differences in communities and cultures? Discussions can revolve around the notion that regardless of the situation, in America everyone deserves a chance to "play the game." Government, and the agencies that comprise it, is theoretically tasked with ensuring that all residents have equal chances to play. Instructors can engage with students to determine if they believe this to be true. For example, the public education system is responsible for educating all children, not just those whose families can afford a private education. Public transportation is designed to allow all people, not just those who can purchase a vehicle, to go from point A to point B. Public libraries are made available to anyone who chooses to use their services, not just those who can pay for Internet or purchase books. Instructors teaching general education courses can use this and other scenes to feature knowledge-based content related to the primary objectives of the course.

Human Resources

All or any of the five seasons of *The Wire* can be used to teach concepts of human resource management. The show features culturally diverse individuals who work in the varying branches of city government including the judicial, law enforcement, and executive arms. Season two is dedicated to stevedores and the inner workings of unions. When discussing Supreme Court actions or decisions on Affirmative Action of federal policies like the Civil Rights Act, instructors can incorporate discussions around the individuals working with the Baltimore Police Department, City Council members, or the States Attorney's Office. For example, instructors may choose to discuss Detective Kima Greggs, an African American female lesbian police officer working in a division of all men, some of whom she leads. Detective Greggs's colleagues often refer to her sexual orientation, even asking about when she realized she was gay. Greggs's interactions with colleagues and experiences as a woman in an all male division can serve as the focus of discussion. Furthermore, the issue of equity around benefits for same-sex couples arose toward the end of season one and the beginning of season two, lending itself to a discussion of job related benefits. Furthermore, the character of Detective Greggs challenges traditional images of a police officer. Again, knowledge- and attitude-based content is delivered through these images presented within *The Wire*.

Budgeting/Financial Management

Through the five seasons of *The Wire*, Lieutenant Daniels and the officers who make up his division struggle with accomplishing the tasks they are given, conducting covert operations targeting drug cartels and corrupt officials. One of the reasons for the unit's struggle relates to the lack of necessary resources to effectively carry out the orders received. The workspace they were given (an empty space in a basement somewhere in a Baltimore police department), the shoddy computers that were provided, and even the questionable manpower allocated to the unit are a few examples of the lack of resources afforded. Instructors of budgeting and financial management courses can use these images to discuss weighing the allocation of funds versus the ability to accomplish unit goals. Students can explore the implications of resource strapped agencies and the (in)effective development of programs and initiatives while considering Pareto's efficiency versus technical rationality. How should/can organizations define and address the concerns of the community with shrinking budgets? How should companies best service/serve their customers with decreased profits? Instructors can also use this to frame exercises around program assessment. These discussions can make tangible the effects of budget cuts and resource reallocation, adding to the knowledge-, skills- and attitude-based content.

Public Management

Season three of *The Wire* presents "Hamsterdam," a story line that depicts the importance of community-based knowledge, particularly as it relates to those with some kind of decision-making authority. Due to the constant pressure felt in ComStat meetings (a CompStat like system) to reduce crime rates in West Baltimore, Major Colvin decided to implement a penalty free zone for drug dealers and users. Drug activity in the "free zone" was relegated to a small section of (mostly) abandoned buildings with police oversight. "Hamsterdam," the colloquial name given to the penalty free zone, removed the dealers and users from the communities and concentrated them into this one section. By essentially legalizing drug use, this part of town embodied a concentration of shared needles (for intravenous drug use) and rampant prostitution. A community activist, seeing the potential for calamity, informed Major Colvin of key details that he had overlooked. Major Colvin began to work with this activist and other community-based organizations to distribute clean needles and condoms with the hopes of limiting the spread of disease. Furthermore, a mobile station was present for anyone choosing to be tested for a sexually transmitted disease. Major Colvin, without the assistance of the community activist, would not have considered offering these services and may have made the issues that he was trying to address drastically worse. Students can learn through "Hamsterdam" that residents and community leaders possess a level of expertise that they, as managers, do not; therefore incorporating aspects of attitude- and community-based content.

Public Policy

The entire series of *The Wire* frames a discussion of the impacts of public policy on urban communities. Season one revolves around a drug cartel and the police unit that is tasked with bringing them to justice. Stevedores, unions, and international trading are subjects of season two. During season three, ComStat in the Baltimore Police Department has a large presence and can serve as the basis for a discussion of the pros and cons of implementing such tools. Season four exclusively focuses on the public school system and how it fails the children of Baltimore. Season five focuses on the role media plays on illuminating the ills of communities and public organizations and the construction of narratives. Class discussions may concentrate on urban inequality as a whole or tackle the individual inequities that are depicted in the series for example, failing public schools, corruption in local government, corruption in the police department, crime, and limited options for residents living in low-income communities. As previously discussed, the show's characters and their experiences can help frame discussions on same-sex partner vs. spousal benefits.

Knowledge and attitude-based concepts are the easiest to incorporate as was evidenced by the study's findings. However, programs and instructors must not neglect skills- and community-based curricula content. Case studies, role-playing exercises, and group assessment activities can serve as avenues for incorporating skills-based content. Whereas guest lecturers, service learning projects, lectures on resident participation, and mandatory internships can help build community-based content.

Cultural competency is vital to establishing a society that embraces and celebrates difference. To effectively achieve this, graduate and undergraduate programs must embody culturally competent curricula so that students are trained to be cognizant of the cultural aspects of the individuals they interact with through their jobs. Competent organizations are only made through a culturally competent workforce. The chain reaction begins with schools and programs. It is thus on the shoulders of program directors and school deans to ensure that faculty teaching all courses believe in the value of a culturally competent curricula, are developing their own cultural competence, and deem the inclusion of culturally competent material in their courses important.

Without a consistent message from deans, directors, and faculty, students will, in the aggregate, not develop these skills.

The future of higher education curricula rests upon the ability of academic programs to acknowledge demographic changes and integrate methods to impart cultural competency to students. It is imperative to understand and recognize the shifting trends as they relate to the required skills for effective leadership. The 21st century student must embody knowledge that goes beyond traditional textbooks and theoretical frames to include an openness to and understanding of alternative experiences and perspectives.

Popular culture can be used as one of many pedagogical tools that can aid in student learning. This essay demonstrates how *The Wire* can be used to build culturally competent curricula and teach the concepts of cultural competence to students. The examination by no means offers itself as the sole, or even best way, to evaluate cultural competence in courses. It does, however, take a very much needed step in identifying tools that can be used to impart aspects of cultural competency to students. Popular culture, primarily television, often mimics the social, political, and economic realities of the world. The fictional imitation of life presents students with opportunities to develop and strengthen the skill of cultural competency. Furthermore, the media synergy experienced in the classroom—the integration of media, print and electronic materials, and traditional face-to-face instruction—(Linebarger) reinforces the concepts of cultural competency from varied perspectives.

Works Cited

Bailey, M. L. (2005). Cultural Competency and the practice of public administration. *Diversity and Public Administration* 171.

Betancourt, J., Green, A. Carrillo, J., and Ananeh-Firempong, O. (2003). Defining cultural competence: A practical framework for addressing racial/ethnic disparities in health and health care. *Public Health Report*, 118, 293–302.

Carrizales, T. (2010). Exploring cultural competency within the public affairs curriculum. *Journal of Public Affairs Education* 16(4), 593–606.

Chaddha, A., Wilson, W.J., & Venkatesh, S. (2008, Summer). In defense of *The Wire. Dissent.* 83–86.

Cross, T., Bazron, B., Dennis, K., and Isaacs, M. (1989). *Toward a culturally competent system of care.* Washington, D.C.: Georgetown University Child Development Center.

Elkmeier, G. (2008). D'oh! using *The Simpsons* to improve student response to literature. *English Journal* 97(4), 77–80.

Gaynor, T. (2014). Vampires suck: Parallel narratives in the marginalization of the other. *Administrative Theory & Praxis* 36(3), 348–373.

Grant, L., and Starks, D. (2001). Screening appropriate teaching materials: Closings from textbooks and television soap operas. *International Review of Applied Linguistics* 39, 39 50.

Hammer, J., and Swaffar, J. (2012). Assessing Strategic Cultural Competency: Holistic

Approaches to Student Learning Through Media. *Modern Language Journal* 96(2), 209-233.

Hornby, N. (2007, August). David Simon: Creator, writer, producer of HBOs *The Wire*, *Believer Magazine* Retrieved from http://www.believermag.com/issues/200708/?read=interview_simon.

Linebarger, D. (2011). Teaching with television: New evidence supports old medium. *Kappan*, 93 63-65.

National Association of Schools of Public Affairs and Administration (NASPAA). (1997). *Guidelines for Baccalaureate Degree Programs in Public Administration*. Washington, D.C.

Norman-Major, K. (2012). Cultural competency across the master's in public administration curriculum. In K. Norman-Major, and S. Gooden (Eds.), *Cultural competency for public administrators* (pp. 310-328). New York: M. E. Sharpe.

Norman-Major, K., and Gooden, S. (2012). Cultural competency and public administration. In K. Norman-Major, and S. Gooden (Eds.), *Cultural Competency for Public Administrators* (3-17). New York: M.E. Sharpe.

Pew Research Center. (2010). *Millennials: Confident. Connected. Open to Change*. Washington, D.C.: Taylor, P., and Keeter, S.

Rapp, D.E. (2006). Integrating cultural competency into the undergraduate medical curriculum. *Medication Education*, 40, 704-710.

Rice, M. (2007). Promoting cultural competency in public administration and public service delivery: Utilizing self-assessment tools and performance measures. *Journal of Public Affairs Education* 13(1), 41-57.

Rice, M., and Mathews, A. (2012). A new kind of public service professional: Possessing cultural competency awareness, knowledge, and skills. In K. Norman-Major and S. Gooden (Eds.), *Cultural competency for public administrators* (pp. 19-31). New York: M. E. Sharpe.

Rivera, M., Johnson, R., and Kodaseet, G. (2012). A dialogic model for cultural competency in the graduate classroom. In K. Norman-Major & S. Gooden (Eds.), *Cultural competency for public administrators* (pp. 276-293). New York: M. E. Sharpe.

Schmoke, K. (2008, January 11). *The Wire* and the real Baltimore: What the hit television drama—having just entered its fifth and final season—tells us about the city I governed and America's war on drugs. Retrieved from http://www.theguardian.com/commentisfree/2008/jan/11/thewireandtherealbaltimor.

Swan, W., French, M., and Norman-Major, K. (2012). Cultural competency around sexual and gender orientation and identity. In K. Norman-Major & S. Gooden (Eds.), *Cultural competency for public administrators* (pp. 141-169). New York: M. E. Sharpe.

U.S. Census Bureau. (2012, December 12). *2012 National Population Projections*. Retrieved March 28, 2013, from http://www.census.gov/population/projections/data/national/2012.html.

Wilson, W.J., & Chaddha, A. (2010, September 12). Why we're teaching "The Wire" at Harvard. *The Washington Post*.

Course: Rel–1

> **Knowledge Based:** "...leave the course with a functioning conceptual vocabulary that enables you to assess a given situation and formulate the appropriate questions to determine to what extent it is a product of structural injustice."
> **Attitude Based:** "...addressing your affective dispositions, and taking you through a process of realization and integration."
> **Community Based:** "There will be an active service learning component in the justice system..."

> **Knowledge Based:** "The critical engagement of the text (in this case *The Wire*), is important in breaking down the underlying structural problems that constrain the imagination and behavior of the characters."
> **Attitude Based:** "The critical engagement of the text (in this case *The Wire*), is important in breaking down the underlying structural problems that constrain the imagination and behavior of the characters."

> **Knowledge Based:** "The critical thinking is instrumental for the larger goal of acting justly. There is no way to act justly in a society that has profound structural injustice ... this course is designed to take you through that process."
> **Attitude Based:** "The critical thinking is instrumental for the larger goal of acting justly. There is no way to act justly in a society that has profound structural injustice ... this course is designed to take you through that process."

> **Knowledge Based:** "You should also be able to identify with the constraint of opportunity that exists in such situations"

Course: FYS-2

> **Attitude Based:** "Critically reflect on their own thought traditions"

Course: FYS-3

> **Knowledge Based:** "...to examine the structural racism that corrupts American institutions"
> **Attitude Based:** "One of the goals of the FYS is to expand and deepen your understanding of the world and of yourself."

> **Knowledge Based:** "...to analyze how *The Wire* makes institutional problems in the U.S. come alive in a novel and affecting way."
> **Attitude Based:** "In this course we will ask, how does *The Wire* get us to see, and to feel, conditions of urban America in a unique and emotionally moving way?"

> **Knowledge Based:** "In this course we will ask, how does *The Wire* get us to see, and to feel, conditions of urban America in a unique and emotionally moving way?"

Course: AS-4

> **Knowledge Based:** "To demonstrate mastery over the major issues, theories, and concepts within the field of American Studies, including urbanization, deindustrial-

ization, failure of traditional urban institutions, the betrayal and pyrrhic nature of the American Dream and the frontier between urban and ex-urban."

Skills Based: "To analyze *The Wire*...to develop effective arguments about the state of the American city, and to present those arguments orally and visually to peers and to the general public."

Skills Based: "To engage in scholarly dialogue with seasoned guest speakers who have experience navigating the systems *The Wire* critiques."

Course: CJ-5

Knowledge Based: "Analyze the history and trends in U.S. drug policy"; "Consider social problems related to the illegal use of drugs"

Attitude Based: "Evaluate various perspectives on the drug policy continuum"; "Explain obstacles prisoners face when reentering society"

Skills Based: "Analyze the code of the street and urban culture"; "Assess foster care legislation and policy."

Knowledge Based: "Explain the politics and limitations of crime rate statistics"

Attitude Based: "Evaluate the roles of schools and limitations of teaching in urban America"

Knowledge Based: "Identify current sentencing and prison practices and their collateral consequences"

Course: CJ-6

Attitude Based: "The nature of community perception of location policing activities and behavior"

Course: Med-12

Knowledge Based: "...we will examine the show's portrayal of urban America as a window into a number of social problems and conditions distinct to contemporary society, including the drug war, the underclass, urban policies and development, post industrial cities, political corruption, urban education, and mass media coverage."

Course: Law-13

Knowledge Based: "students will have the opportunity to critically analyze a host of criminal justice policy issues relevant to contemporary American society"

Attitude Based: "...participation is also fundamental to bolstering each individual's own experiences with the difficult issues the series presents..."

Course: SW-14

Knowledge Based: "Interpret the complex impact that urbanization has had on institutions and individuals."

Attitude Based: "Reflect on their own sources of privilege and personal assumptions regarding disadvantaged populations."

Skills Based: "Apply their understanding of urban issues to the development and critical analysis of programs and policies appropriate to addressing contemporary social and economic problems."

Course: PA-18

Knowledge Based: "Identify the implications of social equity in policy development and implementation"

Course: PS-19

Attitude Based: "...students will develop their critical thinking skills and apply them to their political and social lives, allowing them to grow as persons and as reflective citizens."

Course: PS-20

Knowledge Based: "...the series offers a sophisticated depiction of systemic urban inequality that constrains the lives of the urban poor"; "we plan to use the show as a thread that integrates the range of topics that form the basis of a thorough understanding of urban inequality—with readings and assignments that relate to the themes addressed in the various episodes."

About the Contributors

Matt **Applegate** is an assistant professor of English at Molloy College. He specializes in critical theory, digital culture, digital literacy, and the political economy of media.

Naomi **Crummey** is chair of the Department of English and Communications at Blackburn College where she teaches writing and literature. She earned a Ph.D. in English with a focus in nonfiction writing from the University of Illinois at Chicago Program for Writers.

Karen **Dillon** received a Ph.D. in American literature from Indiana University. She teaches literature and writing at Blackburn College, specializing in 20th century American and African American literature as well as first year writing.

Michael **Ennis** received a doctorate from Duke University, where he specialized in Latin American cultural studies. He teaches at the Program for Writing and Rhetoric at the University of Colorado Boulder. His research interests include utopian literatures, indigenous social movements and alternative literacies, and writing pedagogy.

Tia Sherèe **Gaynor** is an assistant professor at Marist College. Her research interests explore social justice, local government, and resident and citizen participation. More specifically, she focuses on identifying avenues by which the distance that exists between community residents and political issues can be decreased and eradicated.

Nathan P. **Gilmour** is an associate professor of English at Emmanuel College. His research focuses on the intersections between literary criticism, rhetoric, philosophy, and theology. He is one of the co-hosts of the Christian Humanist Podcast, a weekly program exploring the liberal arts.

Alex M. **Kupfer** is a doctoral candidate in cinema studies at New York University where he taught the course "*The Wire*, Quality Television, and the Media of Dissent" in Fall 2012. He is a fellow at the Institute for Research in the Humanities at the University of Wisconsin–Madison.

Daniel **Listoe** teaches in the Department of English at the University of Wisconsin–Milwaukee. Publications include articles in *American Literary History*, *SubStance*, *The Journal of Dramatic Theory and Criticism* and the edited volume *The World and Darfur* (ed. Amanda F. Grzyb).

About the Contributors

C. W. **Marshall** is a professor of Greek at the University of British Columbia. With Tiffany Potter, he has co-edited *Cylons in America: Critical Studies in Battlestar Galactica* (Continuum, 2008) and *The Wire: Urban Decay and American Television* (Continuum, 2009).

James W. **McCarty** III received a Ph.D. in religion, ethics, and society from Emory University. His research focuses on the ethics of reconciliation, peacebuilding, and social justice activism. He has published articles in the *Journal of the Society of Christian Ethics, Theology and Sexuality, West Virginia Law Review*, and *St. John's Law Review*.

Tom **Nurmi** is an assistant professor of English at Montana State University–Billings where he teaches American literature. His research examines the intersection of geography, narrative and ethics in early America. He is at work on a book manuscript on the spatial imagination in nineteenth-century American writing.

Tiffany **Potter** teaches English at the University of British Columbia. With C.W. Marshall, she has written several articles on *The Wire* and co-edited *The Wire: Urban Decay and American Television* (Continuum, 2009), as well as the PCAA award-winning *Cylons in America: Critical Studies in Battlestar Galactica* (Continuum, 2008).

Paul D. **Reich** is an assistant professor of English and director of the American Studies program at Rollins College. His pedagogical work has appeared in *Pedagogy: Critical Approaches to Teaching Literature, Language, Composition, and Culture* and *Teaching American Literature: A Journal of Theory and Practice*.

Todd M. **Sodano** is an associate professor in the Department of Media and Communication at St. John Fisher College, where he teaches courses in television history, video production, and media studies. He earned a Ph.D. from Syracuse University and wrote his dissertation on *The Wire*.

Michael L. **Wayne** is a Ph.D. candidate in the Department of Sociology and a graduate instructor in the Department of Media Studies at the University of Virginia. He is also the managing editor of the *Communication Review* and an adjunct instructor of sociology at Virginia Commonwealth University.

Index

After Virtue 4, 145, 146, 148, 152
Albrecht, Chris 13, 16
"Alliances" (4:5) 143, 150
Althusser, Louis 99
Anderson, Brad 70, 71
Anderson, Christopher 15, 16, 24
Antigone 162, 165
Aristotle 109, 111, 129, 132, 157, 165
Assmann, Jan 183, 184–185
auteur theory 32, 34, 35, 39, 40
The Autobiography of an Ex-Coloured Man 5, 63, 73

Bakhtin, Mikhail 185, 194
Balsamo, Anne 209–211
Barksdale, Avon 11, 18, 138–139, 167, 171, 175, 181
Barksdale, D'Angelo 4, 11, 50–51, 65, 66, 68–70, 73–74, 98, 119, 127, 131, 134–138, 140, 141, 169–171, 175, 179, 181, 189–194, 200
Barthes, Roland 40, 199, 200
Baumann, Shyon 55
Bean, John, 154, 158*n*4
Beilenson, Peter 4, 8; *see also Tapping into The Wire*
Bell, Stringer 11, 44, 62, 99, 131, 135–141, 169–171, 175–176
Bialostosky, Don 185, 194
Bianco, Robert 25
Bianculli, David 24, 25
Boardwalk Empire 53, 99
Bourdieu, Pierre 2, 5, 15, 48, 50, 55, 56
Bowden, Mark 38
Brandon 161, 165, 168–170
Breaking Bad 17, 32, 53, 61, 99
Brice, De'Londa 115
Brice, Namond 49, 79, 111, 114–116, 122, 123, 131, 140, 143, 150, 151, 156, 180

Brice, Wee-Bey 19, 66, 114, 115, 116, 122, 150–151, 167
Broadus, Bodie 11, 99, 115, 117, 118–120, 122, 135, 166, 169, 190
Brother Mouzone 139, 141, 180
Bubbles 36, 110, 124, 127, 131, 140, 161, 180
Buckman, Adam 24
Bug 117
Burns, Ed 20, 33, 64, 65, 66, 69, 70, 72, 73, 94, 95, 102, 106; *see also The Corner* (book)
Burrell, Ervin 161, 171
"The Buys" (1:3) 11, 70, 135, 190

Carcetti, Thomas 84, 85, 110, 113, 114, 121, 128, 131, 147, 156
Carrizales, Tony 216, 220
Carroll, John 37
Carver, Ellis 19, 115, 116, 120, 122, 166
Christensen, Jerome 41
"Clarifications" (5:8) 11
"Cleaning Up" (1:12) 10, 99, 106, 118, 135, 169, 176
Colesberry, Robert 23, 34, 39
Colvin, Howard "Bunny" 28, 49, 88, 101, 114–116, 120, 121, 122, 126, 127, 143–144, 147, 149–151, 156, 176*n*1, 191, 197, 207, 208–209, 226
The Co-op 118, 123
The Corner (miniseries) 34, 36, 37, 64, 95, 97
The Corner: A Year in the Life of an Inner-City Neighborhood (book) 20, 33, 65, 94, 102, 103, 106
"Corner Boys" (4:8) 84, 143–144, 152, 188
"The Cost" (1:10) 9, 19, 70, 169
Crime and Punishment 162, 173–174, 175, 176
CSI: Crime Scene Investigation 52, 55

Index

Daniels, Cedric 62, 121, 125n3, 126n19, 140, 161, 166, 171, 225
Darnell 49
Davis, Clay 85, 122, 182, 200
"Dead Soldiers" (3:3) 127
Deadwood 10, 13
Deleuze, Gilles 35
"The Detail" (1:2) 42, 169
Devar 117
Dickens, Charles 7, 18, 28n6, 57, 98, 115
Distributive Open Collaborative Courses (DOCC) 197–198, 209–210, 211
Doherty, Thomas 2–3, 61, 74n3
Donette 50–51, 68–69, 136–139, 191–193, 200
Dostoyevsky, Fyodor 162, 173–174; *see also Crime and Punishment*
"Duck and Cover" (2:8) 121
Duquette, Ms. 143–144, 149, 150, 151

Edelsky, Carole 112
Edward Tilghman Middle 80, 116, 206, 207
Emmy (award) 9, 11, 14, 26, 27

Felski, Rita 49
"Final Grades" (4:13) 28, 109–111, 113–115, 117–118, 120–121, 123–124, 151, 176n1
Fiske, John 198–200, 202–203
Fitzgerald, F. Scott 181, 192–193; *see also The Great Gatsby*
Foucault, Michel 41, 43, 100, 165, 188–189
Freamon, Lester 38, 167, 171
Freire, Paulo 100, 208, 210

"Game Day" (1:9) 169
Game of Thrones 61, 85
Gans, Herbert 54, 57
Gant, William 22–23, 166
Gee, James Paul 183, 185–192, 194
Genealogy of Morals 4, 145, 146, 147, 152, 155; *see also* Nietzsche, Friedrich
Gilligan, Vince 17, 53
Godard, Jean-Luc 34, 35
Golding, Martin 164
Goody, Jack, and Watt, Ian 183, 184
Gray, Jonathan 32, 43
The Great Gatsby 98, 137, 179, 192–193; *see also* Fitzgerald, F. Scott
Greggs, Kima 9, 11, 18–19, 21, 25, 38, 62, 70–72, 74, 127, 131, 140, 156, 167, 168, 175, 180, 225
Gutierrez, Alma 37, 38

Hamsterdam 114, 147, 151, 176n1, 208, 226–227

Harris, Joseph 97
Hauk, Thomas "Herc" 19, 111, 122, 166
Haynes, Gus 37, 38
"Home Rooms" (4:3) 81, 101
"Homecoming" (3:6) 139, 152
Homicide: A Year on the Killing Streets 20, 34, 94, 102–104
Homicide: Life on the Street 20, 33, 34, 95, 102
"The Hunt" (1:11) 19, 62, 67
Hurston, Zora Neale 5, 69–70, 71; *see also Their Eyes Were Watching God*

The Interrupters 101

Jameson, Frederic 3, 198, 201–201, 204
Jenkins, Henry 41
Johnson, Derek 32, 43
Johnson, James Weldon 5, 63, 73
Joyner v. Joyner 164, 165
Judge Phelan 166–167

Kafka, Franz 165, 170
Kant, Immanuel 129, 132, 134
Kenard 116, 122, 123
Kermode, Frank 108, 109
Klebanow, Thomas 37, 38
Kleinman, Arthur 130, 131–132, 135
"Know Your Place" (4:9) 49, 191, 206
Kozol, Jonathan 82, 96, 100

Lanahan, Lawrence 38
Landsman, Jay 34, 38, 122, 124
"Late Editions" (5:9) 114
Lee, Michael 79, 110, 115, 117–118, 119, 120, 122, 123, 127, 140
"Lessons" (1:8) 62, 169, 175
Levy, Maurice 9, 166
Little, Omar 9, 11, 24, 37, 40, 44, 81–82, 84, 85, 118, 123, 127, 133, 139, 140, 141, 152, 161, 167, 174, 176n7, 179, 181
Lotz, Amanda 24, 51, 28n2

MacIntyre, Alasdair 4, 6, 145, 147, 148–149, 151–152, 154, 156, 157–158
Mad Men 13, 32
Marimow, Bill 37, 38
Marimow, Lt. 38
Massive Open Online Courses (MOOC) 197, 209
McDuff, David 173
McNulty, Jimmy 9, 11, 42, 62, 65–66, 71, 103, 111, 115, 119–120, 122, 125n3, 127, 131, 140, 156, 161, 166–167, 169, 170, 171, 175, 197, 224
"Middle Ground" (3:11) 11
"Misgivings" (4:10) 117, 126n20

Index

Mittell, James 18, 19, 20, 22, 28, 28n1
"Moral Midgetry" (3:8) 138
"More with Less" (5:1) 34
Moreland, Bunk 9, 34, 42, 84, 103, 122, 152, 168, 182, 197
Morrison, Toni 63, 72

Nannicelli, Ted 105
Native Son 4, 64, 72, 68, 72; *see also* Wright, Richard
Naylor, Gloria 64, 67, 72
"A New Day" (4:11) 82, 119, 147
Newcomb, Horace 13, 52, 167
Newman, Michael, and Levine, Elana 48, 52, 53
Nietzsche, Friedrich 4, 145, 146–149, 151–152, 154–158, 165, 184, 201
Noble, Nina K. 34, 116, 120
Norman-Major, Kristen, and Gooden, Susan 224

Officer Walker 118
"Old Cases" (1:4) 9, 103, 176n1
Old Face Andre 84, 118
"One Arrest" (1:7) 161, 166, 177n9
Oz 13, 42

"The Pager" (1:5) 4, 50, 68–69, 136, 169, 191, 200
Parenti, David 89, 101, 114, 121, 143, 144, 149, 150, 151, 158, 208
Partlow, Chris 3, 115, 117, 176n1
Pearlman, Rhonda 122
Pearson, Snoop 3, 40, 181
Penfold-Mounce, David Beer, and Burrows, Roger 21, 58
Petry, Ann 63, 64, 67, 72
Plato 129, 148, 150, 151, 159n6, 183
Polan, Dana 35, 42
Poot 135, 161, 168–169
Potter, Tiffany, and Marshall, C.W. 3, 83, 202, 203
Povinelli, Elizabeth 181
Price, Richard 103, 181, 192
Proposition Joe 188, 122
Pryzbylewski, Roland "Prez" 80, 84, 114, 115, 116, 120, 122, 144, 156, 167, 169, 187–188, 197, 206–208

Rabinowitz, Peter 110, 125n6
Rapp, David E. 214, 217, 218
Raskolnikov 173
Rawls, Bill 38, 168, 171, 182
Rawls, John 129, 165
"React Quotes" (5:5) 121
"Reformation" (3:10) 121
"Refugees" (4:4) 38

Reising, Russell 110, 114
Renaldo 81, 82
Richardson, Brian 110, 113, 125n1
Richter, David 109, 113
Roush, Matt 53

Sabotka, Frank 127
Schaub, Joseph Christopher 27, 28n1
Sennet, Richard, and Cobb, Jonathan 48, 50, 51
"Sentencing" (1:13) 19, 73, 166, 168, 170
Sex and the City 13, 42
Sherrod 180–181
The Shied 13, 56, 57
Simon, David 7, 8, 12, 14, 16–17, 18, 20–23, 25–27, 33–39, 41, 43–45, 47, 64–67, 69–73, 81, 94, 95, 97, 100, 102–104, 106, 110, 117, 118, 121, 124, 125n11, 125n12, 140, 149, 157, 159n5, 174
Six Feet Under 13, 42
Socrates 157, 159n6
Sophocles 162, 165
The Sopranos 13, 14, 32, 42, 52, 61, 99
Stanfield, Marlo 3, 38, 82, 117, 120, 121, 138, 152, 156
The Street 63, 64, 72; *see also* Petry, Ann
Sydnor, Leander 167

Tapping into The Wire 3, 101; *see also* Peter Beilenson
"The Target" (1:1) 19, 22, 65–67, 69, 73, 188, 224
Templeton, Scott 37, 38
Their Eyes Were Watching God 5, 69, 73; *see also* Hurston, Zora Neale
"—30—" (5:10) 118
"Took" (5:7) 180, 200

"Unconfirmed Reports" (5:2) 18
"Unto Others" (4:7) 80, 180, 207
USA Patriot Act 165

Vondas 111, 122

Wagstaff, Randy 79, 110, 115, 116, 120, 122, 123, 127, 140, 144
Wallace 6, 10, 11, 99, 106, 118, 119, 127, 135, 160–161, 165, 168–171, 173–176, 190
Walon 181
Weems, Duquan "Dukie" 79, 110, 115, 116, 117, 122, 123, 127, 131
Whiting, James 18, 37, 38
Williams, Linda 7, 28n1, 36
Williams, Raymond 198–203, 205
Wilson, William Julius 4, 8, 47n2, 141; *When Work Disappears* 96, 100
"The Wire" (1:6) 9, 121, 161, 169

The Wire: Urban Decay and American Television 3, 83, 202
Wise, Dennis "Cutty" 101, 122
The Women of Brewster Place 64, 72; *see also* Naylor, Gloria
Wright, Richard 4, 64, 67, 69, 72; *see also Native Son*

Zenobia 49, 114
Žižek, Slavoj 3, 170, 198
Zurawik, David 25

www.ingramcontent.com/pod-product-compliance
Lightning Source LLC
Chambersburg PA
CBHW030620230426
43661CB00053B/2072